NEW MEGA TRENDS

NEW MEGA TRENDS

Implications for our Future Lives

Sarwant Singh

palgrave
macmillan

First published 2012 by
PALGRAVE MACMILLAN

Palgrave Macmillan in the UK is an imprint of Macmillan Publishers Limited, registered in England, company number 785998, of Houndmills, Basingstoke, Hampshire RG21 6XS.

Palgrave Macmillan in the US is a division of St Martin's Press LLC, 175 Fifth Avenue, New York, NY 10010.

Palgrave Macmillan is the global academic imprint of the above companies and has companies and representatives throughout the world.

Palgrave® and Macmillan® are registered trademarks in the United States, the United Kingdom, Europe and other countries.

ISBN 978–1–137–00808–4

This book is printed on paper suitable for recycling and made from fully managed and sustained forest sources. Logging, pulping and manufacturing processes are expected to conform to the environmental regulations of the country of origin.

A catalogue record for this book is available from the British Library.

A catalog record for this book is available from the Library of Congress.

10   9   8   7   6   5   4   3   2   1
21 20 19 18 17 16 15 14 13 12

Printed and bound in Great Britain by
CPI Antony Rowe, Chippenham and Eastbourne

*Dedicated to the two Mega Trends in my personal life,
my children, Damien and Leyla*

CONTENTS

CONTENTS

LIST OF CHARTS AND TABLES

CHARTS

TABLES

PREFACE

A MORNING IN OUR LIVES IN 2025

Soft music plays gently, just loud enough to awaken me from my sleep. I hear the distinctly calming murmur of my favourite companion, Sarah, next to me, greeting me with a familiar message these days:

> Good morning, Richard. Your breakfast has been warmed to your requirements. I noticed when you awoke that your glucose levels were low; accordingly, I have adjusted your morning nutrients. Please get ready for work; you will require an additional five minutes this morning based on current traffic data.

Sarah has an uncanny ability to know how I feel and to prepare me for my day by seemingly knowing what I need to feel better about myself. I do find it slightly strange that I am guided so much by Sarah, but having been recommended to get her now for the last two years, I finally made the call and took the rebate my new employer was offering. Since then I can surely attest to feeling less hurried in my life and, certainly, life in the house is lot more relaxed.

A few bites from finishing my morning bowl of cereal, I start to ponder the day ahead and wonder what is going on with my family in England and how my soccer team did last night. Fortunately for me I can now combine two of my favourite activities, checking out the latest soccer action and a nice hot shower, into one event. A few weeks ago I had finally donated the last of my Dad's old TVs and, while I am not the last of my friends to do so, I am not the first to go 'TV-less'. This shower view is incredible and all embedded into the glass, voice commanded and integrated to the Web, which is a given, of course. I must admit, though, I won't be making video calls like some of my friends from the shower; I need to remember to keep my privacy settings up to date! Having these portable TVs sure does have some drawbacks!

I also appreciate not needing to carry keys anymore; I always lost or misplaced them. Biometrics has made some huge leaps in the last two decades. Everything from my house door, car keys, personalisation features in my car and office access are all biometric now. Even some of my cooking utensils are biometric, so my nephew and nieces cannot accidentally hurt themselves.

Listening to the news makes me realise that the US has really lost out to Asian economies like India and China. The growth in their economy led by internal consumption and political generational change, combined with an immense young population, has really propelled these nations. We see more innovations and entrepreneurs coming out of those two nations than from California.

The trip to the university campus in my electric car normally takes me 35 minutes but is made all the more pleasurable with the standard gimmicks of my car. My doctor said I would feel the difference, but I truly did not believe that, with a simple new app upgrade, my car would monitor my health (keeping Sarah off my back) and also sense my mood. I have to be honest, though, I am going to have to stop getting so worked up in this traffic: if the player tunes one more time to these calm, melodic songs, I may have to do a software downgrade! Strange thing, though, they say traffic accidents have decreased by 35% in the last five years because of this technology. One thing is for sure: moving around is so much easier despite the fact that we are approaching two billion cars on the road and eight billion people on the planet. Last week my new 'Vidmail' service highlighted the progress made by the new hands-free car that is getting so much attention. As I recall, the first car to meet the new safety regulations will roll off the production line in the next five years. That will take some adjusting, so I think I will wait a while before jumping in. No doubt my good friend Parker will be first in line; he is more of a risk-taker than I am.

Undocking my smart device from the car, rolling it up and placing it in my backpack, I take what is my favourite five minutes of the day: the brisk walk to campus. I enjoy seeing all the students bustling around getting ready for their lives ahead. I often reflect on my time at the university and how rapid change is. My dad still reminds me of how lucky we are to be in such a prosperous country and how, a little more than a decade ago when I was a kid, the country was far different with so many people unemployed. I certainly had no idea I would end up in my field. My, how things change! I see one group of students sitting on the lawn in a circle using a holographic image projector to get ready for a class presentation. It is so different now: our students can virtually project into classrooms around the world, which truly has made global cooperation far more important and removed boundaries. I really believe this is our future.

When I reach my office, I sit to plan out the week's agenda. Creating programs with my remote, global team is quite a challenge; but to be so young and have such a large team to be responsible for is gratifying. It takes most of my morning to check through the safety protocols and programming for the team of 15 robot janitors (Janbots) that are our most prized possessions here in facilities management. As lead programmer, a few years ago it would take nearly all day to program the network, but the speed with which our network can process the updates has increased so substantially that we are now able to program and uplink commands in only a few hours. We often wonder how long it will be before it is down to just a few minutes and then maybe they won't even need programming and would soon become autonomous. This would be an incredible achievement because the Janbots exist in collaboration with our students and faculty members, and the insurance risks can be quite high from rogue robot accidents – not that we have ever had an incident; we are a zero-incident facility, one of only two here in North America!

Before lunch I typically walk the halls to observe the integrity of the facility and focus on assessing the new installations we have made. A significant amount of our infrastructure is old, given we have been an academic presence now for over 100 years. A few years ago I attended a conference that explored the challenge of integrating new materials and technologies into aging buildings, and it struck me just how far we have come. When you replace old with new, it really does strike a true contrast between the advent of technology and the speed with which it is evolving. Take my dad's iPad, for example; I vividly remember how excited he was when he first played with the touch screen. It is almost laughable now to think how those are considered museum pieces. Some of the experts at the event spoke from truly historic cities like London and Paris where the challenge is far greater than ours, yet they have managed to use new materials and micro technologies to transform energy-sucking buildings into energy-generating and, in some cases, fully self-sustaining edifices. That is a key goal for our campus – to be 100% self-sustainable; but Europe began ahead and continues to lead the way, with the Chinese catching up in no time. We are nearly there, and reviewing our renewable fuel-to-shale gas dashboard mix as well as our strategy to transform rooftops into solar generators is starting to pay off. Of course, none of that would be possible without the advancements in energy storage technology, especially the use of used electric car batteries. The system we invested in has only another two years before it has fully paid for itself. Of course, the ultimate goal is to be a certified carbon-free site and 100% sustainable.

With our solar panels checked, it is now lunchtime, and I can tell you it is a vastly different experience to when I was in school; you can see this just walking down the street and viewing how few people are obese these days. Whether I eat at the university cafeteria or go off-site, which I seldom have time for, the focus of food is far more geared towards my exact dietary needs, which means that, when I get to the cafeteria, my precise nutritional requirements are met. Now, I chose this dietary monitoring voluntarily because it lowers my insurance rates substantially, but it can be a bit 'big brother' for me. I do not have any serious predisposition to diabetes, but since developing slightly higher-than-usual glucose levels, our companies' nutrition division contacted me and asked me to participate. I can now go into any restaurant or store and, by scanning the menu into my personal device, it will automatically tell me which is the most suitable and healthy choice on the menu. Sure, it is a little autocratic, but the benefits are paying off already, and it means more money in my pocket, which can't be bad. Of course, the alternative would be higher insurance rates, so I did feel somewhat forced. It makes me laugh sometimes how many supermarkets now stock, and extensively sell, nutricosmetic products that help with growing healthier nails or getting your hair back.

It is now time to get back to my office for my appointment with our supplier from Africa, who will appear on my office video wall. I have a busy evening as well with my friends. The guys want to go out for a drink afterwards and, despite my better judgement, I just might do that, although I am tired of them trying to match me with someone. I wonder what prank they will try to pull tonight to get me married off – perhaps I should consider letting them help, since I am almost 35 now. Not sure how Sarah would react!

RICHARD SEAR

1

INTRODUCTION TO THE
NEW MEGA TRENDS

Of all the chapters in this book, I struggled most to write this introductory chapter. How do you introduce a future that is so uncertain yet so exciting, but possibly also very intrusive? How do you tell your readers that the gadgets they use in their house and workplace will be completely different ten years from now? How do you tell someone that the very city they live in will not be the same at the end of this decade, and their jobs and skill sets will completely change? How do you tell businesses that they can expect new customers and new business models in the coming future simply through the evolution of networks? Well there is one way, but first let me start by asking you something.

Are you someone who ponders on the past and believes in the future? Are you someone who is interested in the future of your industry and company, and often thinks about what your job role will shape into by the end of this decade, or what your next job or the one after it will look like? Do you like to guide the careers of your children and plan your own investments? And do you dabble in the share market? If yes, then you need to read this book to understand the impact of these New Mega Trends on you, personally and professionally.

I head the Visionary Innovation Group (VIG) within Frost & Sullivan, a global growth consulting company which works across 12 different industry sectors. Way back in 2001, when I was a junior project manager, I pushed the managing director of my company to allow me to open a new sector – automotive. He was not convinced and rightly asked me why he should put money in an industry which is mature whereas he could make seven times the return if he put the same investment in the information and communications technology (ICT) sector. It was the dot-com era and anything and everything which had to do with the Internet was booming. Those were good times, and here

1

I was saying, 'Let us put investments into a mature brick-and-mortar business which, if it grows by 2% a year and a car company makes 4% net margin, is termed as a fine performance'.

My managing director needed some convincing, but seeing my passion and motivation, he allowed me to work on it as long as I completed my normal daily responsibilities. And that was the beginning of a remarkable journey. Today, the Automotive and Transport practice at Frost & Sullivan is the biggest of the 12 practices in Europe as well as the most profitable one (and bigger than the ICT practice). To be honest, what my team achieved was not difficult. When we established the business, we made it our mission to focus on the future. Our mission statement was 'we will focus on anything that in cars is a cutting-edge trend, innovative technology or an inventive solution'.

So every time I went to see a car company in Europe or Asia, I told them something new, something they did not know. Most of the times it worked, but at times they thought I was a maverick. In 2008, when I told a world's leading automotive company that they are not in business of making cars but in the industry of personal mobility, and that since car sharing will be an important personal mobility business model of the future, they needed to look at it seriously, I was almost thrown out of the gates. Three years later, the same car company now runs a car sharing business (with our help).

The highlight of my career came in July 2009 when I went for the first time to see the Detroit Big 3 (Ford, GM and Chrysler) in their headquarters and walked away with three six-digit contracts in hand after three meetings of an hour each, during which I presented to them on the future of mobility. Finally, these bankrupt car companies had realised they needed to learn and innovate to survive, and they were willing to spend despite being broke. Here in Detroit the idea of new Mega Trends was born.

The success in Detroit, in the middle of the automotive industry's worst recession, got noticed by both my chairman, David Frigstad, and my immediate boss, Aroop Zutshi, and I presented them with an idea for us to develop a study which looks at the trends that impact, globally, the 12 industries in which we operate. I proposed the idea that it is not the trends that are important but the macro to micro implications of those trends, as applied to diverse industries and sectors, which will be the highlight of our work.

Déjà vu, I was offered another side job; this time, to develop the Mega Trends study. The success of that report first published in 2010 and the work we did in applying the study through strategy workshops with

Fortune 1000 companies has led us to this book. In the last three years, I have worked with some of the world's most powerful companies in sectors ranging from luxury goods to high-cost capital equipment, and in services ranging from branding to outsourcing operations. The same ten trends that you will read applied to all of them, and they developed some serious, new, uncontested marketspace opportunities as a result.

The unique feature of this book, compared to other predictive and future-watch books, lies in its ability to not only identify and evaluate emerging Mega Trends, but to also translate those opportunities to everyday business and personal life. In other words, my work is not just about throwing out predictions for the future, but also showing how those predictions present immediate opportunities and threats in the here and now. As a reader you will be able to paint a picture of how you, as well as your work and personal lives, will be changed in the years to come. This book highlights opportunities for readers to immediately take advantage of – or protect themselves from – these changes.

Please note there is a similar flow and structure to each chapter. Each chapter introduces an important new Mega Trend: defines it, breaks it into sub-trends and their secondary effects, offers evidence for its imminence, provides early examples and predicts its 'macro to micro' impact. All of this is designed to take you, as the reader, not only through the underlying dynamic of this trend, but also shows, based upon the earliest signals, how it is likely to play out over the next decade. The last chapter of the book will help you learn the 'macro to micro' methodology of estimating and evaluating the opportunities, and applying it yourself.

New Mega Trends is not a spiritual or a theoretical book. It is a practical book that is built on the time frame of up to 2020, and it works backwards to define the micro opportunities in diverse industries in the short, medium and long term. The chapters and trends in the book are in random order.

NEW MEGA TRENDS: THE DEFINITION

Identifying and defining a Mega trend is one of the most controversial parts of the entire process, but also one of the most important. Without an accurate definition, we run the risk of over- or under-defining our starting point, which automatically puts us in the wrong position to launch. My colleague Richard Sear likens this to the grip on a golf club, a reference to the importance of placing your hands on the golf club in the most neutral position so that you are giving yourself the greatest chance to make the best swing possible. The grip is key, before you ever make your first graceful swing.

We at Frost & Sullivan defined Mega Trends as global, sustained and macroeconomic forces of development that impact business, economy, society, cultures and personal lives, thereby defining our future world and its increasing pace of change.

Let us break this definition down a little so that you understand why we define Mega Trends in this manner.

> **Mega Trends are global:** The trends that I will cover in this book are global. The point, however, to note is that, although these trends are global, they hold different meanings for different markets, industries and geographical regions; and, yes, even for different communities and individuals. Example: Urbanisation is a global phenomenon. However, urbanisation happens differently across different regions based on population levels, GDP growth and even topography, bringing in different and new implications for businesses, firms, individuals and day-to-day activities.
>
> **Mega Trends are sustained macroeconomic forces of development:** Not every fad is a trend and not every trend is Mega. For a trend to be classified as a Mega Trend, it needs to have a major impact on global economies and needs to be sustained. This begs the question 'is it certain?' because we cannot measure sustainability without understanding if this trend will even occur. The answer is yes, a Mega Trend is a certainty – it will happen. The issue then becomes to what degree and on which timeline this will impact us. For a trend to be considered sustainable, it must have staying power and viability for a broader market.
>
> **Mega Trends are transformational:** Mega Trends define the very labyrinth of our business, markets, industries and even our personal lives. It will alter the way we view certain aspects of our personal and professional lives, and therefore will transform the way we go about our daily activities and even connect with our peers in the future.

WHY ARE THE NEW MEGA TRENDS IMPORTANT?

Let us review some of the trends of the last decade:

- China as an emerging super power
- Internet retail and e-commerce

- Social networking
- Green and sustainability

In hindsight, it would seem obvious that most of these identified trends were quite certain to come to fruition. If we look at the pace of change taking place today, even over the last five years, it is remarkable to think how we, in our personal and professional lives, have changed so dramatically from ten years ago. Organisations are still reacting to China's growth, companies are still trying to enact successful e-commerce strategies and the publishing world is frantically attempting to morph itself into a new business model to survive digital pressures. Look at companies that have created leadership positions by being early adopters of trends. Siemens' infrastructure and city business model is one of the strongest we have seen. Facebook's emergence to take advantage of social trends, IBM's business transformation into a solution provider and Amazon's powerful e-commerce and now hardware strategy have all led to positions of dominance, based on early identification and adoption.

The important questions to ask include: are you reactive or proactive? Do you lead or follow? How will you define your future so that you do not become the negative statistic, but lead the charge?

This book sets the stage for visionary thinking by identifying the most important global Mega Trends, potential scenarios of specific trends in 2020 and the implications of these Mega Trends in transforming businesses, markets and our personal lives.

I hope you enjoy reading it as much as I enjoyed working on it.

2

SMART IS THE NEW GREEN

I predict that this decade the failure of green technology to show a manageable and predictable Return on Investment will lead to a shift towards intelligent products, services and even cities that 'behave' green by adapting and changing to the environment around them. The megatrend of the last decade – Green products – will be replaced in this decade by Smart products and services.

Being 'Green' to individuals normally means 'Switch your light off when you leave the room', 'Reduce your carbon footprint by driving or flying less', 'Pay $14 for an energy-saving bulb which normally would cost you a dollar' or 'Invest in expensive solar heating panels and forget the returns; it will only help your conscience'.

Comparatively, 'Smart' is all about improving efficiency and not changing personal habits. It is also about convenience and savings. Unlike Green products which have no defined payback period and were a dilemma for boardrooms and governments to justify investment, these Smart products have a real business case, can typically provide energy and efficiency savings of up to 30% and boast a typical two- to four-year return on investment.

Examples of the Smart concept already include Smart cities, Intelligent buildings, Smart homes, Smart Energy, Smart cloud computing, Smart citizens, Smart governance, Smart businesses, Smart cars, Smart materials – the list is long.

DEFINING SMART

There are several definitions of 'Smart' floating around, and the definition has evolved over time from a device connected to the Internet to a product which has an embedded intelligence in the form of a microprocessor. Most current definitions relate Smart products to a Smartphone (like the iPhone) which is based on the premise that these products have information and communication technology embedded in them. This is true in most cases and is the direction where most Smart products are heading. But it is not entirely true.

In general terms, one can say that there are three levels of Smart products:

- Level 1: Products which have a basic sensing mechanism and a simple means of communicating any changes in its environment. For example, Smart bandages feature sensors embedded in the mesh of standard dressings that can warn patients and doctors if the wound develops an infection (and possibly in the future also specify which bacteria is causing it).
- Level 2: Products which have sensing ability and a means of data communication as well as the ability to take corrective actions through embedded software. A simple example of a Level 2 product is the Smart lighting controller which, when it senses that there are no occupants in the room, can turn off the lights and, similarly, when one walks into the room, can automatically switch them on. It can also be configured to a preset dim rate, which can save electricity and indirectly extend a $14 'green' bulb's life.
- Level 3: Products which build upon the Level 2 definition by having increased intelligence, a two-way flow of communication, being part of a connected Internet-based network and having advanced capabilities of data collection, processing, reporting and intelligence built into them to sense and take corrective action. For example, a Level 3 Smart lighting control can do all the functionalities mentioned previously but also regulate the intensity of the light in the room based on the natural light levels and keep it constant throughout the day and night. It can also be remotely regulated through the use of a Smartphone, a function which can be useful should you have by any chance forgotten to switch on the security lights at home while on a holiday.

For the purposes of this book, we can agree with the definition that a Smart product is characterised by an intelligent sensing technology that is increasingly being integrated with Internet technologies, thereby allowing the product to react and communicate to the changing environment around it, thereby optimising operations and improving efficiency.

Being 'Smart' in future will mean moving away from closed island solutions and solo Smart products towards cross-linked intelligent solutions. This would mean not just a Smart device but a Smart home, Smart building and also Smart cities. The vision of companies like Siemens and IBM is to use this concept to connect disparate sources to tell you, for example, when and where the next traffic jam will be before you get to it. It makes sense, as it is too late if you are already in one.

Chart 2.1 shows examples of smart products, technologies and concepts.

SMART CONNECTED HOME

Today's concept of a 'Smart home' or a 'connected home' is a progression from what was defined over the last decade as an 'automated home'.

In 2000, Frost & Sullivan did a report on Home Automation. It was a very popular report with significant interest from companies, and had predicted considerable growth in that market. Unfortunately, ten years later, that market has not lived up to its potential.[1] The main reasons for failure were that the technology of the past was not actually smart and hence the automated home was in reality just a load of remote-controlled functions like TV, stereo, blinds/shutters, lights, etc. It turned out that people were not really impressed enough to pay lots of money for what was nothing more than 'cool gadgets' in the house. Home automation therefore stayed as purely a luxury market.

More recently three things have happened which will ensure a repeat failure does not happen: Smart technology means that the home can actually be 'managed' by technology (rather than just controlled); secondly, the issue of energy efficiency has became really important, so there is an additional reason to automate the home; and thirdly, Smartphones and tablet computers provide a perfect platform for consumers to manage their homes through a single source.

The Smart home of the future that has so often been featured in movies and TV serials is almost upon us. It can provide the following services which can be broadly categorised under home concierge, home energy and waste management:

• Virtual butler: Controls the ambiance in the house like mood lighting and scene setting for a hot date, and also scent, air purification, etc.

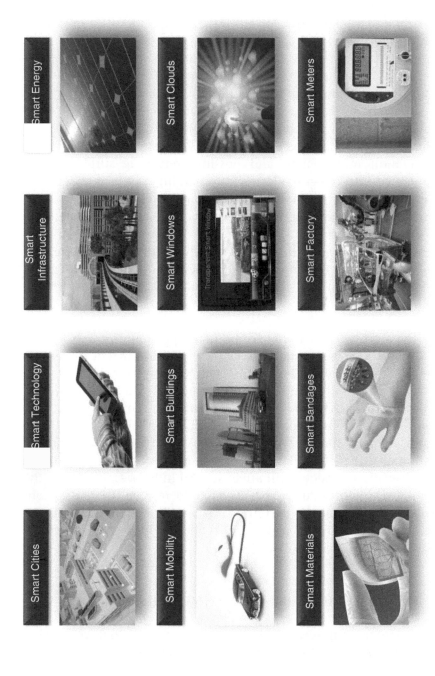

Chart 2.1 **'Smart' is the new green: Examples of Smart products and technologies**

Photo credits: Dreamstime and Connected Digital World.

Source: Frost & Sullivan.

- Virtual caretaker: Can take care of the elderly in the house and also monitor children or dogs remotely.
- Personalised living: Provides an unprecedented level of personalisation tailored to unique habits – for example, providing climate control in each room of the house to suit personal tastes. No more teenagers complaining their room is too cold or too hot.
- Effortless replenishment: For example, in a Smart bathroom and kitchen, the fridge can make its own shopping list.
- Integrated media and entertainment solutions.
- Home energy management – wireless connected home, power generation management and possibly returning surplus power generated into the grid, electric car charging, power management for peak and off-peak hours through Smart meters.
- Virtual waste and energy management: For example, water and energy conservation.
- Remote management through Smart devices like Smartphones.
- Information and education through feedback such as your energy consumption patterns and energy audits using clever software and reporting.

All the aforesaid functions will be made possible through a black box called the Smart home hub, similar to your current digital TV set-top box, also called the Home Area Network (HAN). A HAN is essentially where all the devices and appliances in a home can communicate with each other and can be controlled centrally.

Future Smart homes will also have Smart windows which will go beyond a simple framed structure of glass and will have advanced functionality that will allow smart management of light, heat and air. These Smart windows will affect several industries, including the window treatment industry, where it could replace the use of conventional shades, blinds, curtains and awning systems. It will also have an impact on HVAC players, with Smart windows becoming an integral part of a climate control system.

THE SMART MEDICAL HOME OF THE FUTURE

Another interesting scenario to ponder over is the nature of what the medical home of tomorrow will look like. Patients currently in their late 50s to 60s are a different generation than their parents and their expectations of quality of life and independence are vastly different. Patients in the past were more reconciled to accept the challenges and limitations that go along with aging; their concept of healthcare services were strictly limited to those covered by their government-sponsored or private insurance or extended family. Comparatively, baby boomers born in the 1950s have different expectations for their retirement: they are more inclined to go under the knife and consider cosmetic procedures and surgeries, and they are more willing to dip into their personal expenses to pay for treatments not covered by insurance or government. Accordingly, when it comes to their homes, they will go in search of medical solutions that afford them greater independence and enhancement of their daily quality of life.

Similar to companies that offer services to set up one's entertainment room with the latest gadgets and advances in home media, we could see the rise of medical home experts that customise one's home with the latest home health technologies ideally suited for that individual. Whether one suffers from diabetes, emphysema, arthritis, congestive heart failure or any other condition, there are assistive tools that could aid the aged in their daily lives and ensure they keep up with their daily monitoring and treatment regimen activities.

A room in one's house could be devoted to and equipped with various home tests that might range from basic biometric monitoring to more advanced diagnostic tests. Basic biometrics might involve heart rate, blood pressure, weight and other commonly tracked health metrics. For diabetes patients, it would include their testing strips and readers. More advanced diagnostic tools might involve urine or blood analysis to identify developing issues.

That information could potentially feed into an online system where a caregiver could track the patient's disease state daily, ensure patients' compliance with their treatment regimen and even on occasion provide web-based consultation regarding any questions or concerns.

Simple appliances could give way to a new range of potential for luxury Smart technologies. We could see a time in the not-so-distant future where a Smart toilet could, on programmed intervals, collect urine samples for analysis; Smart fridges could help patients maintain dietary schedules; or even at-home automated pill dispensers could help prevent medication errors.

Emergency alert systems were some of the first home health monitoring services to be introduced nearly 20 years ago. A future system could not only alert emergency responders of an acute event requiring attention, but potentially forward along patient information as well so that responders or hospital personnel could perform prep work prior to the patient's arrival.

Growing old in the future might therefore not be as painful as it seems, as long we have our own personal care homes.

SMART CARS

Cars are no exception to the Smart phenomenon. If five years ago the focus in the global automotive market was on being green and fuel efficient, now it has become entwined with a vision of being smart. The future of driving will be less of shifting from a gas guzzler to driving hybrid or smaller cars, but more about driving astutely and using functionalities like gear shift indicators, the ability to switch the vehicle into economic driving mode and the ability to recognise driving conditions to alter driving behaviour like intelligent speed adaption systems. The premise behind this is that drivers who do not engage in aggressive acceleration/deceleration and drive around the bend four times to find a parking space can save up to 25% off their fuel bill.

Typically a Smart car has three core areas of focus – safety, dynamic information and innovative user interfaces. A Smart car is a vehicle that can interact with the outside environment (road and traffic infrastructure and sense conditions), process it with a brain of its own and sound alerts, warnings and real-time information to the user in a distraction-free user interface to enhance and enrich the driving experience.

Research suggests that vehicle safety systems, which are typically called advanced driver assistance systems in the automotive world, have a typical reaction time of about 600 milliseconds from the time an object or obstacle is detected and the corresponding function of the safety system kicking in: for example, automatic braking. This is one aspect of the Smart car vision in which automakers want to reduce the reaction time of vehicle safety systems, and for that they are resorting to various measures. Some of these measures include installing stereoscopic cameras around the vehicle in addition to the existing sensors, which can dramatically increase the reaction time. An example of this is what is called 6D-Vision in a Mercedes Benz, where the automaker plans in the future to introduce several stereoscopic cameras that can reduce the reaction time to less than 200 milliseconds, thereby aiding in high-efficiency accident prevention.

Another area of research for Smart cars is the ability for cars to speak to roadside infrastructure and each other to communicate roadside traffic and incident information to prevent accidents and ease traffic congestion. In the industry this is referred to as vehicle to vehicle (V2V) and vehicle to infrastructure (V2I) communication, which uses a particular wireless technology called DSRC 5.8 GHz (dedicated short-range communications). BMW already claims that its brand of cars can talk to each other and pass vital information – such as to slow down if there is an accident ahead – using a concept called floating car data (FCD). In the future, legislation could even enforce the use of FCD to share vital data between a Mercedes, a BMW and a Ford. Future will also see vehicle to home (V2H) communication systems linking cars to home area networks.

An interesting function of a Smart car is to provide dynamic information to the user by utilising a connection to the Internet from the car through a super-fast computer to process this information. Car manufacturers are resorting to either using the driver's mobile plan or embedding a dedicated data plan inside the car to achieve connection to the Internet which can provide the drivers with several useful information pieces such as real-time traffic, dynamic point-of-interest information like parking-space availability and booking. By end of this decade, most car manufacturers will take this concept to a cloud-based solution where information of any type can be retrieved at any time and processed accordingly. One example of this approach is Toyota who has partnered with Microsoft to use the Microsoft Azure cloud platform to create a new information platform which links Toyota to its customers and dealers in real time. Ford is also partnering with Google to use its prediction API cloud to do pattern analysis and aid drivers in taking best routes that are derived after careful historical analysis and future predictions. Clearly the car is turning into a dynamic information zone, but this information needs to be provided in a useful manner to drivers to avoid any backlash.

Your car's display in the future will also be the size of an iPad, about 8 inches long, which will be aided by several technologies such as touch screens and voice interfaces that further enhance the experience and avoid any distractive situations. Technologies such as MirrorLink from Nokia, which acts as a remote terminal replicating the smartphone inside the car are also examples that are accelerating these developments.

Apple came up with a perfect innovation in the iPhone 4S – SIRI – which supports natural voice recognition and analysis. Several carmakers, for instance Cadillac, will bring up a very similar technology in 2013 models on a system called Cadillac User Experience

(CUE) which supports semantic natural voice recognition. This means consumers no longer have to speak commands but can speak natural statements and phrases and complete their tasks and applications. This is one example of the futuristic vision car companies have to ensure the information is presented to the user in a very safe, smart manner.

But driving the car will be a whole new experience once we have augmented reality embedded into the vehicle, which will turn any visible environment into an interactive information and safety space. Examples of this today are demonstrated by BMW and Audi, which are using a particular technology called contact analogue displays to turn the windscreen into a safety zone showing vehicles ahead on the road and alerting drivers to possible collision and safe zones. The same technology can also be used to show points of interests and landmarks when the vehicle is not in motion on the windscreen itself, thereby converting it into a fun zone.

While there are so many innovative efforts by automakers to turn the car into a smart James Bond 007-type assistant, they are also fighting hard to find the right balance between what is ideal for driving conditions and what should be limited to idle mode. Also increasing the importance of this fight are issues relating to driver distraction, which further prompts them to invest in the right mix of smart technologies.

Chances are that, in 2020, cars will be a hub of dynamic information and fun features.

SMART ENERGY

Only 30% of the residents of the African continent today have access to electricity. This will reverse and Africa will cease to be the blackout continent, with about 70% having access to electricity by end of this decade. Similarly, in India, a country with about the same population as the African continent, 40% of Indians still live in homes without electricity. China has already become the world's largest consumer of electricity. In all developing regions of the world, the focus is now shifting to generating more power to meet the needs of a population that is demanding refrigerators, washing machines and televisions as standard household items. Ironically, the situation in Europe and North America is different. Power-hungry industries are in decline and energy efficiency is becoming more important.

A change in the mindset in how electricity is generated and transmitted is long overdue. Many of the transmission and distribution networks in North America and Europe date back to almost 100 years. Power grids were built to carry electricity from remote locations to cities. There was little concern about the potential loss of electricity in the process, and the idea of generating electricity on a smaller scale closer to population centres (distributed generation) or of individual households generating electricity (micro-generation) was largely unheard of. This has to change. The wastage of electricity in transmission costs utility companies (and, indirectly, consumers) billions, and the value of these losses has increased as electricity prices have risen. It also means emissions are generated for electricity that is never even used! Renewable energy and localised electricity production has the potential to reduce emissions and cut bills if the potential for both can be realised. To do this effectively across an entire electricity system, the best solution is to create a Smart grid.[2]

High consumption levels across the globe mean higher emissions, unless action is taken to increase the share of electricity generated from low or non-emission fuel sources, such as wind and solar energy. Action also needs to be taken to generate, transmit and distribute electricity more efficiently. Finally, we as individuals need to consume electricity more efficiently, whether through improving our buildings or the household appliances we buy. Smart energy is the key thread that makes many of the goals outlined earlier achievable.

Smart meters: Making home chores intelligent

There is good news and bad news for our home energy bill. The bad news is that days of cheap energy at home are gone; therefore, the cost of energy will continue to rise and so will our bills. The good news is that, thanks to Smart meters already being rolled out in major parts of the world, we can monitor our usage better and lower our bills if we are as intelligent as the meter itself.

All those days of husbands shouting at their wives and children to switch the lights off are about to become part of history. Smart meters will change all this. By incorporating energy monitoring technologies, Smart meters will enable us to track the electricity intensity of a range of household appliances. This is something that is currently unknown by virtually everyone. How much does it cost to boil water in a kettle? Or to power a washing machine for one cycle? Or watch football on the 55-inch plasma screen? As an electrical engineer, I would have had no idea without looking it up online. Knowing the cost of consumption will empower consumers to potentially limit any avoidable usage of high-energy-cost appliances and should make the energy efficiency of domestic appliances a much more significant issue, with manufacturers being pushed to make improvements or risk their inefficient products not being bought by consumers anymore. Utilities will vary their pricing and reward individuals for using electricity at off-peak hours with lower costs. Therefore, the cost of washing a basket of clothes between 11 p.m. and 4 a.m. might be one-fourth of what it will cost during peak hours (although it may upset your neighbour in the flat below, especially if you live in Switzerland where the authorities strictly forbid any noise-making activity in flats). As an individual, I am unlikely to think about it when I watch my football or cricket, but it may lead me to switch on my dishwasher or tumble dryer at an off-peak hour (with all due respect to my neighbours).

Two-way communication between utility and consumer, the so-called Advanced Meter Infrastructure, will also enable consumers who are generating electricity through distributed generation (such as micro wind turbines or solar panels on roofs) to sell the electricity back to the grid.

These are just some of the benefits to us as consumers. There are huge benefits for utility companies. By curbing usage, utilities are engaging in something called demand response. Demand response is a concept whereby you encourage a course of action through incentives – in this case, lower prices. The benefit for utility companies is that if they can reduce demand at peak hours by even a relatively small amount – say 5% to 10% – it can lead to a disproportionately greater reduction in a number of power plants, particularly smaller plants that are only used in times of high demand. Power plants that are used to meet peak demand are often energy intensive, requiring large amounts of fuel because they have to become operational very quickly. Many countries use oil, which has very high carbon dioxide and other emissions, as a fuel. Reduced peak demand should see some of these peak power plants closed.

The global meter rollout is already underway. A number of US states and utility companies are already pushing ahead with roll-out plans, and in Europe, Italy and Sweden virtually every household already has a meter. The European Union (EU) has legislated to ensure that by 2022 every household in the EU will have to have a Smart meter.[3] Japan,

South Korea, Singapore and Australia are also rolling out investment programmes. However, the technology is not just limited to developed economies;[4] Smart metering is expected to be implemented in large parts of Latin America, Asia and the Middle East. As per Jonathan Robinson, senior consultant in the Energy Practice at Frost & Sullivan, 'The global Smart meter market is forecast to be worth $10 billion in 2012, up from just $2.5 billion in 2009. This creates massive opportunities in a market that had traditionally been low growth and conservative. Toshiba's acquisition of Landis+Gyr is evidence of how the big global energy conglomerates are attacking this market.' The forecast for 2020 is for the market to have doubled to $20 billion, providing huge opportunities for a street-smart Smart metering company.

Smart meters also mean that the sight of the meter reader coming to the neighbourhood and getting chased by the dog will be a distant memory. This means massive cost saving for utility companies in sending people out, and far fewer people are needed to handle complaints about dodgy meter readings.

Smart grid

Essentially the Smart grid is about making the 100-year-old electrical grid more automated and more intelligent – bringing it into the modern age. There are some complicated definitions of Smart grid out there; but in layman's terms, it is basically a grid that uses digital technology to enable two-way communication between the consumer and supplier, and deliver efficient, economic and secure electricity. And most importantly, Smart girds also allow integration of diverse power-generation sources and for decentralised power generation. There are several major advantages that the Smart grid has over a conventional grid.

A key benefit of creating an intelligent grid is that it will be easier to balance production and consumption of electricity by using storage supply opportunities such as electric vehicles and domestic refrigerators and freezers. With increasing amounts of generation coming from renewable sources (both residential and utility), balancing power becomes more complicated. As electricity is very hard to store (research is ongoing in this field, but it will take time), having the ability to control consumption is important. In the case of a refrigerator or freezer, new intelligent appliances will be able to have their operations controlled remotely by a utility company. Refrigerators and freezers operate on a cycle of intensity in consuming power; basically, they are on for 45 minutes to push the temperature down, and then off for 45 minutes as the temperature slowly rises to the maximum level allowed. This could be controlled to balance out peaks in demand over a shorter period. By relying on electric cars and refrigerators to help with power balancing, it means we would need fewer expensive-to-maintain and carbon-intensive power plants.

A key benefit of the Smart grid is that it enables renewables to be better integrated into the energy system and increases the possibility that renewables could become one of the major power sources in many countries. Germany, for example, has already invested substantially in renewable energy; but for nuclear to be phased out without reliance on high carbon fuels, such as coal, massive funds need to be invested in the power grid. The Smart grid enables two-way transmission of power, which will enable homeowners to sell electricity back to the grid on a much larger scale than is currently possible. It will also mean that electricity generated by wind and solar power plants located in remote locations (particularly wind, which can be offshore) can be fed into the electricity network more efficiently and effectively, minimising electricity wastage.[5]

Another key benefit of Smart grids is the instantaneous correction of faults and improved reliability of the grid. In the current grid, a fault is often only known when the consumer reports it. The utility must then find the fault, which can be labour intensive and time consuming. While the search to find and remedy the problem is on, the consumer is without power. With a Smart grid, the use of sensors and communication technologies mean that the fault can be located immediately and potentially be resolved remotely. The sensors also enable preventive maintenance so that a weakness can be identified before it causes a fault to occur. This saves disruption and cost later on. Estimates from a study[6] by K. LaCommare and J. Eto show that the annual cost of power interruptions in the United States totals $80–100 billion.

Smart city

In an analysis that we did in the Visionary Innovation research group at Frost & Sullivan, we discovered that Smart cities are widely discussed these days and that many cities label themselves 'Smart', but – if one went by the true definition – there aren't really any Smart cities today.

So, to start, we created a definition (Chart 2.2) and analysed policies and initiatives of major cities globally. Our analysis found that there is potential for about 26 cities globally to be Smart by 2020–5. About half of the Smart cities will originate from the Western economies; but, interestingly, some Smart projects (not complete cities) will be built from the ground up like Tianjin Eco-city and Masdar near Abu Dhabi.

Chart 2.2 gives the key parameters that will define a Smart city in 2020.

It is important to also differentiate and distinguish between eco, green or sustainable cities. Most of these eco cities will implement certain Smart policies, and are important cities for businesses to target, but they are not necessarily 'Smart' as per Frost & Sullivan's definition. Interestingly, we were able to count around 100 cities globally which will be sustainable or eco cities by 2020, and what is fascinating is that about 34 of these will be from developing regions like India and China and most of these cities will be built from scratch.

A city which will be truly Smart and also the first carbon-neutral capital of the world by 2025 is Copenhagen, which is profiled as a case study in Chapter 4, 'Innovating to Zero'.

Amsterdam gives a good glimpse of a major city today which is embracing Smart principles – www.amsterdamsmartcity.nl. The project, which was initially planned to develop a Smart electrical grid within 18 months, turned into an Amsterdam Smart City programme. The project has been set up as a unique collaborative programme with citizens, businesses and government bodies. The project as of today has 71 partners and is using 36 Smart technologies with 16 sub-projects. The city plans to roll out an extensive infrastructure of Smart products which includes high-speed broadband, Smart meters and grid, intelligent green buildings and charging stations for personal transport. The city expects these smarter technologies to achieve a 40% reduction of CO_2 emissions from 1990 levels.[7]

What the Europeans can do, the Chinese can do even better. A trip to Sino-Singapore Tianjin Eco-city[8] will put even the Swiss to shame with its meticulous planning and execution. The Tianjin Eco-city is a 50-50 joint venture, a brownfield, ground-up project between the Chinese and Singapore government with private-sector investment shared between two consortiums. It is located in the Tianjin Binhai New Area, about 45 km away from Tianjin City Centre. It is comparatively a small project enclosed within a 30 sq. km area, about half the

Smart Energy

- A 50% roll-out of Smart meters across cities, Smart grids with over 15% of cities' energy generated from renewable sources. At least 50% decrease in overall energy consumption per capita

Smart Mobility

- Cities' ability to provide support to low-emission vehicles, infrastructure for advanced mobility solutions like electric and fuel cell vehicles,
- Policies to encourage new mobility business models like bike and car sharing.
- Implementation of intermodal and integrated mobility solutions, including sharing of mobility-related data between all forms of public and private transport solutions

Smart Technology

- Roll-out of 4G in city, high-speed broadband, development of Wi-Fi cities and adoption of smart and intelligent technologies and policies (like Smart home solutions), and M2M communication

Smart Health care

- Implementation of policies that encourage health, wellness and well-being for its citizens, use of technology like mHealth and eHealth. Behavioural change to health monitoring and diagnostics as opposed to treatment

Smart Buildings

- Policies to encourage green and intelligent buildings with BIPV, and 10% of the buildings to be carbon-neutral buildings by 2020. Improved energy conservation and intelligent waste management

Smart Infrastructure

- Multi-modal transport hubs for freight and personal mobility, 100% waste recycling, integrating green concepts into urban environment, interconnected and intelligence built into all forms of city infrastructure

Smart Governance

- Government policies that promote and incentivise businesses and citizens to adopt green and smart concepts, including government implementing strongly in public sector Smart policies mentioned here like carbon-neutral buildings

Smart Citizen

- Interest of citizens to embrace smart and green solutions as seen in Amsterdam and Copenhagen where majority of citizens cycle to work

Chart 2.2 **Key parameters that will define a Smart city in 2020**

Source: Frost & Sullivan.

20

size of Manhattan. It expects to host about 350,000 residents by 2020 with the first batch of about 25,000 households moving in by the end of 2012. The city plans to develop green mobility, work and living solutions as a demonstration project for the rest of China to follow. It plans to drive the development and utilisation of non-traditional water and energy resources like solar panels, waste heat recovery and rainwater harvesting. In line with the changing Chinese culture, which is increasingly mixing tradition with the materialistic world, the city developers are modelling the city to be in harmony with its environment, society and, importantly, the economy.

SMART FACTORIES: FACTORIES OF THE FUTURE

When it comes to production and factories, Toyota is the ultimate company. Its philosophy, called 'the Toyota way', which is strongly embedded in its Toyota Production System, has been talked about and benchmarked across the globe. However, in 2009, as a result of the recession, even Toyota changed its production philosophy from 'kaizen' (means continuous improvement in Japanese) to 'kakushin', which means radical.

So here is a company which, for over 50 years, had been preaching kaizen and 'jidoka' (Japanese word for automation) and pursuing a goal of High Quality, large volumes, deciding that it actually needs a radical change, a kakushin, to stay ahead of its competitors. So when in 2009, its new Takoka plant in Japan became operational, the company actually cut production from a capacity of 660,000 cars to 500,000 in this particular plant. It increased the plant's flexibility by being able to build eight high-volume models instead of the three on the original assembly line that had been in place prior to the plant's refurbishment. It halved the lead time to add new models on the assembly line and reduced the assembly lines from three to two, including reducing the length of these two assembly lines to half of what they were originally.

Toyota made some drastic changes to the new plant, such as adding a new welding system that slashes the cost of jigs and other tooling. The new tools that hold steel in place to be welded into the shape of a car do so from the inside, rather than from the outside. It developed stamping presses that use servo motors rather than hydraulics, combined with high-speed delivery robots, which led to a reduction in energy used and, therefore, a lower carbon footprint. It developed

21

a 'set parts system' that delivers a basket of parts to each vehicle. The basket rides down the line with the car that gets the parts. Workers no longer have to rummage through numerous bins along the assembly line to find the right part. Sounds like common sense; but in a flexible manufacturing plant, this enables any car to be built as parts come delivered with the car, not spread along the production line. Toyota ditched huge expensive machinery in favour of smaller, more nimble equipment which resulted in less energy use and expense with the added advantage of faster processes. The new stamping machine uses high-speed conveyor robots that work much faster than older plant robots, thereby drastically increasing productivity. The new paintwork station, by using robotic technology, reduced painting time by 40% by applying three paint layers (primer, colour base and clear colour) one after the other and allowing them to dry at the same time. The list of innovations was immense. As a result, Toyota achieved a Smart plant, that was flexible and agile in reacting to changing market conditions, reducing errors and defects by 50%, as well as halving CO_2 output and lowering the energy required to produce vehicles by 20%.

By doing so, Toyota laid the foundation of the factory of the future: a Smart factory. Since then, the concept of the Smart factory has been taken to the next level. The future factory will cease to be a mere place of work; it will transform into a place for a worker to engage, collaborate and achieve targets efficiently and effectively.

To begin with, the worker in the factory of the future will not require access cards. With the help of RFID technology, coveralls and factory wear will be embedded with microchips that can store access details and authorise entry and exit from restricted zones automatically. This inbuilt microchip will also be supported with sensing technology that determines working conditions continuously, alerting the worker in case of an accident like a gas leak in a process plant.

The worker in the factory of the future will also be entering an age of augmented reality where control rooms don't house workstations anymore. Augmented reality systems will replace conventional workstations, and operating personnel inside control rooms will have an immersive 3D experience of suggestive simulation scenarios that are likely to emerge in case of an emergency. This will enable predictive action, reducing the probability of downtime considerably.

The next-generation factory worker will be aided with smart tabs that can help him track production output, perform maintenance operation and monitor process issues on the move. In addition, field assets in future factories will transform from static devices into dynamic systems with embedded intelligence that can interact with other devices, pre-empt accidents and perform corrective action in case of hardware defects. The advent of such Smart devices will change the colour and texture of factories, bringing in a wave of dynamism that was hitherto unknown to the factory floor. In essence, field devices in the factories of the future will transform into vibrant physical entities that can interact with a worker as if the devices were a fellow colleague.

As much as it benefits the common worker, the future factory will benefit higher management as well. Through an integrated approach, the factory of the future will become part of a broader framework called the enterprise ecosystem. In this envisioned ecosystem, the factory floor will be seamlessly interlinked with engineering design and boardroom operations, providing a platform for increasing transparency and efficiency throughout the enterprise.

Smart factories will also capitalise on dedicated cloud servers that reduce operating expenditure significantly. The emergence and adoption of cloud computing will enable factory workers access-relevant strategic data from the Internet to execute real-time decisions that will enhance operational efficiency. Cloud computing will gradually become the major means of data storage, information access and intelligence building in future Smart factories.

With the advent of robotics, the manpower in future factories will be minimal and restricted to selective disciplines, and a worker's role will be more intelligent and less task-driven. Smart robots will complement workers in plant operations and be programmed with decisive powers to take remedial action in case of an emergency, which could also be a source of dispute and possible strikes as it could lead to unions complaining against robots 'taking over my job'.

The future factory, smart as it may sound, is also going to become very competitive for current suppliers. The future Smart factory will see the entry and entrenchment of new players like commercial IT vendors marking their presence in different spheres of factory activity both through software and hardware. This future landscape will blur the lines of separation between industrial systems and commercial IT players and create a homogeneous environment where IT vendors and industrial vendors come together to offer advanced products at competitive prices. This is good news for the manufacturing sector, which always wanted cheap and efficient factories.

The pursuit of perfection is an inherent aspect of creation. In fact, the need to pursue perfection is fundamental for survival and the industrial world is no exception. In this path towards perfection, the future factory is poised to imbibe the Smart concept as a three-pronged strategy that includes technology, commerce and competition. This comprehensive development will transform the factory of today into an advanced organism that functions as a single, unified entity of high efficiency and productivity.

MACRO TO MICRO

Smart products provide abundant commercial opportunities across a wide cross section of the industry and will alter the competitive landscape of existing industries.

The components and technology necessary to facilitate Smart products touch on a variety of industries. Key elements include:

1. Sensing and measurement instrumentation: This includes different types of sensors, power supplies and analysers, data acquisition, calibration and standards, bus analysers and industrial PC solutions.
2. Devices: These include all consumer electronics gadgets, from Smartphones to tablets to e-books to non-telecom devices such as digital cameras, Smart meters, display screens and personal healthcare gadgets.
3. Networks: This includes both core and transport networks. There is a wide choice of communications networks, from the mature mobile and fixed connectivity to WLAN and all-IP transport networks. There are also niche technologies such as WiMAX, satellite and powerline broadband networks.
4. M2M/Consumer Device Connectivity: Short-range technologies used, for example, in a HAN. These include technologies such as ZigBee and Wi-Fi, and could also include sensor networks.
5. Service and Application Enablement: Network enablers from an OSS/BSS (operational support systems/business support systems) perspective but also additional enablers such as those that allow interaction with different types of networks.
6. Industry-specific Value-added Services (VAS) and Enablement: Interfaces and enablers that will communicate with industry-specific networks, where protocols and application program interfaces (APIs) may differ.

7. Applications: Smart solutions that application developers create using the information obtained from the network and devices, leveraging status, location and predictive analytics to address an industry-specific, operational pain point.
8. Others like energy-storage devices, energy-management software, data analytics, consultants, turnkey solution providers, to name a few.

Convergence of Mega Trends leads to convergence of competition

One thing that I have learnt from the macro to micro analysis methodology is that convergence of these trends leads to convergence of competition. And it applies very strongly to the Smart industry structure.

One of the most competitive and major market growth sectors within the energy sector is the Smart grid industry. Frost & Sullivan forecasts that the global Smart grid market will be worth $100 billion by 2015 and will double to approximately $200 billion a year by 2020. As the market doubles, so will the competition and the rivalry, especially from new entrants.

With the advent of Smart buildings we are now witnessing a repositioning of automation and building management companies like Schneider, Johnson Controls and Honeywell into rebranding themselves within the Smart space through acquisitions. Schneider labels itself an energy specialist today, compared to its position of a tier 2 supplier ten years back, mainly in selling low- and medium-voltage equipment. Similarly, Honeywell, which has had a background mainly in building controls, now provides energy and utilities efficiency-improvement services. Similarly, within the energy industry structure, the transmissions and distribution companies like Siemens, GE and ABB are facing new challenges as a result of the grids going intelligent.

When, in 2010, the Singapore's Energy Market authority released a tender for companies to bid for the Smart grid pilot project, it was fiercely bid by many companies. Siemens thought it was in a good position to win this contract given its transmissions and distribution background. To its shock, the project was won by Accenture and ST Electronics. As primary contractor, Accenture was asked to project manage a cross-functional team, provide system integration services, implement a meter data management system and support the change management process.

This came as a shock to Siemens, and to all traditional players in this industry. Since then they have all been on an aggressive shopping spree making acquisitions to bolster their software and IT capabilities. Swiss grid giant ABB spent about $1 billion to buy Ventyx in 2010, while Schneider Electric made a suite of software purchases, notably its $2 billion purchase of Telvent, a European Smart grid software provider, to develop capabilities in outage management systems, advanced distribution and asset management systems. Siemens, who has been fairly quiet for a period of time, at the end of 2011 bought its Smart grid software partner eMeter. Combined the big four in this industry – GE, Siemens, ABB and Schneider – have made about 25 acquisitions worth about $8–10 billion. A key aim here is to link buildings to grids by combining low-voltage and high-voltage business groups within their organisations, and add some intelligence through IT.

Is this the end of their shopping trip? No. This is only the start and is expected to accelerate. Siemens is sitting on an approximately $27 billion bank balance to spend on strategic assets. It is expected to make more strategic acquisitions, perhaps focusing on specific products where it has gaps in product portfolio or in regional markets where it can gain market share with utilities. For sure it will have to pay a lot more now to gain share at the expense of low single-digit profit margins in its Smart grid division.

But Accenture is not the only IT company positioning itself as a hero in this market. Other companies, such as IBM, SAP, HP and Oracle, are currently seen as the main project owners for Smart solutions deployment, especially when it comes to complex solutions like Smart cities.

CASE STUDY: SCHNEIDER ELECTRIC GOES SMART

A good example of a company that has rapidly evolved its strategy to focus on smart energy solutions is Schneider Electric, the €20 billion global diversified energy management company that is headquartered in Paris. Having been one of the first companies to see the potential of smart solutions in the field of energy management, the company has spent the last five years successfully positioning itself as a leader in the development and deployment of smart grid solutions across the energy chain. Schneider Electric has a long heritage in energy-related products and systems and, up to the middle of the last decade, was largely known as a supplier of automation, power distribution and management products. However, it is within its most recent history – with energy efficiency being linked with so many global Mega Trends – that the company has become a visionary innovator in the field of 'intelligent energy'.

The Schneider Electric approach is built on the convergence of digital intelligence with the products, technologies and expertise from across the company focused on applications in utilities, industry, buildings, datacentres and networks, as well as residential homes.

Designed around an open architecture to facilitate systems integration and interoperability, the company has expanded during a period of targeted, strategic acquisitions and with a historically strong product range to become a global specialist in energy management. Schneider Electric uses the slogan 'from Power Plant to Plug™' to define its comprehensive solutions package that covers the entire energy cycle from the point of power generation to the point of use. The results of this strategic transformation have clearly demonstrated that the company has made the right decisions.

Schneider Electric's revenues have continued to increase through a period of financial crisis, including 9.3% organic growth in 2010 at a time that many players were struggling. They believe that new market opportunities will ultimately create a category of technologies and services that deliver intelligent energy and this is already beginning to be realised.

Since the concepts of Smart grid and Smart energy became mainstream around five years ago, one of the key challenges has been to define the way the different elements of the infrastructure will be connected and managed to create the so-called energy Internet. On the premise that you can't manage what you can't measure, Schneider Electric has developed its own architectural approach to deliver actionable data to drive energy efficiency, security and improved business results. This approach is the foundation of the company's intelligent energy management offering and is entirely scalable, as well as being appropriate for both new build applications and retrofits in all markets.

Recognising the need for open communication protocols between devices and systems in the Smart grid, and the need for sophisticated yet user-friendly energy management software, Schneider Electric made its most significant 'smart' move to date in 2009 with the launch of its EcoStruxure architecture. This is the company's integrated system solution – a suite of hardware and integrated software programs that address the design and management of the energy systems. The EcoStruxure approach uses software to measure, control, aggregate and animate the energy data flowing from all components within the architecture, displayed through one dashboard. As an umbrella platform, it is designed to support the convergence of Schneider Electric's key domains of expertise: power management, process and machine management, IT-room management, building management and security management. In all of these areas, the company is able to offer complete systems integration by providing solutions from complex enterprise level systems down to individual hardware components.

In 2010, Schneider Electric made eight strategic acquisitions across the world with the express goal of expanding its range of energy efficiency solutions, broadening its Smart grid expertise and increasing footprint in emerging economies. These included Areva Distribution, which has annual sales of around €1.9 billion; Uniflair with sales of €80 million; the French energy monitoring software provider Vizelia (€4 million); and D5X (€4 million), a specialist in solutions to optimise commercial space utilisation.

More recently, in mid-2011, the company made perhaps it boldest step yet in committing itself to leadership in Smart energy management with the acquisition of the Spanish software firm Telvent for approximately €1.4 billion. This move would have been unthinkable in the traditional energy industry a mere five years earlier, but with Smart energy poised to boom, this will give Schneider Electric a massive boost in its solution capability for the Smart grid. The real synergies and benefits will not be proven for a couple of years yet, but the acquisition has immediately doubled Schneider Electric's overall software development competency and enhanced its IT integration and software service capability – all critical elements of a truly smart solution. By the end of 2011, the company had already announced a joint offering between Telvent and

Schneider Electric for its next big growth target – Smart cities.

In the battle for supremacy in the converging world of smart energy, Schneider Electric is not one of the biggest players. It is up against the likes of Siemens, ABB, GE, IBM and many others. But one thing is certain: they have staked a large bet on Smart energy markets taking off and delivering sustainable growth for the decade ahead.

Enterprise Resource Planning (ERP) has made many IT companies, like SAP, rich. It has made them globally well known, multi-billion, household names in less than two decades. As much as ERP solutions are mature in most industries, the utility enterprise management market is still in its nascent stage. With the Smart grid, the Smart city integration market is expected to have huge growth in the coming decade and the likes of SAP, IBM, Oracle, Alcatel-Lucent and Microsoft will benefit from combining their existing relationships with the utilities by joining their back-end services (like customer billing/relationship management, workforce and asset management solutions) with grid-facing devices and integrating the current siloed IT systems of utilities with operations, management and administration.

There are exciting days ahead as these enterprise giants fight it out for supremacy. A particular battle to watch out will be between SAP and Oracle. While SAP is following a mix of do-it-alone as well as partnership approaches, Oracle has been building on its current capabilities just like a new football coach would do, which is to first gauge and build on the capabilities of the existing team before bringing in new players to fill the gaps. Oracle is trying to provide a completely integrated service by leveraging its existing position in meter data management services and distribution grid management services.

However, the current small skirmishes that have been fought by these transmission and distribution, building management and IT companies is set to move on to a full-blown battle with the advent of the Mega Trend in connectivity called cloud computing. There are early signs already of the troops lining up as GE, Honeywell and others are launching or preparing cloud-based Smart energy services because their customers, the utilities, don't want to manage and store the heavy weight of IT integration.

And then there is the big giant IBM, which – very cleverly through a policy of branding, marketing and creating utility (Smart grid) communities globally with platforms to share experiences – has carved itself the position of a mega integrator. Its service-based business model makes it a good partner to companies traditionally shown in the automation and building controls market in Chart 2.3.

If you are in this industry and following the roller coaster movements, don't just rest yet. The ride is going become more unpredictable and you will soon be losing your ability to tell which way is up with the telcos getting into this space. Companies like Verizon, AT&T and Deutsche Telekom will play a bigger role in all Smart markets, including Smart homes, grids and cities. I predict a strong shift in supplier dynamics in the future, and particularly within a Smart home and Smart energy concept towards the telecom sector. The development of smarter applications that exploit network assets for better end-user processes and decision-making will raise the profile of the telecom sector in this space.

A key area of growth within the Smart concept is within the sub-segment of machine-to-machine (M2M) communications, where the traditional M2M players will find that they have received a new lease on life, thanks to the telecom service providers reorganising their traditional M2M solutions to enable a world of interconnected

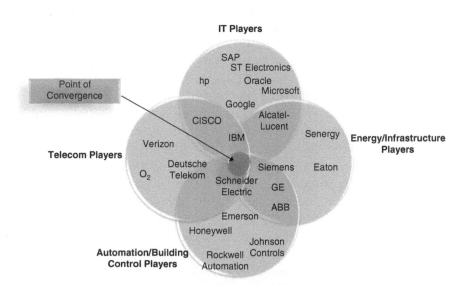

Chart 2.3 'Smart' market opportunity: Convergence of technology will lead to convergence of competition

Source: Frost & Sullivan.
Note: This is an illustration and does not show all market players.

30

machines and objects. The M2M market is expected to have high double-digit growth as is evidenced in the last two years within the EU27 countries based on demand for M2M SIMs.

As per Frost & Sullivan analysts, the EU 27 achieved almost 60% year-on-year growth, with around 20 million M2M SIMs deployed in that year.[9] This was followed by a 2009 performance of around 45% year-on-year growth from 8.6 million to 12.6 million M2M SIMs. This strong momentum in M2M SIMs' growth in the past two years was enabled by many tier 1 telecom operators reorganising their M2M operations into centralised units that benefitted from economies of scale and successful targeting of customer segments within existing and new geographies. This growth is expected to continue as we connect 80 billion devices globally in the future, including our homes.

The telecom industry, thanks to the huge market growth for M2M SIMs, have realised that they have huge prospects in this market. Within the telecom industry the telecom service providers, telecom equipment vendors, telecom software providers, device manufacturers and Internet service providers all should benefit from this growth.

The telecom industry players, especially the telcos, will step up their pace in entering this industry and will jockey for position with the traditional competitors. Telcos are exploiting their existing enterprise relationships to establish first-mover advantages in such readily available functions as telematics, Smart metering, Smart grids and even M2M communications in consumer electronics. They have an inherent competitive advantage over other players as they have a track record in direct customer relationships with huge amounts of people, because their communications infrastructure can be used to carry much of the data that a Smart system will generate and that most of the remote control functions will be enabled by Smart phones/tablets. In the future, telcos could play a directly disruptive role in the sector: for instance, Vodafone would be unlikely to want to own and operate its own power plants, but it could establish a retail relationship with customers buying the power for producers and selling it on. Virgin, in the UK, sells television, telephone and Internet packages – it is certainly possible in the future that gas and electricity sales could be added to these. This is made possible by the liberalisation of the gas and electricity markets in major parts of the world.

The consequences of telecom operators entering into the Smart space is not necessarily bad for the industry and other players as it will lead to symbiotic relationships – 'you scratch my back and I'll scratch yours' type of relationships. Some telcos, like Deutsche Telekom, are aggressively driving cross-industry collaborations with industrial equipment vendors and specialist application providers to be relevant in a world of interconnected machines and objects.

Last year Deutsche Telekom forged a cross-industry alliance with German energy providers E.ON, EnBW, appliance manufacturers eQ-3 and Miele to develop a HAN for Smart homes called Smart Connect. This year it added new partners – Samsung and photovoltaic systems installation specialist Winkel Solarsysteme. More are expected to join. This HAN provides control of home appliances, windows, lighting, shutters/blinds, alarm systems, etc., which can be controlled through a Smartphone or tablet PC. The company is set for mass-market launch in Q3 2012 in Germany for its Smart Connect HAN.

HANs offer major opportunities to new businesses for a range of different companies currently operating across different sectors, not just for telcos. As of 2012, these companies are facing major challenges as they grapple with developing a sustainable business model. With the implementation of Smart meters, Smart grid and cloud computing, coupled with the collective will of many of these companies, a viable solution will be found. Some of the other new players I see entering this HAN market are commodity consumer goods companies like Procter & Gamble and appliance manufacturers like Bosch and Whirlpool Corporation. Whirlpool is targeting to have all of its electronically controlled appliances to be able to have two-way communications from the grid through the Smart meter or other control devices.

The rate of the Smart market's development and success will depend upon the extent of collaboration between the industry traditionalists, IT players and telecom operators to design relevant end-user M2M applications.

As the industry witnesses the full deployment of end-to-end Smart solutions over the next decade, it is inevitable that a new wave of suppliers, with advanced technology solutions, apps and services, will make way into this market. Therefore, the competitive landscape will further evolve and lead to newly defined ecosystems of suppliers, grid infrastructure providers, telecom providers, value-added services providers and other partners who will have to service this market, either singly or in collaboration with one or more players. All in all, one can expect to see a mega ecosystem forming to match a Smart city concept as shown in Chart 2.3. At the point of convergence in the middle will sit the winner, most likely someone like IBM or Siemens who has the ability to mega-manage the massive projects with its demanding and long list of stakeholders, implement change and connect silos. If the Smart city concept thrives and we see growth as predicted, the success of the market will accelerate cross-industry integration, transformation and creation of new players.

Any company operating in the Smart sector will need to carefully review this new mega ecosystem as some of these new players could be potential partners or even competitors. For a company like Philips Lighting, it is certainly a dilemma because it needs to decide whether it should treat these new Smart operators in this industry as partners, potential future customers, possibly competitors (if it is bold enough to compete with them) or perhaps even a merger.

The question most companies need to ask is where they fit in the 'Smart' value chain. If you are Procter & Gamble or its competitor Unilever, and you make thousands of consumer products, which of the products you make should be Smart, tracked and communicate for automatic replenishments? Do you become a full home integrator and move out of your core business? Do you provide some energy tracker services? Or do you create a Smart Duracell battery?

The opportunities are unlimited. Everything we see, touch or feel can be Smart – from Smart traffic lights to Smart remote control. If you go on IBM's website, it talks everything Smart – from Smart transport, Smart energy and Smart retail to a Smart planet. Interestingly, the company even released a Smart game in which it allows gamers to experience some of the complex problems facing cities. The game, called CityOne, offers players the opportunity to optimise four major Smart issues – retail, energy, water and banking. It is an interesting game and free for you to download. What is attention grabbing is it talks about, for the first time that I have ever heard, 'Smart banking'. Now this is what we could surely do with to avoid recessions and job losses worldwide – a Smart banker.

So what does all this talk of Smart mean to you, and where do you fit into all this? Could there be a scenario in the near future where when you reach home on a cold winter day to find that the Smart home hub has shut off your heating based on a command from the utility to conserve energy; your Intelligent fridge ordered groceries despite you picking some up on the way home; your Smart TV did not record your favorite show; and you can't charge your electric car for your journey tomorrow as the Smart hub cannot connect to the wireless charging station? Disaster! And you look at your expensive investments in all the Smart devices and think, 'I am not that Smart after all.'

Hopefully, this scenerio will never happen, although one cannot rule out its possibility in a future Smart world.

3

eMOBILITY

THE ELECTRIC REVOLUTION

If the last half-century has taught us anything, it is that when it comes to commuting to work human beings will put up with considerable expense and discomfort to congregate in one place (the city) to work and disperse to another place (suburbia) to live their private lives. And, if given a choice, most of those people will drive an automobile to have control of their own transit in between the two places instead of using public transportation.

Finally, almost no amount of prodding, threats, rewards or punishments will change that behaviour for the majority of people – in other words, the age-old dream held by city planners and utopians everywhere of convincing the entire population to commute en masse in low-polluting buses, subways and trains will remain just that: an unfulfilled dream.

But, that said, there is no reason to believe that we won't soon find an alternative solution: that of individual vehicles, powered by low-polluting electrical batteries and alternative fuels, capturing an ever-greater market share from increasingly expensive gasoline-driven vehicles. This tipping point, when the average consumer finds an electric car more appealing than a gas car – even without having to factor in the common good – once seemed an impossible goal. Now, with innovative new vehicles from Tesla as well as from established automotive giants like BMW, General Motors and Nissan, that moment seems likely to happen within this decade.

It is estimated that more than 45 million electric two- and four-wheelers, from electric cars to electric buses and electric unmanned aerial vehicles (drones), will be sold annually around the globe in

2020[1] – and, coupled with technological innovations and governmental subsidising of necessary infrastructure, the number could be several times that. Over 300 million electric two- and four-wheelers will be driven around daily with more than 80% of two-wheelers being pushbikes, which are used in countries like India and China.

In the next five years, 54 car companies are expected to launch more than 115 electric car models globally – precisely the kind of explosive entrepreneurial growth we've seen in the past in 'hot' tech industries from computer disk memory to personal computers to smartphones. Chinese Vehicle Manufacturers alone are planning 30 new electric car model launches by 2015.

If the stories of past tech booms are any indication, electric vehicles will quickly become a fiercely competitive industry that is characterised by a lot of innovation, fortunes made and lost overnight, plummeting prices (of batteries) and an inevitable industry shakeout that will kill-off a majority of the players. But the companies that emerge from this trial by fire will be rich, powerful and will define their era. And the rest of us will be the beneficiaries.

eMOBILITY IS ABOVE AND BEYOND CARS

Electric mobility (eMobility) will redefine personal movement for much of the rest of the twenty-first century. For example, and most obviously, the trip to the gas station will be replaced by some new habit of either plugging the car in overnight at home, or using wireless charging by parking the car over a mat buried in the concrete in the driveway, for a trickle charge, or at a public station for a fast one – and that will in turn subtly, but also profoundly, change our driving behaviour. So, too, will the (at least for now) limited driving range of electric vehicles. How we will 'solve' these new challenges (swapping out batteries at stations on long trips? Roadside fast-speed chargers on freeways?) is as yet unknown. But they will come, and we will assimilate them, almost seamlessly, into our lives.

Whatever inconveniences these changes represent, the good news is that electric vehicles will fulfil the human ambition of zero-emission vehicles: the only CO_2 emissions emitted by an electric vehicle come from the driver.

Here is one likely scenario for the near future of eMobility: the cost of the battery in today's electric car – about $12,000 for a 22–24 kW car like the Renault Fluence or Nissan Leaf – is almost equal to the price of the conventional car. This suggests that the growth of electric mobility will create the opportunity for a major new industry: leasing electric cars, similar to pay-as-you-go mobile phone contracts, whereby the price of your annual lease will be dictated based on actual vehicle usage. Thus, if you drive 100 miles per day, you might pay $500 per month for a car, battery and energy; whereas, for the same car, a 40-mile-per-day driver might pay $350 a month.

As you might imagine, given this burst of demand, the market for Li-ion batteries is likely to grow exponentially over the next decade, making this technology the fastest growing clean-tech industry of the new era. If an electric light-commercial-vehicle maker, such as the UK's Smith, buys 100,000 packs of batteries every year for its vehicles, its battery volume will be the equivalent of all of the Li-ion batteries used in cellphones all over the world annually. Now, extrapolate those numbers to the ten million electric four-wheeled vehicles that will be built annually by 2020 – and you'll recognise one industry whose stocks you'll want to bet on. That said, however, be careful: like every high-tech industry before it, the battery industry is also likely to experience a boom/bust cycle of its own, with a lot of companies lost in the final shakeout.

As always during major technology-driven discontinuities, electric mobility will bring to the surface a new set of players, with new business models and offering new and highly innovative infrastructure and technology solutions. I call these companies 'eMobility integrators'. Just as oil companies make most of their money in the automotive ecosystem (e.g. Shell made a $31 billion profit in 2009 and the average profit margin of oil companies in 2007 was 23% of total sales, compared to 1.1% for car companies), in the eMobility market, by comparison, the major investment opportunities will lie with utilities, charging-station manufacturers and companies that can create integrated vehicle/leasing packages.

Another interesting example of an established organisation venturing into the eMobility business is the electronics giant, Best Buy. In April 2010, Best Buy, which already dominates independent electronics retailing in the US with its 1100 stores, declared that it will upgrade from selling Brammo electric motorcycles in a handful of its stores to full-fledged sales of electric car charging equipment and related services for car companies like Ford and Mitsubishi. For the mega-aspirational, Best Buy will even showcase the super-fast 'Tesla Roadster EV', priced at over $100,000.

CASE STUDY: BETTER PLACE AS AN eMOBILITY INTEGRATOR

The best example to date of this new eMobility business integration model is Better Place, which was founded by Shai Agassi in Israel. Led by HSBC bank, Better Place managed to raise one of the fastest and largest cleantech funds ever in 2010 which they topped up with series C equity financing in November 2011 – valuing the company at $2.25 billion merely on an idea, and before it had even sold its first electric car. Better Place plans to sell electric vehicles (in select markets/cases), complete with charging stations, as well as swap batteries for its customers using an intriguing new innovative business model dubbed 'pay by electrons (miles)'.

Better Place is already finding a market for its products in Israel, thanks to an agreement that took place after Agassi met Israeli President Shimon Peres at a conference on Middle East Policy in 2006. Agassi's vision of a world free from oil dependency was stirring and piqued the interests of listeners present. Shimon Peres, in particular, connected with Agassi's vision, as he himself was obsessed with energy security, the greening of Israel and its burgeoning solar industry. Agassi's vision of a future without oil dependence needed a cooperative government which would subsidise electric vehicles – at least initially – to pull consumers on board. Agassi convinced legislators in Israel to reduce the tax on electric vehicles to just 10%, compared to 72% for a traditional gas guzzler.

That deal translates into 100,000 electric vehicles running on Israeli roads by 2015 as their owners' primary vehicles (the total number of cars sold annually in Israel is only about 200,000), supported by 200,000 charging spots and 100 battery swapping stations. This is a very different business model compared to that presented by most other car companies, which are built upon selling electric cars to drivers as a *second* car for driving kids to school or weekend shopping.

By comparison, Agassi plans to market his cars to mainstream, high-mileage, daily commuting, corporate leased cars or taxi fleets. This is a smart move in a market like Israel, where as many as half of all cars are leased and there are only a handful of popular models, such as the Mazda M6 and Ford Mondeo, available – thereby making it easier to swap them with the physically similar fully electric Renault Fluence ZE.

Soon after convincing the Israeli government of the viability of his business plan, Agassi made similar inroads into Denmark via a partnership with Dong Energy, the nation's biggest utility. There he convinced the government that it could make more money selling its excess wind power at higher prices to Better Place, who will then convert it into cheaper miles for drivers, rather than exporting it at production costs to neighbouring countries.

Most recently, Better Place and General Electric have announced a technology and financing partnership to accelerate the deployment of electric vehicles into the rest of the world. Better Place's projects in Israel and Denmark became operational in early 2012 and the company will begin selling electric vehicles, charging stations and 'pay by electrons (Kilometres)' contracts to drivers through customised packages that are based on driving characteristics.

Is Better Place's business model the best possible solution? History suggests not, but I'll bet it's close – close enough for both Better Place and its competitors to find success through trial and error, customer feedback and technical innovation. I also believe many companies will adopt some version of this eMobility integrator model. If that's the case, Better Place has a four-year head start over its competitors. If Shai Agassi is as clever as he appears to be, that should be enough of a lead to keep Better Place in the front of the competitive pack for years to come.

THE MACRO TO MICRO OF eMOBILITY

Where do you fit into this eMobility revolution? The opportunities are, in fact, everywhere. The automotive industry currently employs one in nine people around the world – an astonishing figure. And with the threat of extinction of the more than 100-year-old internal combustion engine finally at its doorstep, the automotive industry is already racing to adapt. That will mean new jobs at almost every level at the major global car manufacturers. But history also argues that most of these dinosaurs will never fully catch up to this new world – and that will leave the door open to thousands of other eMobility-based businesses developing not just new cars and automotive powertrains, but also – along the supply and retail chains – new infrastructure, batteries, charging stations, etc., and there the game is wide open to new competitors.

Thus we can expect many new players to enter these markets with the 'eIntegrator' business model (refer to Chart 3.1 for an eIntegrator business model), which is designed similar to business models in the telecom industry. In the eIntegrator business model, companies will sell electric cars to the customer using customised 'usage' packages. The contract will include the car, battery, charging station and, in some limited cases, even a contract for battery swapping.

What's missing from this chart is an even more lucrative opportunity in what might be called the 'secondary' and 'tertiary' automotive markets. Look around you at the gigantic global industry that is based upon the gasoline car 'culture': magazines, television, repair books, retail items, after-market upgrades, even the location of gas stations, restaurants and motels based upon gas engine mileage numbers. Even the way we design our homes and communities are, in some small part, based on the gasoline engine. These too are now at risk for replacement –or at least a rapid adaption to the new eMobility world. And that means nearly innumerable business opportunities.

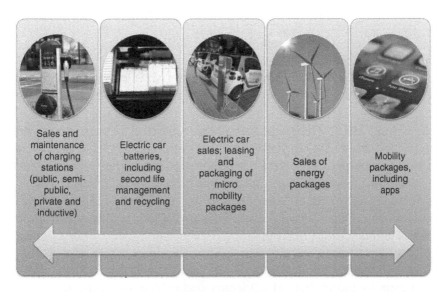

| Sales and maintenance of charging stations (public, semi-public, private and inductive) | Electric car batteries, including second life management and recycling | Electric car sales; leasing and packaging of micro mobility packages | Sales of energy packages | Mobility packages, including apps |

Chart 3.1 **Examples of products that can be offered by an eIntegrator in the eMobility market**

Photo credits: Dreamstime.
Source: Frost & Sullivan.

Two- to six-wheelers all go electric

One of the key prospect markets in the emerging eMobility-based global economy is one that we in the developed world rarely ponder over: two-wheelers. Great fortunes are about to be made there.

In 2010, there were more than 25 million electric two-wheelers sold in the world. More than 90% of them were electric pushbikes – and more than 90% of those pushbikes were sold in China.

Electric scooters and motorbikes of up to 1000 watts are gaining traction (so to speak) and more than one million of these will be sold in India alone by 2020. There is also potential for electric bikes to gain as much as a 50% market share in China, the world's biggest maker of motorbikes where more than ten million bikes are manufactured every year. There is also a strong likelihood that China, in this decade, will make it mandatory in megacities such as Shanghai and Beijing that all bikes below a certain power range (probably under 100cc) must be electric. Just imagine what this will do to the demand for electric bikes – as well as the significant noise and pollution reductions in these cities as a result.

You probably haven't noticed yet, but these same Chinese-made electric bikes can easily be bought today in Walmart and many other retailers (including Best Buy) across the US and in several countries in Europe. Don't be surprised if you buy one yourself in the next few years. Here, too, is a ready-made business opportunity in electric motorbike repair, add-ons, etc.

By 2016, we will also start noticing electric buses on the world's roads. Most electric bus manufacturers are aiming for buses with seating capacity of 35 to 45, but an American company called Proterra has already successfully developed a 65-seat, fully electric, transit bus – and is already struggling to meet demand from numerous metropolitan transit companies. A Proterra bus is expected to cost between $500,000 to $750,000, complete with a fast-charging station. These buses will function exactly the same as conventional buses, and with comparable cost of ownership – but of course with a whole lot less noise and pollution. The company's business model even convinced General Motors' private equity arm to invest in electric bus manufacturing, perhaps showing that electric buses and cars will have many technologies in common, including batteries, motors and vehicle electronics.

Putting all of these trends together, I predict that 2018 will be a watershed year for the automotive industry: electric cars and trucks will replace gasoline-powered vehicles as the heart of automotive OEMs' business. From there the adoption curves of hybrid and electric bikes, cars, trucks and buses will only accelerate. Automakers are going to get a legislative boost as well: due to strict global emission legislation that is expected to take effect around this time (including the European Union's strict mandate to have under 95g CO_2/km around 2018), the high price of oil and the maturing of battery technology, we will likely see a scenario when every full hybrid vehicle (like the Toyota Prius) will become a plug-in-the-wall-to-charge hybrid. Meanwhile, second-generation electric cars will hit the market around this time, all of them featuring much higher mileage per charge. This will, for the first time, make electric vehicles not just 'second' cars, but the average family's primary vehicle.

When that happens, the world's car culture will become an *electric* car culture, with all of the changes in lifestyles, mores, etc. that will follow. As a result, we will see sales volumes for electric cars rising sharply around this time.

Note that, contrary to the popular view that electric vehicles will take off in the first half of the decade, I predict the growth to mainly happen in the second half of the decade. This follows what is known as Malone's Law, which states that *significant technology revolutions always take longer than we predict, but arrive sooner than we are fully prepared for.* The second half of that law is as important as the first, because it is from that lack of preparation that great opportunities, great companies and great fortunes are made.

Wireless charging

The most lucrative, as yet unmet, opportunity in the future eMobility world is in building, selling, installing and maintaining charging stations. For every electric car sold in the market, about 2.5 charging stations will need to be sold during the first few years, with the ratio coming down to about 1.7 charging stations per car by year seven. So, for the ten million electric four-wheelers that will be sold annually in 2020, more than 17 million new charging stations will need to be sold. These charging stations will be mainly installed in private homes and apartment complexes, in semi-public places such as offices and in public locations such as train stations, markets, airports and – most of all – parking lots.

Meanwhile, the charging stations themselves present a huge business opportunity. Today, the hardware cost of a typical Level 2 semi-public or public charging station (installed in public places) is between $2000 and $3000 – and the cost of installation is almost the same as the purchase price. Being an electrical engineer myself, I can tell you the cost of making this electrical system cannot be more than a few hundred dollars. However, due to the public–private partnership involved in setting up these charging stations and subsidies given by governments, there are huge profits to be made right now in this market. It is an opportunity that won't last forever.

One innovation which will change the way we view electric cars in the future will be wireless charging, usually known as inductive charging. It will allow you to charge your electric car without plugging it in every evening. All that's needed to do is drive your car into your driveway and park it at a given spot. A system embedded into the driveway's concrete will automatically make a connection with your car and, based on your charging contract, will charge your vehicle while you sleep with a full 100 miles of battery power for your next day's average commute. Inductive charging is expected to be one of the most exciting technologies of this decade, and will do to electric cars what the mobile phone did to telephony. That is, it will make usage both simple and seamless with everyday life – and most importantly, easier to use than existing technology, the crucial last step to mass adoption. Just as mobile phones made a billion people disconnect their landlines, induction charging will make you swap your internal gasoline engine for an electric car. (Interestingly, wireless charging is coming to our mobile phones as well, making wired chargers soon a thing of the past.)

Cradle to grave

Another major opportunity is in battery second life and recycling. After roughly 2000 battery cycles – which equates to four–five years in the car – the typical electric car battery, now operating at 80% of its capacity, will be no longer suitable for in-car applications. Nevertheless, it will still be an asset worth up to $4000 (for a 22 kW battery). This battery will therefore find second-life applications as vital backup power for remote installations such as offshore oil-drilling platforms, for rural areas to tap/store power generated from renewable sources, in commercial vehicle idling, recreational vehicles and as a fail-safe power source for HVAC in public transportation or commercial vehicles. Batteries will also find applications for powering data storage centres, in wind and solar plants, and in limited cases in utilities for load-levelling. Someone is going to have to broker all of these transfers and transactions.

After another ten to 12 years, this same battery will be recycled to extract metals such as nickel, copper, cobalt, lithium and other precious metals. The global battery-recycling market, analysed by Frost & Sullivan, is expected to be worth more than $2 billion by 2020 – making it an attractive source of revenue for the recycling industry.

At the other end – the beginning – of the battery's life, important changes are already taking place that, once again, present huge opportunities. The eMobility market is already having a profound impact on some precious metals and raw materials like Lithium; so imagine what it will be like a decade from now when demand is ten times higher. By then, more than 40% of the world's lithium will be used for making batteries, thereby making it an important chemical of the future. With 70% of current lithium deposits in South America's ABC region (Argentina, Bolivia and Chile) and current precious metal mines needed for making important motor and battery parts mainly located in China, some countries are about to be made very wealthy – and geopolitical tensions over its ownership are likely to rise in the coming decade. Fortunately, contrary to popular belief, there is no threat of the world running out of lithium as current production of this metal accounts for less than 1% of the identified global reserves.

Will utilities be the new oil barons?

Meanwhile, there is a general belief that electric utilities will be the biggest beneficiaries of the eMobility trend, and will become the new oil companies of this century.

Well, maybe not. With electricity priced at 8 cents per unit in the US and about 18 cents per unit in Europe, there is as yet no real business case for utilities selling energy to cars. There is also no threat in the next ten years that utilities will need to build new power plants to deal with the advent of electric cars. That's because, even if a region or city had 250,000 electric cars on the road, the power consumed by those vehicles would not be enough to warrant new power generation capacity.

That's only one of the surprises about utilities in the eMobility market. Over the years, I have worked on several management consulting projects for utilities. I learnt that the most lucrative business case for utilities is in selling, installing and managing charging stations or using customers' charging profiles to balance loads around off-peak hours. In a project for an Austrian utility, I learnt that the typical electric vehicle customer is also an early adopter for a home solar combined heat and power (CHP) plant. A typical CHP domestic plant costs close to €15,000, with a healthy 25% margin – a far more interesting prospect than getting directly involved with electric cars. So, though it may *seem* that there is a logical connection between electrical power plants and electric vehicles, in real life that may not be the case. In fact, for many utilities, the advantage of doing nothing may prove greater than that of entering the market.

*

Once you think about it, this eMobility megatrend will likely affect – and almost always benefit – just about every industry in the modern economy. Even a light bulb manufacturer like Philips stands to gain from this market as, in the future, LED bulbs will be preferred in electric vehicles due to their energy-saving characteristics. Similarly, a testing and measurement equipment supplier will now be able to sell new electrical and electronic testing equipment in the automotive market. An IT company can develop and market mobility IT platforms. Moreover, companies such as Duracell can license their brand names to charging stations – even make second-life batteries for home applications. The opportunities are only limited by the imagination.

I recently met with a venerable company which makes electric motors for elevators. While studying the changes taking place in the car industry, this company's executives suddenly realised that their elevator motors might have a competitive advantage as car motors, given their high torque, zero noise, ability to work in arduous and stressful conditions, and excellent safety and reliability record. A century of experience in lifting people vertically had suddenly made them perfectly positioned to propel people horizontally.

If, indeed, every industry can benefit from the eMobility mega trend, then it behoves all companies to run an internal macro-to-micro exercise to determine where they fit in this new regime and when they should enter it. The study should not only focus upon new opportunities in their existing businesses, such as current customer needs they can now fulfil, but also opportunities to move laterally (and unexpectedly) into brand new markets where their current skills can overwhelm an unwary competition.

As for one's personal life, it is easy to see how driving an electric car or bike might slightly influence one's daily behaviour: the added planning for trips of more than 100 miles, the switching from the weekly trip to the gas station to plugging in the car at home each night. But consider that the implications might be far greater. After all, much of the architectural and infrastructural design of our homes, offices, schools and cities are based upon the fact that cars are noisy, smelly, potentially explosive and producers of toxic chemicals.

So, ask yourself: what happens when those unappealing and/or dangerous characteristics of cars, trucks, buses, motorboats, ATVs, vans, taxis, and scooters and motorcycles go away? Do you still need a detached (or at least firewalled) garage? Open-air parking lots? How long will it take you to more than make a quick glance – and depend upon your ears – while crossing the street?

4

INNOVATING TO ZERO

This chapter and trend is very different from all others discussed in this book. 'Innovating to Zero' is not a mega trend in its true sense. It is a Mega vision; it is more a concept than a real happening. It implies the desire for perfection in our society: a 'Zero concept' world with a vision of Zero carbon emissions, Zero crime rates, Zero accidents and carbon-neutral cities. Although this seemingly perfect world sounds almost impossible, the point is that governments and companies today are moving towards this 'picture perfect' vision of eliminating errors, defects and other negative externalities, and along that very journey creating for themselves huge challenges and opportunities. We might not achieve this goal in this decade or ever, in some cases, but because we humans can make this as our ultimate goal – even if we achieve half of the set objective – it will be huge progress. It will make a real difference to society.

'Innovating to Zero' is a term I have borrowed from Bill Gates to describe the Zero Concept World. In his TED 2010 talk, Bill Gates coined the phrase when he advocated a technology called the 'Travelling Wave Reactor', which uses depleted uranium. Ever since hearing him, I have come across several examples of Innovating to Zero manifesting itself in different words like PepsiCo's 'Path to Zero' programme, Volvo Car's 'Zero Car Accidents', Nissan's 'Zero Emission' (electric) cars and recently with Marks & Spencer (a retail store in UK) which even established a 'Carbon Neutral' underwear factory in Sri Lanka.

Discussions with experts like Shai Agassi, founder of Better Place (refer to Chapter 3, 'eMobility') and David Frigstad (Chairman of Frost & Sullivan), and further research have led me to envisage a much bigger Innovating to Zero trend than just the 'Zero Emission Technology' that Gates spoke of. I foresee a 'Zero Concept World' in the future, where Innovating to Zero can be made applicable to almost anything: Zero emission technologies, Zero waste, Zero accidents, Zero defects, Zero security breaches, Zero carbon emissions (carbon-neutral buildings and cities), Zero obesity, Zero crimes and even Zero diseases. I expect and forecast organisations working towards this Innovating to Zero goals this decade and embracing this concept in their research and development, planning, and execution.

NET ZERO CITIES: CARBON-NEUTRAL CAPITALS OF THE WORLD

Zero waste, Zero pollution, or Zero carbon emissions are perhaps the most commonly used and talked-about 'Zero-based' initiatives which have been around for years and will be pertinent for eons to come. Their thread of commonality is, of course, reduction of energy and climate change – all linked to the common labyrinth of sustainability. It is interesting to note, however, how the Zero waste trend has expanded from its erstwhile extremely basic waste-reduction measures for a single economic unit to be applied to an entire building and, fascinatingly, even to an entire city.

ZERO WASTE: FROM CRADLE TO CRADLE

Zero waste, as its name suggests, simply conveys complete recyclability; and complete recyclability as a concept, again, is not new. Companies, households, buildings, and even cities and governments have been, time and again, advocating the importance of carbon dioxide emission reduction and, with it, the need to reduce waste. Perhaps the best definition of Zero waste is the one coined by the Zero Waste Alliance in 2004, which defines it as 'a goal that is ethical, economical, efficient and visionary, to guide people in changing their lifestyles and practices to emulate sustainable natural cycles, where all discarded materials are designed to become resources for others to use'.[1] In fact, they go even further to say that 90% diversion of waste from landfills is considered to be Zero waste, or darn close to it. However, I believe that a true 100% waste reduction is possible.

The concept of Zero waste has been adopted on various scales by different economic units and organisations globally. The European Union's 'European Pathway to Zero Waste' (EPOW) programme,[2] which runs through 2012, has undertaken ways to achieve Zero waste in south-eastern England as a benchmark for other EU regions. This programme, funded by Life+, the financial arm of the EU, focuses on sustainable utilisation of resources through the '4Rs – Reduce, Recycle, Reuse, and Recover' programme, which reclaims energy from waste. It runs eight projects in south-eastern England with a sole aim of creating a 'recycling society' at the end of the programme in 2012.

NET ZERO BUILDING: ZERO 'HOME IMPROVEMENT'

Now moving on to a much bigger Zero concept, a 'Net Zero building', as the term suggests, is a building with net energy consumption or carbon emissions per annum equal to Zero. Some of these buildings can be 'off-the-grid' and can harvest energy on-site. The entire operation of the building is made carbon neutral through intelligent systems, renewable energy such as solar and wind, and other energy-saving features. Companies, cities and even national governments have made many efforts towards this goal.

The most commendable of all Net Zero building efforts, however, is found in the United States. Not only is the country one of the few nations that can boast a host of designated building codes that ensure carbon emission reduction but here is an instance where the government sector leads the industry by example. On October 2009, President Barack Obama's Executive Order 13514 set a target that all federal buildings (a whopping total of 500,000 federal buildings) must be carbon neutral by 2030.[3] Additionally, the US DOE's Net-Zero Energy Commercial Building Initiative (CBI) requires all commercial buildings in the US to be carbon neutral by 2050. These pioneering national-level efforts are ably supported by United States Department of Energy and research organisations and laboratories in the country, making the country a front-runner for this Zero-based initiative.

CARBON-NEUTRAL CITY: ARRIVING AT 'DESTINATION ZERO'

A carbon-neutral city is a city that completely offsets the carbon emissions that it generates. In other words, the net carbon emission that is emitted by the city per annum is absolutely Zero. As ambitious as it may sound, many governments globally have bravely adopted this strategy which, though it might have found its humble beginnings in a simple Zero waste initiative, is now being made applicable to the entire city. With this move, city authorities expect to create 'Zero related opportunities', improve infrastructure, reduce carbon emissions and construct a sustainability business case – one that will stand as a prototype for many other similar cities to follow globally.

CASE STUDY: COPENHAGEN 2025 – FIRST CARBON-NEUTRAL CAPITAL OF THE WORLD

Imagine an evening in Copenhagen in the near future. After enjoying a few carbon-neutral beers and a low-calorie meal (Copenhagen levies a high tax for junk food and is also aiming for an informal target of Zero obesity) in a carbon Zero restaurant, you return – on your bicycle – to your carbon-neutral building, where all energy is powered by solar and wind. A car journey would have taken you ten minutes, but the bicycle journey is much shorter as the city provides direct routes and access through its five-minute drive programme. Drive carefully, though, on those beers, as in Copenhagen you have more of a chance of being run over by a cyclist than a car or a lorry with over 36% of Copenhageners commuting by bike. You get home to a flat heated by a hot seasonal thermal store (technology designed to retain heat during the hot summer months for use during winter weather) and you set your washing machine timer to start while you sleep during the off-peak hours as your intelligent energy meter halves the cost of one bucket wash. You have just spent a truly carbon-neutral evening during which the only device that has harmed the environment and emitted carbon dioxide is you yourself.

The city of Copenhagen, capital of Denmark, has an ambitious plan to be the world's first carbon-neutral capital by 2025. To make this goal realistic and attainable, the city has set itself an initial target of attaining 20% reduction in CO_2, roughly a reduction of 500,000 tonnes, by 2015 – then to attain complete carbon neutrality in 2025. There are around 50 specific initiatives that have been set up to achieve this target and six exceptional initiatives (also called lighthouse projects), each with its own set of emission reduction targets for 2015 as shown in Chart 4.1.

Some of Copenhagen's key initiatives to meet this target include:

- Have 50% of its citizens bicycle to work/school.
- Develop 14 new gardens by 2015.
- 14 wind turbines are currently in the city. Have more than 100 wind turbines by 2025.
- Shorter journeys through dedicated direct routes for public transportation and bicycles.
- Buy 200 electric vehicles (85% of municipal vehicles running on electricity by 2015).
- Push for electric and hydrogen infrastructure for transport and provide 100% car registration tax exemption to Zero-emission vehicle buyers.
- Set up car sharing clubs and drive car ownership down.
- Set up intelligent meters and give its citizens the ability to use green energy during the night.
- Shift from coal power plants to mainly wind power, but also to solar and geothermal energy for heating/electricity.

Copenhagen's energy initiatives have spurred collaboration between the public and private sector; have led to multiple opportunities, especially in infrastructure development; and have set a best practice example of how to implement such an initiative. The city authorities are pushing partnerships with energy companies, infrastructure developers and public authorities, especially in the areas of transportation, energy supply and renovation of buildings. They are also working closely with the community to educate and seek its cooperation in implementing the initiative.

If you have not done so yet, planning a holiday in the first CO_2-neutral city in the world, which is rated as the number one cleanest as well as one of the most attractive cities to live and work in Europe, would be worthwhile.

ZERO INITIATIVES AT WORK: FASTER, SAFER AND FLEXIBLE ZERO WORK CULTURE

Zero papers (paperless office), Zero downtime, Zero delays in delivery, Zero client complaints and Zero waiting time are some obvious examples of Zero at work. However, in the future we can see more 'Zero-based' working harder in the employment arena with some examples listed further.

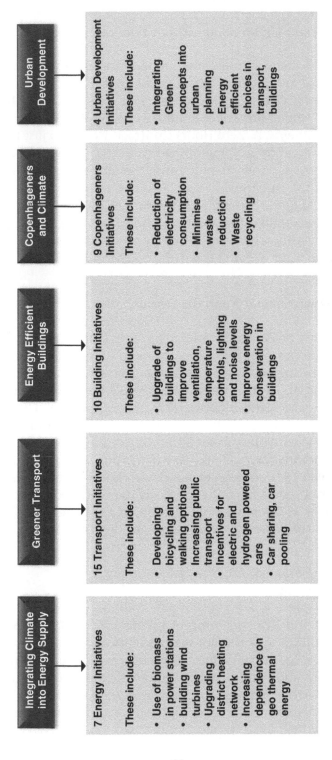

Chart 4.1 Case study: Copenhagen to be world's first carbon-neutral city by 2025

Source: Frost & Sullivan.

The chart contains the following boxes:

Integrating Climate into Energy Supply

7 Energy Initiatives

These include:

- Use of biomass in power stations
- building wind turbines
- Upgrading district heating network
- Increasing dependence on geo thermal energy

Greener Transport

15 Transport Initiatives

These include:

- Developing bicycling and walking options
- Increasing public transport
- Incentives for electric and hydrogen powered cars
- Car sharing, car pooling

Energy Efficient Buildings

10 Building Initiatives

These include:

- Upgrade of buildings to improve ventilation, temperature controls, lighting and noise levels
- Improve energy conservation in buildings

Copenhageners and Climate

9 Copenhageners Initiatives

These include:

- Reduction of electricity consumption
- Minimise waste reduction
- Waste recycling

Urban Development

4 Urban Development Initiatives

These include:

- Integrating Green concepts into urban planning
- Energy efficient choices in transport, buildings

Zero hours contract: Working without time commitment

Innovating to Zero will also become applicable to work culture in the future. In the previous chapters we looked at how technology and new social demographic trends, such as Gen Y and the aging population, would increase demand for different types of flexible work environments. A 'Zero Hours Contract' would do just that. This contract would allow an employer to call upon the employee on an on-demand basis, rather than defining the number of working hours per week in the employment contract. The employee is expected to be available as and when required (or 'on-call') and will be paid both a fixed retainer and for the number of hours put into his or her work. In particular, this scheme could be beneficial for retired people or students who want to earn something on the side.

Zero accidents: Super Zero to the rescue

'Zero accidents' or 'Zero occupational hazards' is now a popular strategy geared towards a safe working environment for employees, especially in manufacturing industries. So it was not a surprise to me when I read that Shell, in the wake of the BP oil spill disaster, had implemented a Zero accident initiative. This programme, titled 'Goal Zero', has been set up within Shell's operation with a target of no fatalities and no accidents within its facilities. By continuingly improving its safety culture, Shell hopes to achieve this vision. To enforce this, Shell has developed 12 lifesaving rules and even holds 'Safety Days' within its facilities. A testimony of its success is the Pearl GTL (gas to liquid) project, based in Qatar, which has recorded an impressive 77 million working hours to date without a single accident.

Zero at work: Zero latency, Zero emails and Zero incubation period

On-demand and live streaming of media and need for instantaneous data retrieval at work will see concepts of 'Zero latency' in the corporate world. This trend implies no time lapses between receipt of critical information and the ability to analyse and act on that information. This trend, mainly driven by ambient connectivity, will lead to 'Zero turnaround time', making business decisions and processes faster and perhaps even on a real-time basis.

In a move to curb unnecessary downtime in sending and receiving emails, a France-based tech company, Atos S.A., recently adopted a 'Zero email™' policy, as they have stipulated that only 10% of the emails received a day are useful. The policy, which is currently applicable for internal emails alone, will see the use of innovative collaborative social media tools (Atos Wiki), instant messaging, videoconferencing, application sharing and a copycat Facebook interface as alternatives to emails. The case study on zero emails outlined below gives more details on their 'Zero Email' initiative.

Advanced technology will also enable ideas to be created, implemented and commercialised on 'Zero time', leading to 'Zero Time Business Incubation' (ZTBI). This will see new types of cutting-edge infrastructure, IT and professional services that would enable ideas to be converted into strategy implementation and perhaps even new products or businesses in 'Zero time'. ZTBI will see tools such as online networking interfaces, file sharing, instant market research, etc. coming into the picture and a host of other Zero-related trends such as 'Zero management gaps', 'Zero processing time' and 'Zero learning gaps'.

Other uses of Zero-related concepts at work include 'Zero tolerance' policies that are formulated to prevent inappropriate behaviour in the workplace. Proved to be successful in many organisations, 'Zero tolerance' policies keep a check on harassment, discipline and even quality control issues in the workplace.

ZERO EMAILS: A BEST PRACTICES CASE STUDY

I started my career in India in 1993 working in a government organisation in which the key means of internal communication was written or typed memos via files. Twice a day, every day, I would receive a pile of files, which I had to review and act upon. When emails arrived as means of office communication, I was excited and appreciated the efficiency improvements over handwritten notes. However, a lot has changed in the last two decades: we have now become slaves to emails. On a typical day, I review over 250 emails, with only about 15% of them really relevant. I check emails from 7 a.m. till midnight, on weekends, in the bathroom, in the car or train, or waiting at airports, even during commercial breaks when watching television. I am desperately trying to keep up as my colleagues and clients expect response in zero time. I have what I call email fatigue. I am sure that when Ray Tomlinson, an MIT graduate, sent the world's first email in 1971 from one computer to another that was one meter away he did not anticipate his creation could have such dramatic side effects. Interestingly, some companies have thought of a solution to tackle this challenge – a policy of having absolutely no email communication.

Zero Emails is one 'Innovating to Zero' concept that will gain popularity in the work environment in the coming decade. The aim of any Zero email initiative is not to reduce communication, but, on the contrary, to enhance and improve enterprise communication through the use of innovative media tools that can enable each employee to work from everywhere, anywhere, using several devices, with the most efficient communication media tools.

According to Duchenaut and Watts,[4] the functions of email can be described in three ways: a filing cabinet, a production line and a communication genre. When one adopts a 'Zero email' strategy, one might wonder how the multiple functions described here can still be maintained. To illustrate, Atos S.A., Europe's largest IT services firm has cleverly thought of alternatives when it adopted its Zero email™ policy in February 2011. By using new collaboration and social media tools that can completely replace all email communication, this company hopes to fully achieve its Zero email™ target in 2013 for all internal purposes (not external). Through this initiative, Atos S.A. aims to promote social well-being, increase productivity, and create sustainable business and greater innovation for their clients, not to mention reinvent its work environment in the bargain.

To achieve its Zero email™ target Atos is developing a scientific approach to deploying Enterprise 2.0 technologies which represent next generation of communication and social networking tools available for the workplace. In the mean time Atos is promoting better email etiquette and behaviour and the wider use of its existing toolset. This toolset includes a micro blogging platform called Yammer, an online mindmapping tool called Mindmeister, an enterprise wiki and a document management system. This set of tools helps with communication, project management and collaboration, community writing, and even the review and approval process. Atos envisages that its Enterprise 2.0 solution will integrate all the functions of the tools described previously and eventually replace all electronic mail.

Atos is taking care to ensure the adoption of Enterprise 2.0 follows the natural and evolving communities which exist already within its business. For the function of filing and documentation, each community will be able to reference a single repository of all files and communication. Everyone will have access to all information and collaborative filtering will help a user to locate a particular file or data. For production lines or project management, the Enterprise 2.0 solution is expected to transform all email communication into signals using data mashups. Additionally, the wiki interface will help employees communicate through a social networking platform with 'updates' from team members enabling project

alerts, reviews of reports by peers, and collaborative project management. And for the final function of emails which is communication, micro blogging and discussion forums, Enterprise 2.0 platforms will completely eradicate the need for communicating using email.

For Atos, the goal is not just to become The Zero email Company™ but will also use this journey to improve processes and aptly identify the restraints of email overload.

Last year, a global campaign was run on 11 November 2011 to have a no email day. I would love to be part of such a campaign, but I dread the day after when I have to catch up with all the unanswered emails from my colleagues and clients who did not participate. I would rather follow Atos' vision of Zero emails every day.

MACRO TO MICRO

The concept of Innovating to Zero can be applied in different industries. For the purpose of this chapter, we have taken the concept of 'Zero' to six popular industries – namely, retail, manufacturing, energy, automotive, health care and logistics.

Retail

A shopping trip in 2020 might entail patronising 'Zero carbon shops', or shops practising 'Zero design to shelves response time', and – much to the dismay of avid shoppers – even shops practising 'Zero discounts'.

'Zero carbon shops', as the name suggests, are retail establishments with Net Zero carbon emissions.

'Zero design to shelves response time' relates to continuous modification of clothing based on demand so the clothes in the showrooms never go out of fashion. This could entail in-house design, cutting and finishing; continuous speedy deliveries via air (not ship from China) to stores two–six times per week; direct point-of-sale data collection from stores; and daily analysis of product sales and customer feedback using software analytics. This is extending Zara's businesses model which ensured new, fashion-attuned designs twice a week – that is, 20,000 styles per year – hit its shops.

'Zero discounts' is, perhaps, pushing it; but imagine what it could do your brand and bottom line if every store of yours worldwide practices a same-price policy with Zero discounts all year around.

Shops could also practise 'Zero shrinkage', which is a complete absence of loss of inventory due to shoplifting, employee theft, vendor fraud or administration error.

Manufacturing

'Carbon-neutral factories' or 'Net Zero factories' were first introduced into the market when Volvo Trucks announced the world's first carbon-neutral factory in Ghent, Belgium, back in 2007. The plant's sole source of energy is renewable. Volvo Trucks expects all of its other factories to be CO_2 neutral in the near future. Similarly, Marks & Spencer, a major retailer in the UK, has a goal of becoming completely carbon neutral by 2012 through the use of renewable energy, power-saving devices and waste minimisation techniques in its factories and other establishments. Its factories are currently set to consume 40% less electricity than a standard factory and will be completely carbon neutral by 2012.

From Zero defects to producing perfect products

'Zero defects' is probably one of the oldest Zero-based concepts in the manufacturing sector. Initially coined as a concept in Philip Crosby's

Step 7/14 Quality Improvement Program in 1982, 'Zero defects' has come a long way from being a mere concept to a quality improvement mechanism to a full-fledged business strategy that many organisations utilise today. The first implementation of 'Zero defects' concept recorded in corporate history is, perhaps, the quality control programme deployed by the Denver branch of Lockheed Martin (then Martin Marietta Corporation) in late 1960s on the Titan Missile project. However, it was launched more as a motivational exercise than a quality control programme, as the 100% defect-free vision was then perceived as an impossibility by quality control professionals. The programme did fizzle out because it was understood to be just that – a mere 'programme' and not a way of running one's business that one would innovate to.

Today, variants of this 'Zero defects' concept, however, have found their way into different business and production strategies, the most popular one being the 'Six Sigma' strategy made popular by Motorola in 1986. According to this manufacturing strategy, which is typically a statistical model, 'Six Sigma' would yield 99.99966% of goods produced to be defect free (an impressive calculation of 3.4 defects for every million products produced). 'Six Sigma' soon became and till today is a buzzword in the manufacturing industry with its facilitators flashing their black belts as if they have won a world martial arts Judo championship.

The essence of the 'Zero defects' or 'Zero faults' or 'Zero errors' concept is simple: you innovate towards manufacturing a perfect product without defects, a strategy which would need highly strict quality control standards. 'Zero defects' is particularly important for drug manufacturing or medical devices, which, if implemented correctly, can be lifesaving too.

Energy: Zero carbon countries

As mentioned earlier, Innovating to Zero was first attributed to Zero emission technology (an advanced nuclear solution) to describe TerraPower's Travelling Wave Reactor (TWR) in Bill Gates' TED speech. TerraPower, which is a start-up backed by Bill Gates himself, has adopted a unique way of approaching countries, rather than financiers or utilities, for their nuclear conversations. Gates recently held talks with the Chinese Ministry of Science and Technology in December 2011 to promote this fourth-generation technology, which uses a reactor that slowly burns depleted nuclear fuel for 40 years. TerraPower is expected to have its first plant in operation by 2020. Setting aside advanced nuclear technology, other popular forms of Zero emission technologies are, undoubtedly, wind energy, solar, geothermal and ocean energy, to name a few.

Moving on to the Transmission and Distribution (T&D) side of the energy industry, 'Zero transmission and distribution losses' coupled with 'Zero load-shedding' and 'Zero energy thefts' are concepts that are increasingly being implemented on an ad hoc basis in cities that are aiming towards no losses during distribution of energy.

'Zero Carbon Britain 2030' is a similar policy vision in the UK[5] for an energy progressive society free from fossil fuels and dependence on imported energy and 'Zero Carbon Australia 2020' is a similar initiative in Australia run by a not-for-profit organisation, interestingly called Beyond Zero Emissions.[6]

Automotive and transport

Innovating to Zero is already well-practiced in the automotive industry and is a source of competitive advantage which also helps sell more cars for car companies, thereby providing a true business case. Volvo and Mercedes already benefit immensely from their Zero accidents vision. Continental Automotive Systems, a leading supplier of driver assistance and safety products, showcases a vision of accident-free driving with its 'Vision Zero' strategy by incorporating products that not only help save lives after an accident has happened through new sophisticated airbags and seat belts, but also through active technology which avoids accidents in the first place. These driver assistance and active safety technologies override drivers, if required, like the emergency brake technology which brings the car to a halt even if you do not press the brake. When you try the technology for the first time on a test track, it will give you shivers – but it saves lives (and your car from damage).

Japanese car companies like Toyota and Nissan have taken the concept of emission-free driving to the next level, developing and achieving a goal of Zero emissions. When Toyota stole the industry's thunder by launching the world's first hybrid car, the Toyota Prius, its competitor Nissan did not just want to copy Toyota and also develop hybrids. It therefore placed a $5 billion bet on developing electric cars that are 'Zero emission' vehicles. 'Beat that, Toyota', said Nissan, 'as your hybrids still emit emissions.' Watch out now for Honda to come up with a Hydrogen car to give itself an advantage over Nissan and Toyota to have a truly 'Zero well to wheel car'.

Health care

In a quest to reduce health care expenses, hospitals globally are now toying with the idea of 'Net Zero hospitals'. The concept, however, today exists more at the 'Net Zero building' level during construction of hospitals (such as increased daylighting, solar control, smart HVAC systems and so on) rather than being made applicable to the actual functions of a hospital itself (such as Zero medical waste, Net Zero surgery errors, etc.).

Other Zero-related concepts that will be introduced in the health care industry include 'Zero invasive surgery'; even more importantly, 'Zero surgery errors'; and, amazingly, even 'Zero diseases'. WHO has set a target of achieving 'Zero deaths by malaria' by 2015 and a polio-free world.

Many nations in the future could aim for 'Zero obesity' by increasing taxes on fatty foods and providing incentives through either gym memberships or lower insurance premiums for those who are healthy.

Already certain Zero-calorie foods are very popular and we have also seen success with branded drinks like Coke Zero. I expect more branding of foods and beverages around the Zero concept in future.

CONCLUSION: COUNTDOWN TO ZERO – MUCH ADO ABOUT 'NOTHING'

Innovating to Zero is definitely a Mega vision. It is not a trend that is incorporated by individuals or companies overnight. It is a gradual process, a journey that will create opportunities, demand investments and yield long-term returns. The most remarkable feature of this Mega vision is that the ultimate opportunity lies not in attaining the actual goal itself, but in capitalising on the opportunities that would lead to it. Success in Innovating to Zero requires an innovation agenda that bravely talks of breakthroughs in the face of radical goals – goals that intend to create a better world, a Zero concept world, which is free of unhelpful externalities and defects. It also needs a strong culture from the people within that ecosystem. Copenhagen would not have set its goals and achieved its milestones had it not been for 40% of its population agreeing to give up its cars to bicycle to work, even in the city's extreme winters.

While presenting this trend at a conference, I was once asked by a gentleman, 'What about "Innovating to negative" or "Beyond Zero", which is actually develop buildings and cities that are not carbon neutral but carbon positive?' Perhaps one will need to consider it once we achieve true innovations that are Zero.

Do you and your company have a Zero vision?

5

URBANISATION: FROM MEGA-CITIES, MEGA-REGIONS, MEGA-CORRIDORS AND MEGA-SLUMS TO MEGA OPPORTUNITIES

MEGA-CITIES, MEGA-REGIONS, MEGA-CORRIDORS AND MEGA-SLUMS

Mahatma Gandhi once said, 'India is to be found not in its few cities but in its 700,000 villages.' Though that may at one time have been true, it is no longer the case. With about 30 country bumpkins moving lock, stock and barrel every minute from Indian villages to become city dwellers, not many villages will be left in India by the end of this century.

Towards the end of the last decade, our planet achieved a remarkable feat. For the first time in human history, 50% of the world's population was living in urban areas. Indeed, the UN predicts that by 2030 60% of the world's population will live in cities.[1] A study I recently led at Frost & Sullivan actually summarised the urbanisation trend to be growing faster than the UN's prediction, and forecast the urban population to reach 4.6 billion globally around 2025 – about 60% of the total world population.[2] In other words, the world is creating a city the size of Barcelona as five million people become urban residents every month.

This extraordinary growth will lead to the merger of core city centres or downtowns with suburbs and daughter cities, resulting in the expansion of city limits. As a result, we will see the emergence of Mega-cities, Mega-regions, Mega-corridors and – sadly – even Mega-slums.

More than 35 cities globally by 2025 will merge with their suburbs and become Mega-cities boasting populations in excess of eight million and a GDP contribution of $250 billion. A good example of a Mega-city is my home city, London. The city has expanded to its suburbs and sprawls all the way to the outer motorway – the M25, one of the world's longest orbital roads – which some of us call the longest and biggest parking lot in the UK.

Almost all major global cities, like London, have an inner and outer orbital road, typically within a 20 to 25 km radius from the city centre. The cities are set to expand beyond these orbital roads to a 40 km radius by 2025 and merge with their daughter cities to form Mega-regions. A Mega-region will be characterised by either two large cities sprawling and merging with each other or a Mega-city merging with smaller daughter cities to form a gargantuan region with a population in excess of 15 million. A good example of a Mega-region is the area around Johannesburg – the East Rand, Pretoria and Midrand region – which is fast becoming one inseparable Mega-city. Locals have already nicknamed the region 'Jo-toria'.

Jo-toria, which continues to attract citizens from neighbouring states as well as other countries, will be home to over 15 million people by 2025 and will be the business capital of Africa. The region will need two new airports, bringing its total number of airports to four by 2025, and will need massive investments in infrastructure despite huge improvements made when it hosted the World Cup football tournament in 2010.

Jo-toria will not be the only Mega-region in Africa. It will have to compete with Lagos (Nigeria), Kinshasa (capital of the Democratic Republic of Congo) and Cairo (capital of Egypt), and will be a distant fourth in terms of population and size.

Gandhi's India will have four Mega-regions greater than 15 million in population, 11 cities with populations larger than five million, and around 60 cities with more than one million people by 2025. Comparatively, China will be a concrete jungle, with a 50% urbanisation rate, and over 200 cities with populations of one million or greater in the same time frame (to put it into perspective, in Europe there are 25 such cities today).

These Mega-regions will not only be relegated to the developing world. They will be just as large in the developed world. The US will have two Mega-regions by 2020 (and four by 2030): Greater Los Angeles and New York City, which will extend into three main neighbouring states – New Jersey, Pennsylvania, Connecticut and New York State – to form the greater New York Mega-region.

Just when you think you have gotten used to the idea of Mega-regions, you will be trying to wrap your mind around the concept of life in a Mega-corridor.

Mega-corridors will connect two or more major cities, 60 km or more apart, and feature a combined population of 25 million or more. An example of a gargantuan Mega-corridor today is the Hong Kong–Shenzhen–Guangzhou corridor in China with a population of 120 million and spanning a distance of 100 km.

But nothing beats what Gandhi's country and, in particular, his home state, Gujarat, is planning. India has announced plans to develop a 1,483 km Delhi–Mumbai Industrial Mega-corridor that travels through seven states, including Gujarat, and will house a population of 203 million, one-sixth of India's population, by 2025. It will have 24 green cities along its length and will cost over $100 billion by the time it is completed. It will include development of nine Mega industrial zones as well as a high-speed freight line, three ports and six airports, including upgrades to transport and electricity infrastructure.

Other examples of emerging Mega-corridors include Tel Aviv–Jerusalem (Israel), Mumbai–Pune (India), BosWash (Boston to Washington, DC in the US), Dubai–Abu Dhabi (UAE), Nagoya–Osaka–Kyoto–Kobe (Japan) and Rio de Janeiro–São Paulo (Brazil).

What is most ironic about the rise of urbanisation and the development of world-class cities and regions/corridors is the disparity in the proportion of 'Urban Poor' and the 'Urban Rich'. The urban poor proportion ranges from anywhere between 20% and 60% of the population in major cities and in some cities like in Addis Ababa and Luanda it is higher than 70%. With the population growth in the jhopadpattis, favelas, bastis and bidonvilles higher than any other environment in the world, we are seeing the emergence of Mega-slums, where one million urban poor live in an area measuring just 1.5 square miles.

Kibera in Nairobi, with an estimated population of 2.2 million people, is the world's largest Mega-slum. Favelas in Rio de Janeiro and the jhopadpattis in India's Dharavi also have over one million people living within a square mile. A UN Habitat report measures over one billion of the seven billion people on this planet living in slums, an absolutely appalling and painful statistic.

THE VERTICAL CITY

This massive rise in urbanisation will lead to the redefinition of our cities and, in turn, our society.

For a start, our planet will look spiky from outer space, as high-rise buildings will dominate city architectures. The cities will go vertical and, in some cases like Shanghai, even have multiple layers of infrastructure. Cities will be integrated, networked and branded. Just as Salzburg is known as the music capital of the world and Milan as the fashion capital, we will see cities vie with each other to woo tourists by branding themselves around a key theme. In the future, just as countries do today, cities will compete with each other aggressively to attract investors, tourists and businesses through differentiation.

Mega-cities and Mega-regions globally will have multiple downtowns, and witness transit-oriented development which will create new opportunities for housing and business within these areas as new land is created by building platforms over highways and rail yards. While less than 70% of New York's population lives within a half-mile of mass transit, 80% of the housing unit capacity created since 2000 is transit-accessible. To push this further and to reduce the commuting time to the city, most governments will pursue transit-oriented zoning and the creation of opportunities within the same zone. This will move certain businesses from the city's key business centres to these newly created zones. One such example is Hunts Point, which has become a key food processing zone to which New York City's food processing business has relocated from its traditional home in Manhattan (New York).

'Built, not building' will be the major opportunity for property investors in future. Shrewd developers will reclaim old power plants and soldiers' barracks to develop flats for the wealthy. Fortunes will be made here as prices of properties in the Mega-cities near scenic views will grow at a faster rate than in the city outskirts. In particular, in the Western world there will be a transition to rebuilding and maintenance rather than infrastructure expansion.

The impact on our society will be profound.

In major cities around the world today, wealth and poverty coexist in close proximity, but with the development of Mega-cities we will witness a redistribution of wealth that will create significant economic divides within cities. People living in the inner city or downtown will most likely be people with high income and no kids (HINK). The inner cities will become a service-based economy, while manufacturing relocates to the city's outskirts. The income inequality gap will particularly be accentuated in the cities of developing economies. The family unit in the developing world will experience significant stress and cohabiting will extend to not only students and young people living together but also to couples sharing flats and multiple generations (grandparents, parents and kids) living together.

In the future, town planning could evolve to place offices and homes adjacent to each other or within a small compound area. In a study in which I was involved, the research team worked for Nissan Motor Company to help them understand the impact of socio-economic changes to demand for cars and vehicle technologies and found that in certain Mega-cities like Tokyo, Chennai and São Paolo traffic, security and long commuting patterns led to a tendency for residents to live and work in the same area. We found interesting evidence of this in São Paolo, where we discovered two multifunctional buildings side by side – one building was the house and the one next to it was the office. In India, we found new satellite and commercial townships being built next to Mega-cities, which include offices, housing and recreational activities in an enclosed area. This meant people in these were buying cars not for commuting to work but to drop children off at school or for weekend shopping. Nissan therefore had to rethink its product strategy which has now led it to develop electric and urban cars.

With rezoning in cities and new working practices like telework/ telecommuting, flexible and compressed working hours, and working from home becoming widespread by 2020, we will see new traffic patterns. The volume of traffic going into the city and coming out of the city during peak hours will become equal, as already noticed in Chicago. The other day, my regular taxi driver in London declined to pick me up on Thursday evening, noting that he now takes Thursdays off, instead of Fridays, as Thursday afternoons/early evenings are the new traffic horror days in London (due to people returning to their countryside homes on Thursdays and working from home on Fridays). 'Thank God it's Thursday' is the new saying.

URBAN MOBILITY 3.0

Urbanisation and growth of Mega-cities will have a profound impact on personal mobility and on the car of the future, and will lead to new mobility business models and some exciting business opportunities. In the future, instead of cities designed around cars, we will have cars designed around (Mega-)cities and car companies will not just be selling cars but also new micro mobility solutions like two-wheeled, single-seat or two-seat Segway-type vehicles.

Concepts like bike and car sharing, integrated door-to-door transport solutions, intermodality, smartphone-based urban mobility solutions and app store applications will become commonplace in the urban world.

Car sharing is a concept that has taken off in last two years from its beginnings as a cooperative model in the rural areas of Europe and for students in North America to a very effective new personal mobility business model for the urban world. Car sharing is a self-service, on-demand, pay-as-you-use, short-term (by the hour or mile) car rental. One can become a member of a car-sharing club by paying a fee of about $75 per year and renting cars for short periods, typically one to two hours, at a fixed cost of about $8–10 per hour (inclusive of fuel). The cars are generally parked walking distance from your street and can be booked on the Internet or through smartphone applications. You don't need a key as normally you will be sent a code by phone when you book your car to access the vehicle. Most car-sharing operators also provide personalisation by allowing you features like the ability to plug your iPod into the car and play your own music instead of listening to the non-stop chatter of the taxi driver. Car sharing is different from carpooling (which involves two or more people sharing a ride in the same vehicle that is most likely owned by one of them). Carpooling is successful in California where one can hire a college student for $20 a journey to allow you to get into the express (or high occupancy) lane.

In a study conducted by Frost & Sullivan[3] on the car-sharing market in 2010, we tracked an abnormal growth in the number of cars being sold to car-sharing fleets and a rapid rise in membership in these car-sharing clubs. In 2009, there were less than one million members in car-sharing clubs in Europe and North America combined. This number is expected to grow to over 25 million members in both regions by 2020. Over 40% of members of Zipcar, the world's largest car-sharing club, have given up ownership of their personal vehicles. We noticed that for every car that went into a car-sharing club, about seven to nine cars were removed from the streets.

What was most interesting is the valuation of Zipcar when it went for an IPO in April 2011. The company, which was founded in 2000 and at the time of the IPO owned under 9000 vehicles – mostly compact and medium cars in the US – was valued at $174 million. The share value on Zipcar's first day of trading surged by almost 75% to $31 per share, boosting the valuation of the company to about $1.2 billion, about $133,000 per vehicle. The company does not rent a fleet of Ferraris, but the investment community does seem to see it that way.

With entrepreneurs taking a lead in car sharing, the governments have decided they are not to be left behind with this exciting opportunity. Paris' Autolib' car-sharing scheme, similar to the already very popular bike-sharing scheme pioneered in Paris called Vélib', is the first major instance of substantial government support for car sharing and is expected to be up and running in 2012. The proposed Autolib' scheme plans to provide about 3000 electric vehicles in and around the city of Paris, with about 1400 charging points. The scheme also proposes cars-on-demand (no reservation) and one-way trips, services that have long been missing in most traditional car-sharing organisations (CSO). The Vélib' programme has been a huge success and it has since then been replicated worldwide with London launching a similar scheme in 2010, often called Boris Bikes, after its oddball mayor. In US and Canada there are similar bike-sharing schemes picking up, which already have over 50,000 members across all programmes.

Car manufacturers are bracing themselves for the inevitable threat presented by car-sharing schemes by transforming themselves into service providers offering integrated mobility solutions. Major car companies like Peugeot and Daimler are unveiling integrated mobility-on-demand solutions and using car sharing both as a branding exercise and also to determine consumer perceptions and attitudes towards their vehicles. Daimler today operates car-sharing fleets in seven cities in Ulm, Austin, Vancouver, Hamburg, San Diego, Amsterdam and Vienna with its Smart vehicles. 'The less space the city has, the more it is a target market for car2go,' notes Robert Henrich, the CEO of Daimler's car2go.

One of the most innovative mobility solutions launched by a car company is the 'Mu' concept developed by Peugeot. It offers a glimpse of what could be an attractive business model of the future for car companies that wish to boost their presence in large cities. The programme is designed around the loyalty card concept that allows one to combine micro-mobility solutions, such as bicycles and scooters, with rental cars and vans. It also allows one to rent vehicle accessories such as roof-boxes, cycle racks and child seats. If you own an electric car that has a full charge mileage of only 100 miles and you want to travel long distances on weekends, in theory it allows you to rent a Ferrari.

Mu is actually a very clever ploy from Peugeot as the only investment it has made is in creating an IT platform and hiring a few people to run it. Most of the cars that Peugeot offers under the scheme are their demonstration cars with dealerships, which are normally idle during the evenings and weekends. Such programmes will become more popular and exciting as was recently evidenced by BMW launching a similar scheme that allows one to have short-term rentals. BMW's 12-month pilot programme, called 'BMW on Demand', allows drivers near its Munich headquarters to rent various models from its model line-up, from its compact 1 Series (about €16 per hour) to its flagship, luxury, 7 Series sedan (€32 an hour). Customers will be able to pick up and drop off the cars at BMW World – the company's exhibition, event and car delivery centre next to its headquarters.

As number of cars per thousand people declines in the cities of the developed world, we will see car sharing spread to smaller cities, and by 2020 car sharing will evolve to provide solutions like peer-to-peer car sharing, in which a private individual leases a vehicle to a car-sharing operator (e.g.RelayRides). Car sharing will also integrate with carpooling/ridesharing schemes, as in the case of Zimride, which creates a larger target population for car sharing. Current Zipcar members can post their travel time on Zimride's reservation centre and offer ridesharing. This solution is becoming very popular with college students.

Car companies, as a result of future urbanisation, will realise that they are not in the business of making cars but in the market for providing personal mobility. They are not the only ones thinking that way; a plethora of other companies are gearing up to compete in the 'Mobility' space, integrating different transports modes from bikes, scooters and cars to trains and planes.

Car sharing, therefore, is not the only game-changing urban mobility business model of the future but rather an element of what will constitute the integrated door-to-door mobility platform of the future. The concept of a dynamic transport solution integrating different modes under a single entity will make intermodal transportation easier for city dwellers in the large Mega-cities of the future. Although the concept is still in the nascent stage and the stakeholders are operating independently, the future will see an integrated approach.

So what is this integrated mobility? Imagine this scenario: you are travelling to Paris for business. As you exit your home, your phone directs you to turn left and walk 250 metres to the nearest bus stop, take bus no. 150 to Vauxhall tube station and then hop into the Victoria line to King's Cross St Pancras international station. The phone informs you that your train to Paris is running ten minutes late and that your check-in has now started. Once in the train and on the other side of the pond, in Paris, the phone directs you to the nearest car-sharing parking spot, where you had booked your electric car to travel to your meeting. It even books your parking spot near the client's office, which is normally a very congested area in which the waiting time for a parking spot can be hours if you just drop in. The procedure is seamless and consists of one mobile ticket that connects international transport and all travel modalities. This is the future of mobility and the new battlefield for 'mobility integrators', which will be fought over fiercely by existing players and new entrants.

According to Mohammad Mubarak, senior mobility specialist at Frost & Sullivan who leads the research in this field, 'We will witness transport operators (rail and bus companies), mobile phone operators, IT services providers and on-line booking agencies providing door-to-door, multi modal solutions. These mobility integrators [MI] will take transportation solutions to the next generation by fully integrating the existing long and short distance transportation providers to create a single solution.' Mubarak's research found that mobility integrators will partner with various online service providers to offer travel scheduling and ticket booking options to customers through an online web portal similar to the existing models of Travelocity.com and Expedia. Customers will be able to register with the MIs and use them as a one-stop shop to book tickets for journeys that encompass both local city transport and long-distance travel on intercity trains or flights. MIs will use mobile communication systems to update customers about various information related to their trip such as departure/ arrival time, bus/tube/train platforms, pickup points for car/bike sharing, and so on. General packet radio service (GPRS)- and global positioning system (GPS)-enabled phones will also help in alerting customers about upcoming destinations, traffic information and other navigation features.

The increased penetration of Smartphone and mobility apps will take this notion of mobility integration to the next level with the MIs developing dedicated Mobility Web 2.0 platforms to provide a suite of services ranging from dynamic intermodal transport planning, including traffic guidance, journey planning, scheduling and routing, ePayment using mobile phones,location-based services, and fleet optimisation (for B2B).

'Beam me up, Scotty' might not happen in our Mega-cities soon but we will certainly experience seamless travel using multiple modes in this new urban mobility business world. Car companies and most mobility service providers will begin to measure their success through 'mobility share' and not 'market share'.

THE NEW HUB AND SPOKE ENTERPRISE MODEL

An interesting urban business enterprise model of the future will be the hub and spoke model.

A hub and spoke model typically involves arrangements whereby one site acts as a principal base that provides centralised support to satellite sites which are connected to the principal site. This system was pioneered by the airline industry, which designates certain cities as hubs, schedules long-distance flights with larger capacity planes to these hubs, and offers connecting shorter flights from the hubs to smaller cities, which can be served by smaller aircraft.

With the rise of urbanisation, this hub and spoke concept will spread to various industries and be used in defining the future of urban health care, supermarkets, retail centres, and logistics and transport companies.

Here is a possible logistics scenario for urban development: double trailers and Mega-trucks, as much as 25 metres in length and weighing up to 60 tons, will travel from all four compass points of a country/ continent and drop one trailer on the outskirts of the city centre at the hub (refer to Chart 5.1), while only smaller trailers will then be allowed access to the city centre. This is because cities of the future will have congestion zones or low-emission zones that will force polarisation of vehicle sizes – smaller trucks in cities and larger super or Mega-trucks outside cities (currently the European Union is considering introducing such Mega-trucks in Europe, although there is a divide among EU states regarding their acceptance). In Europe, by 2020, it is expected that more than 13 cities will charge a tariff for congestion and that more than 150 cities will have declared low-emissions zones. Some Smart cities (refer to Chapter 2, 'Smart is the New Green', for a definition of and trends affecting Smart cities) like Amsterdam already have policies in place that will permit only electric light commercial vehicles to deliver bread to bakeries inside city centres in the future. So if you are trying to supply commercial goods to a city centre, you will need to either have an electric vehicle or work with a transporter who has one. Similar policies are also being considered in France, where mayors of towns and cities could be empowered to restrict city-centre access to only certain types of vehicles.

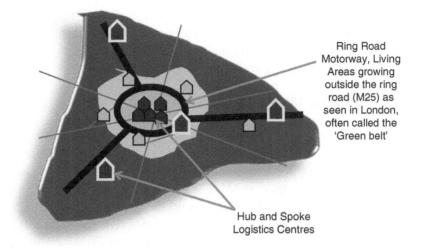

Ring Road Motorway, Living Areas growing outside the ring road (M25) as seen in London, often called the 'Green belt'

Hub and Spoke Logistics Centres

Chart 5.1 How Mega-cities will expand in future behind their outskirts and have hub and spoke type enterprise model (with example of hub and spoke logistics centres)
Source: Frost & Sullivan.

The hub and spoke model will also apply to health care. Most health care centres and hospitals will work on a similar hub and spoke concept and already do so in some Mega-cities globally like in London. This concept will benefit both the state as well as the patients. The concept can provide efficient, high-quality, specialised and sophisticated medical services in select locations (the hubs), while simultaneously providing easy access to regular health care and attend to low complexity cases through the satellite spokes. At the hubs, the hospitals can offer specialised services like complicated surgeries, intensive care facilities and offer Mega-hospitals with more than 1000 beds for patients (e.g. UCLH, London; Necker, Paris). The spokes can be smaller hospitals with limited beds or even smaller spokes like health centres, GP centres, lifestyle health centres in high population density places, airports, central railway stations, retail spaces, etc.

The hub and spoke retail model is already very prominent in big cities with large Mega-stores or shopping malls located outside core downtown areas and smaller convenient 24-hour shopping stores situated inside the city centres. With the strong shift to online retailing, the trend will accentuate and it will become even more important to retailers to try new store formats.

This hub and spoke model allows lower investment and operating cost, optimum utilisation of expensive equipment and, most importantly, enables companies to reach out to the populations of densely populated cities, airports and railway stations.

THE MACRO TO MICRO OF URBANISATION

The development of Mega-cities and Mega-regions is actually a blessing for the well-being of both society and business. Urbanisation provides unique opportunities for all types of businesses, including entrepreneurs and pioneers.

In the future these Mega-cities and Mega-regions, rather than nations, will drive wealth and economic prosperity. Cities like Bogota and Seoul account for about 50% of the country's GDP; Budapest (Hungary) and Brussels (Belgium) each account for roughly 45%. London, with 12.5% of the UK's population, accounts for 20% of the country's GDP and 15% of the jobs, which some forecast to contribute to about 30% of the UK's total GDP by 2030. The BosWash corridor will have 58.2 million in population and is expected to account for one-fifth of the United States' GDP in 2025. Jo-toria houses 20% of South Africa's population but contributes to around 34% of the country's GDP. So make your own decisions regarding who is more important and easier to do business with: Seoul with its area of 605 sq. km or South Korea, which spans a 100,032 sq. km area, for both contribute equally to the nation's GDP.

Today's cities use three-fourths of the world's energy and generate over 80% of the world's carbon. Although the major source of income in cities will be service-based economies, urban areas will consume more than two-thirds of all types of manufactured goods. Cities in the developing world will need huge infrastructure spending. For example, India will need to invest over $500 billion in this decade to maintain adequate infrastructure to accommodate the citizens of its cities. Cities will need health care for aging populations and to keep up with younger people's changing lifestyles; investment in Smart grids, urban transport, city security, water and building management to accommodate energy demands; and huge expenditures in IT hardware and services. Cities, therefore, will make all businesses and business people rethink their strategy of manufacturing, distributing and servicing their customers.

I predict that, in the future, as the mayors of Mega-cities become more powerful, there will be a huge shift in how corporations and governments view the market opportunity presented by these cities. The Mayor of London sits on a budget of more than $120 billion every year, and with London's GDP contribution of over $600 billion, it – like many other similar cities – deserves a change in how organisations structure and position their businesses around cities.

Some forward-looking organisations like Siemens (refer to the Siemens case study later in the chapter) and IBM have already taken a giant leap in this direction. For IBM, the future world is getting *instrumented*, *interconnected* and virtually all things, processes and ways of working are becoming *intelligent* (read more in Chapter 2, 'Smart is the New Green' on IBM's Smart city strategy). IBM paints a picture of the *instrumented* city that incorporates sensors, cameras and connectivity into all forms of infrastructure, including cars and humans. IBM believes in linking and *interconnecting* everything, including linking information on roads, in cars and railways, throughout the supply chain, the electricity grid ('the Internet of things') and, most interestingly IBM predicts the world becoming *intelligent*. In an *intelligent* world, cars talk to each other (a phenomenon called Floating Car Data is already being trialled in Europe, Japan, North America and China). Moreover, sensors talk to each other and predict the location of traffic jams, both before and during your drive. Similarly, a delayed train can talk to the local buses to optimise their timing, and carriage loadings are displayed in real time on platforms so people know where to stand to get a seat.

IBM believes a lot of this data is in silos. The left hand of the city does not know what the right hand is doing. If the IT systems in the city could connect the data and convert it into information, especially if the information is available in a number of standard open formats for third parties to create services, it could enable multiple hands in the city to work in unison to provide better transport planning, manage the grids smartly, make the cities safer, provide better incident and disaster service management and make life more fun for millions of urban residents. The key to this for organisations like IBM and Siemens is to move away from providing single products and solutions to cross-linked intelligent urban infrastructure solutions.

A macro to micro analysis of this Mega Trend provides a plethora of opportunities for all types of businesses.

I managed a project for one of the world's largest lighting manufacturers during which we looked at how urbanisation would impact our client's business and what opportunities it brings. We looked at the opportunities based on their lighting market segmentation, which was split

CASE STUDY: SIEMENS FOCUSES ON CITY AS THE CUSTOMER

One company that has been visionary in understanding the potential of Mega trends over the past decade has been Siemens AG, a highly diversified €73.5 billion German giant.

In 2008, the company reorganised itself around the major Mega trends of the decade – changing global demographics, urbanisation, climate change and globalisation. It reduced its board from 11 to eight members and organised itself around three business areas – industry, energy and health care.

Approximately two years after the new organisational structure was established, CEO Peter Löscher realised that urban infrastructures provide huge business potential if addressed appropriately. In late 2010, he started a strategy process that led to the announcement, in October 2011, of a fourth sector called 'Infrastructure and Cities' (IC). The objective of creating this new division was to exploit the opportunity posed by city infrastructure spending.

Siemens' strategy seems quite simple. It has combined 80% of its business, which is targeted towards cities, chiefly in the power distribution, mobility and building technologies, to form five new Divisions within its city Sector: rail systems, mobility and logistics, low and medium voltage, Smart grid and building technologies – products, solutions and services which are all essential to a city's survival. Through this move, Siemens has now opened its doors to a €2 trillion market of annual global city infrastructure spending, out of which Siemens has an addressable market of around €300 billion. Some €225 billion of this is addressable by Siemens' broad portfolio of technologies from the IC sector, with the remainder targeted mainly by their other divisions in health care, water and their Osram Lighting subsidiary. Siemens expects a growth with CAGR between 3% and 5% over this decade, an increase in demand in the Americas and Asia, and well-balanced market growth across their full product line.

This newly formed IC division, with €16.5 billion in revenues and some 87,000 employees in 2011, not only offers research for unique urban solutions but also provides innovative and customised city concepts for mayors and urban planners ranging from integrated mobility solutions to security technologies and Smart grid applications. It expects Mega-cities to provide three-digit million-Euro revenue opportunities to them. In some cities like London, it is already realising this vision (Siemens in London already has a substantial three-digit million-Euro range, which excludes the current large orders for new rail vehicles).

The performance of this unit in Q3 2011, during the first few months after its birth, has quite a story to tell. Not only has the division proved its worth by bagging the largest contract in Siemens' 160-year corporate history with Deutsche Bahn at €6 billion, it also now boasts the world's broadest portfolio of urban city solutions, far outdoing its rivals. This new Sector will be a strong contributor in the Siemens Group and plans to achieve the €100 billion revenue target in the coming years.

The company does not plan to limit its scope only to Megacities (>ten million population), but to expand its entire spectrum of city solutions to smaller cities globally as well. In this manner, Siemens plans to increasingly locate its respective business areas closer to its city customers. When interviewed for this book, Dr Roland Busch, CEO of the Siemens Infrastructure and Cities Division and member of the Managing Board of Siemens AG, commented, 'A key element of our strategy is the investment and expansion of the City Account Manager programme [CiAMs]. We now have approximately 70 city account managers installed in cities across the world and, we will continue to ramp up our resources according to the city potential. Our CiAMs offer the entire Siemens portfolio and strive to be involved as early as possible in the city planning process and through consultative selling. It is clear that the earlier we can contribute our know-how, the better our chances are for landing business opportunities later in concrete projects.'

The company understands that, to tap into the public sector funds in the future, it needs close partnership with a vast number of stakeholders and, has therefore developed a city-based organisational structure, with a city business development account management structure at its head, to allow for easier and quicker decision-making and, most importantly, forge strong partnerships.

The company's go-to-market strategy includes an increased focus on the so-called vertical markets. Siemens has identified data centres, hospitality, Smart buildings, rail infrastructure, airports, harbours and logistic hubs, road and city mobility, and municipalities as additional focus markets for the IC Sector.

Not only is Siemens expected to benefit with top-line growth through this initiative, it also expects large gains through synergies, economies of scale and efficiency improvements in its operations. For a start, the hugely diversified conglomerate expects savings through a shared-service approach for certain key corporate functions such as accounting and IT. Within some former divisions, like low-voltage and medium-voltage groups, it sees benefits in combining them through optimisation of the factory footprint and the supply-chain process. Siemens is also witnessing better market coverage by merging sales channels, especially within its Low-Medium Voltage and Building Technologies divisions. As a result, the company has a more robust portfolio strategy with enhanced management focus on specific markets, technologies and business types. A good example of this is their decision to reorganise the old Mobility Division into two separate divisions: Rail Systems and Mobility and Logistics. While Rail Systems focuses on manufacturing of trains, the Mobility and Logistics Division's business model is an IT and software-based solution that manages the flow of traffic and goods in cities. Separating these areas provides enhanced management focus, is more aligned to customer needs, is based on clear value-add, and has a distinct business model (assembling a rail vehicle versus the IT-driven e-vehicle infrastructure).

When I asked if this is a risky strategy given that cities in the developed world are struggling due to the economic crisis, Dr Busch commented, 'We support cities through providing finance [through Siemens Financial Services], performance guarantee programmes like our energy performance contracting and also solutions that can generate additional income for cities, like tolling systems.' Given that they provide finance, payback guarantees on their work and help generate income for cities, it indeed sounds like a compelling business case.

To show off its 'urban' capabilities, Siemens has decided to develop a $46 million visitor attraction and global knowledge hub – the Crystal (www.thecrystal.org) – which will open to the public in 2012 to showcase Siemens' offerings to make the world's cities better places to live and work in.

Designed and developed in two dramatic, crystal-shaped sections, the Crystal will be an eye-catching new landmark for London's Royal Victoria Docks, hopefully replicating the success of the similar Gherkin building in London's financial district.

No wonder, when Doha was chosen as the venue for World Cup football in 2022, Siemens was one of the first companies to rush into the country by opening a local office. With Doha planning to spend over $40 billion on infrastructure-related projects, including a new airport worth $10 billion, one cannot fault Siemens' strategy to put cities as top seed in its strategy for growth.

With an order book in January 2012 of €24 billion for this sector alone and a substantial bank balance, Siemens expects to make strategic acquisitions in this sector to boost its product and services portfolio.

Siemens, for sure, has been much smarter than its rivals, such as General Electric, Schneider or ABB, who are still wrestling with the idea of establishing a city division and have at most created a job function or a small department. The first-mover advantage for Siemens here could be critical in its becoming the world's first €100 billion 'urban' enterprise. However, what confuses me is that, instead of choosing a Mega-city like London (the only Mega-city in Europe) as its global headquarters for this division, which would have been appropriate for this Mega vision, the company decided to be conventional and stick to its roots in Munich.

into fields like outdoor lighting, retail lighting, etc. We made some interesting findings and presented our client with a bucket full of opportunities. Some of the changes and the opportunities urbanisation provided to our client's outdoor lighting business are as follows:

- Public places remaining open 24/7 as people in cities prefer things 'on demand', which means more lighting in places like zoos, park gyms and late opening of museums.
- A city's expansion from 25 to 40 km in diameter enables funding for and necessitates the installation of more street lighting.
- City transport infrastructure expansion by more 50% will require

lighting in public transport, streets, stations and retail centres for city dwellers.

- Beautification schemes to build a city's image and differentiation with lighting becoming central to it are more commonplace: for example, Istanbul's famous Bosphorus Bridge.
- Sport/event/outdoor facilities to increasingly be used at night (e.g. the golf club in Singapore is open at night) and for multiple purposes for night sport and social/virtual gathering events (e.g. rollerblading or skiing at night, urban bingo)
- Security to push more lighting in dark places, especially since high-rise buildings block moonlight (by 2020, the sky in densely populated areas will not be bright during the full moon).

An interesting opportunity we realised is that a possible smoking ban in China by 2020 could push 300 million people out in the streets to smoke, which means more lighting will be required. Interesting!

URBAN SHOPPER WILL NOT COME TO STORES, BUT STORES WILL NEED TO COME TO THE SHOPPER

The retail sector, in particular will benefit immensely from urbanisation, but at the same time will need to make serious investments as the retail industry urban business model changes. As cities expand, they will create multiple city centres with varying retail atmospheres. The urban retail model will shift from mom-and-pop shops, whose incidence is typically very high in the developing world (as high as 90% of retail businesses in countries like India today and often termed the unorganised sector) to the chain stores (organised sector). In particular, a key impact will be on channels to market, and retail owners will need to think of smaller and more exciting stores in busy areas like train stations, similar to what we see in Tokyo, Japan, where a whole community of retail and hospitality industry – a station within a station – thrives in its subway system. Subway stores might even go virtual as seen recently in an experiment by Tesco in Seoul with its new Homeplus Subway Virtual Store where busy Koreans could order groceries in subways using smartphones and get home in time to pick up the delivery. An average store is expected to physically shrink by up to 20% and leading brands will run and staff their own mini stores within a Mega-store (already very popular in China) – literally a store within a store. In Mega-cities of the future, retailers need to realise that shoppers will not come to stores, but stores will need to come to the shoppers.

Kiosks or pop-up stores only make 1% of the current European market but these will increase to over 20% of total channel share. Kiosks will help retailers counter the higher rents and general overheads associated with bigger stores. Kiosk manufacturing is an opportunity I have recommended to several friends in Asia, as the current Rehri (small table-type booths/kiosks) used for selling wares will be substituted with modern kiosks.

At the same time, we will see increase in flagship stores by leading brands and there will be intense competition for space in the up-market area within a city. Over 75% of Hugo Boss' profit and volume is made in B, C and outlet stores, yet future plans include an increase of 12% in flagship and high-end, company-owned branded stores.

We will also see huge growth in the franchised business model in the hospitality industry as hotels and restaurants fight to gain mind share as well as market share. Three in five hotels are expected to be franchised, and investing in two- and three-star hotel chains in the developing world which cater to the middle class will be highly profitable. Dedicated hospitality venues will need to diversify to make ends meet; therefore, they will open more locations to weddings, conferences and lectures only to compete with non-dedicated venues like football clubs offering weddings on their premises in the future. All building assets will need to sweat harder as estate prices, energy costs and overheads will impact profitability. Hotels will be considering usage or pay-by-the-hour business models.

*

In the developing world, the opportunities presented by urbanisation are immense. Even in Mega-slums, banks can secure microcredit financing which helps not only their corporate social responsibility tag but also their bottom line. Image-conscious countries like Brazil have hired more than 40 architects to redesign Rio de Janeiro's favelas to make them presentable for the 2014 World Cup football tournament and 2016 Olympics. Countries like India and China, in the coming decade, will need over 900 million square metres of new housing space annually. That's an area equivalent to two large Mega-cities. Most new buildings, for instance in China, have to be designed according to strict new energy standards. Construction companies, green material suppliers and property developers are expected to have a field day.

Water consumption per capita in the developing world's cities will increase by 40 to 50 litres a day and energy use will double in next ten years. Power generation and water infrastructure equipment and service providers like Siemens, GE and many others will benefit hugely.

Even governments are expected to get savvier in supporting their industrial bases' attempts to win contracts from cities for infrastructure development. Japan, in particular, has been rather wise. For the $100 billion Delhi–Mumbai Industrial Mega-corridor (DMIC) project, Japan has very cleverly provided the funding but has also bargained with India to ensure the tenders have a clause that makes it mandatory for a Japanese company to be selected as the lead partner in the major infrastructure projects. As a result, Japanese companies like Hitachi, Mitsubishi Corporation, Toshiba, JGC, Itochu and Tokyo Electric Power Company are expected to benefit immensely. And they will also pick up many peripheral projects, like a small task of setting up 24 green cities in the DMIC area. And we thought Siemens and IBM were the clever ones. Perhaps other countries (including the European Union and the United States) can learn the lesson here that investing in infrastructure abroad might provide better return on their investment than in their home countries and still creates jobs for its nationals.

One could even argue that in the future the UN should admit Mega-cities, and not countries, as member states.

As for our personal lives, we humans will either move to different cities as our careers develop or move within cities as we progress through different stages of our life. I have personally moved seven times within London, starting in the more chic areas of Fulham and Clapham in my 20s, to now living in a suburban house with my children. As urban dwellers we love our cities for the diversity, entertainment and socialisation they provide, but at the same time we hate the traffic, the overcrowding and the competitive behaviour of our fellow urbanites. As investors, we exploit the vast opportunities the city affords, both in opportunities for entrepreneurs and in their vast service-based economies. The opportunity is immense and the change it brings, globally, is massive.

Charles Dickens portrayed the eighteenth century as a tale of two cities; the twenty-first century will be a tale of Mega-cities.

6

SOCIAL TRENDS THAT WILL
MODEL OUR FUTURE SOCIETY

This chapter discusses the six major social trends that will have a profound impact on our society in this decade. The six trends covered here are Geo Socialisation, Robo Slaves, Decade of the iPad Generation and Little Emperors, Reverse Brain Drain and Global Talent Wars, Middle Bulge, and Girl Power.

SIX DEGREES APART: GEO-SOCIALISATION

It took the radio 38 years to reach an audience of 50 million, the television 13 years, the Internet four years, but it took Facebook less than two years. If Facebook was a country, it would be the third largest in the world today with over 800 million members; and with eight people joining Facebook every second (its birth rate is twice that of the world's), it is also the fastest-growing community in the world.

One of the mega-mega trends of the past decade was social networking as can be evidenced by the success of sites like Facebook and LinkedIn. I believe the next platform of social networking will rely on geographic services and capabilities such as geocoding and geotagging to allow social networks to connect and coordinate users with local people or events that match their interests. This collaborative web-mapping technique will result in new trends in networking and digital marketing and innovative ways of socialising, furthering the evolution of interactions between people and their surroundings. It will allow users to interact relative to location and time on a real-time basis.

Geo-socialisation allows a user with a smartphone (or other portable device), based on his or her preferences and contacts to stay informed about local deals, the locations of their contacts and interesting events in their immediate vicinity – thereby allowing this user to create a 'customised social life on the go'. It gives a user the ability to leave a mark on the places where he or she has visited and allows 'showing off' personal interactions and other geo-updates in the name of technology. It is an example of socialisation leveraging on geographic services and capabilities, such as geocoding and geotagging (i.e. the geographic identification of data).

We have named this trend 'six degrees apart', taking our inspiration from the concept originally set out by Frigyes Karinthy of 'six degrees of separation' (also referred to as the 'human web'), which implies that everyone is, on average, approximately six steps away from any other person on Earth and this chain of connected friends can be made to connect any two people in six steps or fewer. Geo-socialisation can definitely convert this theory into reality.

Geo-socialisation: Who is on your block?

In a real-life scenario, geo-socialisation would mean if you are shopping on Oxford Street in London, you could be pushed towards certain discounts. These alerts could range from a 'Buy one get one' Gucci handbag free in Selfridges between 5 p.m. and 7 p.m. today, or receiving a notification through Facebook that you have an old friend from your university having a drink at a local bar 500 metres away. By connecting and coordinating preferences, contacts and geo-locations, your mobile phone will have the power to keep you abreast of 'who is on your block'.

The possibilities and opportunities of this geo-socialisation are endless. We are now talking about a world where markets, businesses and individuals are driven by the need to interact, advertise and promote in real time. For personal lives, this feature would now open a whole new dimension for socialisation – the ability to meet and greet new contacts and find deals on a location-based pretext.

With concepts like Foursquare and Facebook with their new geo-social feature 'Places', geo-social networking is already on its way to be the new wave of socialisation.

Geo-social commerce: Connecting while buying and buying when connecting

Geo-socialisation will go beyond mere socialisation, just as Facebook has done today. It will manifest itself to a fully fledged marketing strategy that companies have to reckon with, particularly while targeting digitally empowered and socially mobile connected consumers. Connectivity through personal portable devices might become the sole means of getting through to the customers of the future and companies are getting increasingly cognizant of this trend. Social utilities and businesses would need to push alerts to create touch points with digitally predisposed customers for initiation of transactions and purchases of local deals.

To capitalise on real-time demand from a whole new spectrum of geographically tagged customers, businesses will soon need to be equipped with new infrastructure and resources. This will also force investments from the retail, entertainment and hospitality industries to upgrade their systems with new IT software to enable these services, thereby bringing a new source of revenue to mobile operators and IT software and system houses. It will allow these industries to manage their inventory in real time and push promotions when inventory piles up or fills capacity – for example, in restaurants, when they are relatively empty.

Geo-socialisation will also be used in disaster scenarios to allow users to coordinate information and rescue operations during natural calamities.

Macro to micro implications

As of 2011, the global location-based markets is valued at $2.9 billion and is expected to increase to $8.3 billion in 2014, according to Gartner.[1] Not surprisingly, majority of the revenue for this market will not be generated from mobile operators or social networking sites, but through consumers like you and me. While companies are trying different ways to tap into this trend and app developers are moving towards a more sophisticated and customised geo-socialisation software, let us look at some of the new business models that this Mega Trend would usher in.

Location-based incentives: Check me out when I check in

Today Yelp, Foursquare and Facebook offer check-in incentives where local businesses can send alerts to geographically close customers, inviting them to stop and claim incentives and creating a gaming scenario for geo-socialisation. These incentives range from free gift cards for Starbucks, free restaurant deals or even loyalty points for a restaurant review. In 2010, Foursquare reported over 381 million check-ins, which translates to people checking in 23 times per second 24/7 globally.[2]

I recently had the opportunity of obtaining such an incentive one night while sitting at a bar with a friend. I noticed a small placard on our table generously offering the customers free cocktails if we would 'check in' on Facebook and 'liked' the place. Although I was searching for 'a catch' in this freebie, the entire exercise was pretty simple. The instant we checked in, we could order the most expensive martinis, and, as promised, they were free. Although we were not sure who exactly was winning in this case, we did make a mental note to do it again and perhaps spread the word, too.

The business model here is quite straightforward. Business establishments, such as this bar, hope to lure in new customers who had viewed the 'like' update on their friend's newsfeed and perhaps visit the place themselves. The 'like' in the newsfeed acts as a free advertisement or a five-star rating among a group of friends. This location-based incentive simply translates to more business for the bar, a business model costing them a couple of cocktails per customer, but that has the potential to bring in at least few more new ones. For such businesses, mobile advertising is now conventional advertising.

Catch me if you can: The Jimmy Choo campaign

A fantastic marketing gimmick riding high on geo-location services was orchestrated by footwear powerhouse Jimmy Choo in 2010 here in London. This world-renowned retail brand organised a real-time treasure hunt titled 'Catch A Choo' campaign[3] wherein Jimmy Choo trainers checked in various spots in London and around 4000 Foursquare users tried to follow and hunt them down. If they were lucky enough to 'Catch A Choo', then contestants could get any pair of Jimmy Choo shoes for free. This brilliant marketing strategy resulted in a 33% increase of sales of the sneakers in-store with one in 17 people in London hunting for a Choo.

Gigwalk: Walking is my business

Geo-socialisation gets even more interesting when it becomes a paid pastime. Gigwalk is a mobile app that acts as a real-time job board that pays people to complete random gigs for businesses that demand real-time attention.[4] You could be walking down a road and get paid to do a task, which could be as random as taking a photo or confirming stock in a store or verifying the name of a restaurant or street. Businesses would advertise the gigs that needed to be completed and interested gigwalkers would complete the tasks at their own pace. The only requirement is that the gigwalkers must be digitally empowered. This digital mobile workforce is paid anywhere from $3 to $100 per gig.

The resounding success of this mobile app in the United States proved itself when it celebrated 1.5 million completed tasks with 100,000 individuals in December 2011, just seven months after its launch. The highest earnings in a three-month period were around $11,713 by a single individual. Gigwalk has not only taken geo-socialisation to the next level, it was has also provided supplemental income for thousands of Americans.

Virtual dollar: Invisible good, visible me

Many heads turned in November 2011 when Zynga, a social gaming company, announced its intention to go public, with an anticipated value of a whopping $7 billion. This gaming company has adopted an innovative business model that relies heavily on the popularity of Facebook. Its sneaky pop-up adverts on Facebook entice users to spend real money on virtual cash for their games, a concept that accounts for a cool $826 million in revenue for the company per annum. Now, if we extend this scenario to a location-based concept, Zynga has definitely nailed a cool business model for companies to adopt. In the future, we could receive alerts to spend real cash on virtual items or gain loyalty points based on the 'here and now' concept. These micro-transactions can range from sales of digital gifts, virtual data or even personalised widgets that are based on the location of a connected customer.

Augmented reality: I digitally manoeuvre my world

While geo-location services seem to invade the very fabric of social networking, there is still scope for new technological developments which would make it seem extremely generic. Geo-socialisation is primarily dependent on mobile technology or apps, but as manufacturers of mobile phone companies and tablet PCs get more innovative, we will soon welcome new aspects of social networking. Augmented reality (AR) is one such technological development that would, again, revamp the way people interact with their surroundings.

AR is defined as a real-time augmented view of the environment through digital data via the use of text, audio, graphics, videos and navigation systems that increase users' interactivity with the local environment. It would literally change the way people look at their world, bringing in a fresh layer of digital information which can be viewed in real time through any screen, be it a mobile phone camera or even a bionic contact lens. This will extend business and mobility options, social interactions and experiences, making the entire world interactive and digitally manoeuvrable.

Augmented social networking: I connect with people I see

Now AR can be extended to geo-socialisation. AR will allow users to access pre-submitted information on people in a particular location – be it on a shopping trip, or a sports game, or while driving on a road, or even while walking around the city – on a camera or a computer screen. An augmented and digital view of the surrounding people with their information, preferences and other data would inform AR users of potential new friends in that immediate vicinity through a cool camera-like view.

Imagine shopping in Harrods. Now, through AR, you could not only receive visual sales alerts on your favourite goods through your camera view (on your phone), but also a flashing 'social alert' that a potential date or business contact is a floor above or sitting in the Starbucks next door. While you might have to think of a spontaneous opening line each time, AR would literally 'visualise your geo-socialisation' options, fuelling the fun levels of a typical daily routine in our lives in 2020 (refer to chapter 9 on "Connectivity and Convergence for more information on Augmented Reality).

Online communities: Together we influence

People's innate tendencies to share, imitate and cooperate in a group have inevitably entered the realm of social networking. Online communities or blogs represent the convergence of strong ideas, similar passions and interests to advocate something borne out of a common shared purpose, popular forms of which are blogs, wikis, micro-blogging or even subgroups on social networking sites. The interesting feature to note, however, is that the power of the social group has transformed itself from a mere knowledge-sharing portal to a full-fledged support group or a marketing forum, calling the shots for new product development, or feedback on certain services, or even coming together to support a common social cause.

Crouching social tiger, hidden digital dragon: Social appetite from Chinese consumers

Urban Chinese consumers today are more digitally sensitised than their Western counterparts. With over 50% of the 500 million online

Chinese consumers having more than one social networking profile, social media claims to be a more powerful media channel in China than in countries, such as the United States. However, the Golden Shield Project (also nicknamed the Great Firewall of China) which acts as a censorship and surveillance gatekeeper has successfully blocked access to prominent websites such as Facebook, YouTube, Foursquare, Twitter and Google. So what do these digitally empowered consumers with a penchant for social networking do? Enter social platforms copycats – the answer to the Chinese's appetite for social media. These digital dragons have thought of a cool new way of creating local versions of the legendary websites. Renren and Kaixin001 are loosely based on the same layout as Facebook, and Sina Weibo and Youku are similar to Twitter and YouTube, respectively. Not to be left behind in geo-socialisation, China now also has Jiepang, which is the equivalent of America's Foursquare. Like every other industry, China sticks to the same old moral: 'Be global, stay local'. Their landscape of social networking is no different.

Social networking today has moved from merely creating new contacts to being at the right place, right time and with the right people. Social groups are no longer a huge cluster of acquaintances. They are now an elite class of digital users who share similar preferences, customising the entire social experience for people. Ambient connectivity, coupled with geo-location options, will make our social life in the future a digital serendipity. This digital empowerment will create a multifaceted view of our environment allowing us to record our social life on a real-time and a location-specific bases very much like a live video stream. Check-ins, geo-socialisation options and AR will allow us to leave a mark wherever we go – a geo-footprint in the sands of time that will be recorded on social networking platforms for generations to come.

ROBO-SLAVES

During the American Civil War, Abraham Lincoln helped his country abolish slavery, but by the end of this decade it will be back. We will all have personal slaves in our households; only this time we will not fight a civil war over them. These slaves, which will act as butlers in our everyday lives, will be androids that are developed from a combination of robotic technology and artificial intelligence.

The US army predicts that 30% of its army by 2030 will be robotised. The government of South Korea predicts a robot in every Korean kindergarten by 2013 and, by 2020, a robot in every household. Now these government statements might be a bit farfetched, but for sure we will start seeing first applications of robots in domestic life by the end of this decade.

In November 2008, I visited Honda's global Headquarters (HQ) in Tokyo. To my utter shock, I was greeted at the HQ by ASIMO, the Honda robot, and led to a waiting room. When I ordered a drink, ASIMO brought it to me, even though I was sitting a good 20 meters away and not easily visible or identifiable. This was the first time I became interested in robots, and the experience led me to research them and the role they could play in our futures.

Research on Honda's ASIMO, which stands for 'Advanced Step in Innovative Mobility', started around 1986, and the robot was officially brought into the world in 2000. It took Honda's engineers about ten years, beginning in the mid-1980s, to get ASIMO to walk, but the latest version of ASIMO, which was showcased in November 2011, has developed very well during his formative years by having advanced artificial intelligence built into him, which allows him to sense and make independent decisions without the need for an operator – indeed, the current version of ASIMO[5] is very close to being a human. Honda believes that robots will one day play an important role in our personal lives and, in particular, they will help humans with special needs to be more mobile, as shown by some of its new innovations like walk assist and stride management assist devices. One could argue, with the Japanese population declining, the Japanese would do better making babies than robots.

Robotic technology development started in the 1950s and '60s, and today it is already assisting humans in the manufacturing, space, military, civil security and transportation sectors. Robots have already taken over human roles in the manufacturing industry, where they have significantly reduced worker injuries, accidents and manufacturing defects. In the automotive industry, robotic technology allows a car to be made with much more precise welds and almost zero errors – better than could be ever achieved by humans. In the health care industry there are numerous successful examples of very precise, minimally invasive, surgery done by robots, and in some cases with the doctor as far as 200 miles away from the patient's bed. Robotics has enabled surgeons to perform micro-cuts and operations beyond the scope of human ability.

In the Afghan and Iraq wars, robots have made giant leaps into the battleground. QinetiQ, a British defence and technology company, is the world's leading supplier of military robotics. The company has sold more than 3000 of its TALON robots, which have been deployed for detecting and disarming mines laid down by Al-Qaeda and Taliban militants. To market its products, QinetiQ impresses its customers by showcasing the capabilities of these robots. When it was marketing its Dragon Runner robots to the Canadian army, it organised a grand show where the robot made its entrance by climbing the front stairs of the embassy, manoeuvring its way through doorways, and travelling up and down a flight of stairs to the theatre dais, where it greeted the Canadian ambassador by waving a Canadian national flag. It then showed off its dexterity by dropping a ceremonial hockey puck into the Ambassador's hand. So impressed were the Canadians that they ordered the robots without further ado.

The successful shift of robots from industrial applications to homes will be driven by improvements in artificial intelligence, and we can expect the first applications of robots to enter domestic life by the end of this decade. Chart 6.1 shows examples of applications of robots in our day-to-day life.

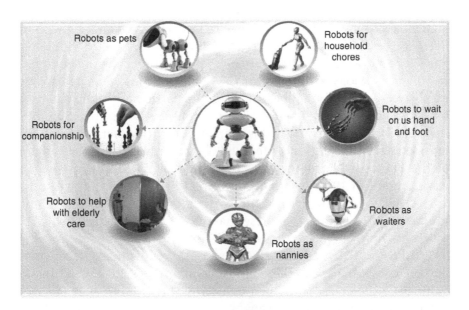

Chart 6.1 **Future Robo-slave: Pervasive robotic technology in 2030 that will 'act as a slave' in everyday life**

Photo credits: Dreamstime and GeckoSystems International.
Source: Frost & Sullivan.

Macro to micro implications

There are fortunes to be made in this robotic industry as robots will be used across diverse applications.

In a study conducted by Frost & Sullivan,[6] the revenues of the global welding robotics market were $1,426 million in 2009 and expected to double to about $2,945 million in 2016, growing at a CAGR of almost 11% from 2009 to 2016. The applications of robots in health-care will witness even more impressive growth, making huge fortunes for entrepreneurs and pioneers. In particular, robot-assisted surgery (RAS) will witness significant growth with CAGRs of over 30% in next ten years. Frost & Sullivan analysts, who have been tracking this industry, project the market for robot-assisted surgery to grow from a mere $495 million in 2007 to an industry worth $2.8 billion by 2014. The RAS systems covered in the Frost & Sullivan study included robots that aid surgery by offering endoscope holding, positioning or controlling, and remote surgery systems (also termed telesurgical systems), which are robots that are manipulated by the surgeon dur-ing the surgery so that technically the robotic arms perform the procedure while the surgeon, seated at a console, operates by using sensor data from the robot.

Of this $2.8 billion revenue generated in the RAS market, by 2014, over 75% of the market is expected to originate from the United States, with Europe just now starting to catch up and appreciate the potential of this technology. Companies in this business are expected to see explosive growth with fantastic margins. A particularly good example of a company making fortunes in this industry is Intuitive Surgical, Inc. (ISRG), the pioneers in this market and the owners of the well-branded da Vinci surgical system. ISRG currently has over 95% share of the market in Europe and North America. The company, which was founded in 1995 and went for an IPO in 2000, has grown to be a $1.41 billion company in 2010, with sales up by 34% from 2009. It expects 2011 figures to represent about 25% of growth. Operating profit of the company is a healthy 39.3% of sales with net income in 2010 about 27% of total sales. Now tell me how many companies do you know that make these kinds of margins? With the company cultivating the market internationally, and the installed base of these machines growing, ISRG's revenues will see a good 25%-plus sustain-able growth, both for new sales as well as servicing of the existing fleet of robotic machines (refer to Chapter 7, 'Health, Wellness and Well-Being' for further analysis of this market).

Robo-etition

I envision fierce competition in this industry with many new players entering the robotic industry from diverse backgrounds ranging from industrial robot manufacturers, health care medical devices suppliers, IT and Internet power houses like Google and Microsoft to my favourite auto manufacturers like Honda.

In 2008, Honda's fierce global competitor and local neighbour, Toyota, decided to go back to its roots of making robots (before Toyota starting making cars in 1936, it manufactured automatic fabric looms using the principle of 'jidoka', which means that when the machine detects a problem it will shut down automatically). Toyota plans to make robots in four main fields: manufacturing, short-distance personal transport, nursing and medical care, and domestic help. Volkswagen is similarly working in its labs to develop robotic technology, but is keeping it more under wraps. It mystified me in the beginning as to why car companies want to make robots. On further deliberation, I realised that the connection is obvious: they are in business of providing mobility and robots can support that as evidenced in both Toyota and Honda's vision for providing medical care. Also, their experience in making electric and hybrid vehicles is priceless as electric motors, electronics and batteries are greatly needed in robots, too. Most car companies have the capability today to make semi-autonomous and autonomous cars, which can drive on their own as evidenced by the plethora of advanced driver assistance system technologies already in today's cars, such as lane management systems or emergency brake assist systems. Combine this with the sensing, mapping, navigation and connectivity technologies in cars, and the puzzle is complete.

Google's foray into robotics is by experimenting with driverless cars for the last two years. Makes you wonder that if car companies in the future will make robots and IT houses (like Google) will make driverless cars, how blurred the lines of competition will become.

Robots in our bodies and in our homes

Imagine you are visiting your local surgeon in 2020 after having contracted an illness. Instead of suggesting a blood or urine test, your doctor implants a tiny robot into your bloodstream. The robot travels through your body to the appropriate area, detects and – with the doctor's help – diagnoses the problem, and provides a dose of medicine to the infected area. These robots are called nanorobots and, although the market is still in its nascent stages, the first generation of applications for these nanorobots is not far away from commercialisation.

Nanorobots, constructed using nanotechnology, are close to the scale of a nanometer (10^{-9} meters) in size. Nanomachines are in embryonic stages of the research-and-development phase and the first useful applications of nanomachines will most likely be detecting cancer cells, targeted drug delivery, cell repair and, possibly in the long term, even in surgery. Potential additional applications, outside health care, include working in chemical and hazardous environments, where they might be called upon to detect and measure toxic chemicals in the environment.

Once they have entered our blood streams, it won't be long before robots move into our homes. And, unlike our domestic maids, robots do not need sick days, holidays or experience other human problems.

Robots in homes will provide huge business opportunities once the transition starts. Most robots will be linked to Smart home hubs, a technology already being developed by many organisations to link all Internet-enabled devices in homes from refrigerators and coffee machines to electric cars. Regulators will need to develop regulations in case a robot hurts a human, and possibly there will be debates for rights of these machines. One could imagine a scenario of Trekkies saying, 'I'll only have an android that has free will'. And if we asked Steven Spielberg to build robots for homes, he would even put emotions into them.

The era of robotics has clearly moved from performing simple tasks in assembly lines to advanced intelligent systems capable of performing complex tasks, just like humans. The question now is: how long before we start seeing robots in homes?

I say it will be before the end of this decade.

DECADE OF THE IPAD GENERATION AND LITTLE EMPERORS

The term 'Generation Y' is used to describe the offspring of the 'Baby Boomers'. The members of Gen Y were born between the mid-1970s and the mid-1990s. Gen Y is often referred to as Millennials, the iPad Generation and at times as also the Peter Pan generation. 'Generation Z', also referred to as the Internet or Digital generation, is used to describe the generation born in the early '90s through to the present. In my view these two generations – Gen Y and Gen Z – will be two of the most defining and important generations of the next two decades, globally. This age group will be the most adaptive to change, most willing to experiment with new technologies and products, and will prefer information and services real time and on demand. This new generation has very different values, beliefs, interests and lifestyles; most interestingly, we will find the young will teach the old, with the mature world learning and adapting to the new Gen Y lifestyle and products.

One of the most interesting presentations I remember viewing a couple of years back was given by a group of Millennials at NASA, who were asked by NASA's leadership to find out how the USA's space programme could better appeal to Gen Y. This presentation, called 'Gen Y Perspectives,' is still available at SlideShare[7] and is worth watching for any organisation that struggles to connect with this audience. What is even more interesting is how NASA has adapted since then and adopted new marketing techniques to reach out to this generation. Refer to the case study 'Earth Calling Gen Y' for more information.

CASE STUDY: EARTH CALLING GEN Y – NASA'S STRATEGY TO REACH OUT FROM MARS TO MILLENNIALS

In 2007, NASA realised that Gen Y is not interested in space exploration and a majority them between 18 and 24 were neither aware of nor engaged in NASA's mission. About 40% opposed NASA's missions with 39% believing that nothing worthwhile has ever come out of NASA. Opposition from Gen Y Hispanics was the highest, while Asian Americans' opinion was slightly more favourable. NASA had a serious problem. NASA was performing better at reaching out to Mars – 225 million km away – than to its future workforce and, most importantly, its future funders and donors. (NASA will need over $300 billion of cumulative funding in the next 20 years which will need to be approved by Gen Y decision-makers. Therefore, the negative perception of NASA by Gen Y was a serious problem.)

NASA realised that the problem was that it was not engaging Gen Y. So NASA leadership turned to four Gen Y members of their own team to help them decipher how the space organisation could appeal to the Millennials.

The Gen Y team helped NASA understand why it wasn't 'connecting' with their age group: the first observation they made was the population demographics in NASA were too much skewed towards those aged 45 years and older (about 3:1 in favour of over 45-year-olds). These four young employees helped NASA understand the values, beliefs and perspectives of Gen Y and advised them, 'Instead of telling us what you want us to hear, facilitate a discussion with us and allow us to participate in the NASA mission. Share a compelling story; touch our lives in ways familiar to us. Utilise social media. Spark conversations. But please be timely and reclaim an image as a leader of innovation.'

The presentation was disseminated and debated fiercely within NASA and led to a number of new initiatives, including NASA's decision to embrace social media more openly and make headlines like 'Astronaut tweets from space'.

In October 2010, NASA made one giant – geo-socialisation – leap when it teamed up with Gowalla to create a Moon Rock Scavenger Hunt virtual game in which users pick up virtual space memorabilia at various agency-related venues around the country.

The whole exercise led to NASA leadership closely examining and reviewing its marketing, public relations, recruitment and other management principles. NASA become one of the first public sector organisations to embrace social media in the country and to develop its own internal networking site, similar to Facebook, called 'Spacebook'. Its culture has since changed and the dad's army of scientists, which was at one time perceived as a group of stuffy, out-of-touch old people by Gen Y, is now lot more collaborative and engaging.

Most importantly, it managed to explain to the generation of the future that, after all, what NASA does is uber-cool: it is indeed rocket science!

This digital generation is like chalk and cheese compared to its parents, the baby boomers. I work with many car companies and they have noticed a distinct trend with Gen Y: its members want personal mobility to travel from A to B. However, the mode of transportation they want as they pursue personal mobility is not necessarily a car, it is more often public transport or micro-mobility solutions like scooters. Cars, for baby boomers, meant individuality and celebration of liberation and freedom, as was widely shown in 1970s-era movies like *Grease* and *American Graffiti*. Thanks to these baby boomers, the US auto industry reached its peak when it sold 16 million cars in early 2000s. In the late 1970s, one in two 16-year-olds applied for a driving licence in the US; by 2010, this ratio had declined to one in three. Meanwhile, car ownership trend among 18- to 29-year-olds in the last few years in Germany, UK, Japan and France is showing a decline of 4–10%.

In Tokyo, Japan, there has been such a drop in new driving licences that driving schools are rolling out incentives to lure customers. Incentives range from a massage to driving a BMW for highway lessons or, for bikers, a chance to try a Harley. Car companies like Toyota even grease the palms of the driving schools by offering them subsidised rates on their Prius hybrids and new models to attract the attention of Gen Y buyers.

Many industries, including automotive, have developed and marketed new models like the Toyota Scion, Nissan Cube and Kia Soul, which are specifically designed to attract the Gen Y customer's attention. Fiat, which was losing brand loyalty with the youth in its home market of Italy, came up with a feature called 'eco drive'. Using eco drive, a customer could plug a USB into a port in his or her car and download his or her driving behaviour onto a computer. Fiat was so surprised by the uptake rate of the feature and the rich data it gave them for analysis of their customers' driving behaviours that it decided to fire ten test drivers. The test driver's job was superseded by the digital generation – an Italian Job that was gone in 60 seconds.

So what are the characteristics of this generation and how do we sell to them? I managed two customer studies in Frost & Sullivan covering five major European countries and the US where we ran online focus groups and interviewed 3600 Gen Yers. This is what we found:

- A larger number of the Gen Yers tends to live with only one parent, which makes them more open minded than their parents, the baby boomers, who have taught them the importance of being socially conscious. Therefore, sharing, giving and participating in non-profits are important to them. Sustainability and environment are also important to them. Of the Gen Yers, 90% favour companies that support good causes.
- Attitude and beliefs: Comfort, status and money are most relevant to Gen Y, with environment and sustainability closely behind.

- Technology savvy: Over half own (or regularly use) broadband Internet at home, along with stereo systems, laptop computers, flat-screen TVs, portable MP3 players and home gaming devices. They are digitally empowered.
- Personalisation: Gen Y males, in particular, exhibit a high willingness to personalise. Willingness to personalise increases with income. Sound system (speakers, output, etc.) is the top feature members of Gen Y 'would like' to personalise on their future vehicle. It is also the feature they are most 'willing to pay for'.
- Influences and self-expression: Friends, TV and social media, in that order, best influence them to buy new products. Print media and radio are a distant last as a source for information and news. They employ multiple touch points for self-expression.
- Demanding and impatient – 'fast and the furious': They want instant messaging, discussions and response; and increasingly want to have voice/speech control with devices.
- Individuality: Products that appeal to their ego and personal values are preferred.
- Price conscious: They like to stick to budgets and prefer online research, online price comparison and social media marketing.
- Influencers: They are strong influencers of the purchasing decisions of baby boomers due to their intimate relationship with them.
- Collaborations, rather than connections, are more important for them.

Macro to micro

Look East, not West, for this game-changer generation

It is my strong belief that Gen Yers and Zers in the Asian and developing countries will be the most influential in times to come, and much more important than their counterparts in Europe, the US and Japan. Of the projected 7.5 billion world population in 2020, around 2.56 billion will be from the age group of 15–34 years, out of which 61% will be from Asia alone. This means that Asian Gen Yers and Zers – particularly from India and China – together will constitute about 1.01 billion people by 2020. Similarly, other developing countries like Turkey will have a very young population base (half of Turkey's 75 million population is younger than 29 today). Chart 6.2 gives the breakdown of the global population by age in 2020.

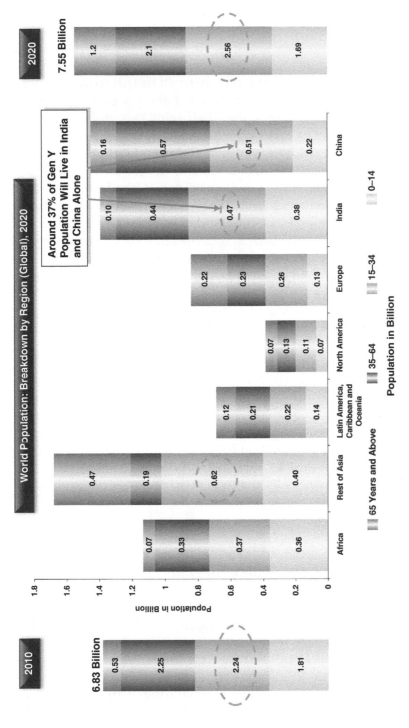

Chart 6.2 Global population in 2020: Out of 2.56 billion people between 15 and 34 years (Gen Y today), around 61% from Asia alone

Source: US Census Bureau, 2010 and Department of Economic and Social Affairs of the United Nations.

Note: Gen Y population is between 15 and 34 years.

Due to their sheer size and growing digital tastes, the Millennials of the Eastern Hemisphere will be one of the most important, influential and noteworthy consumer group in the world. The Chinese 15–34 age group is often called 'Little Emperors' as they are born out of the single-child policy and were thoroughly spoilt by their parents as well as their grandparents. Unfortunately, for them it is payback time, as not only will they need to look after their aging parents but also their dependent grandparents.

In my interactions with the youth in China and India, I found they have much more aggression, dynamism and entrepreneurial flair than their counterparts in the Western Hemisphere. When I went on a tour of China a couple of years ago and gave strategy presentations to several Chinese car companies, I was initially shocked that about 90% of the audience consisted of 25-year-olds. I doubted that they were picking up on my suggestions, especially with the language barrier. How wrong I was: I discovered that, in almost all cases, they implemented my technological and strategic suggestions in their vehicles within 12 to 18 months. Comparatively, when I present in Detroit, I find an audience of primarily baby boomers and Gen Xers (age group of 35–64 years) who are more concerned about their jobs than entrepreneurship.

If you have experience of doing business in Asia, you will find it is a different ball game. Most likely in the ASEAN region, India and China you are dealing with a 30-something person. You go from proposal to implementation within hours or days, not weeks or months, and from recommendations to implementations in a matter of a few months, not years. And as this generation becomes more entrepreneurial, like we had in the past in the West, don't be surprised if the next 'Facebook' originates in the streets of Chengdu (China) or Bangalore (India).

End of China's single-child policy

I predict that in this decade China will roll back its single-child policy, which was first introduced in the country in 1979 after a huge growth in the Chinese population in previous decades and widespread famines. The policy is said to have reduced China's population growth by around 400 million, although these figures are debatable given that countries like India have been able to reduce birth rates through other means. However, one significant problem this single-child policy has caused is the reduction in China's working population. India's working population will see growth of 17.4% during 2010–20, compared to a modest rise of 0.3% in China. In other words, about 120 million

Indians will attain working age in this decade compared to about 12 million in China. In absolute terms, China will still account for a greater level of population in the 15–64 age group (988 million) compared to India (923 million), but this trend will give India a competitive demographic advantage over China, helping to increase demand and collective economic growth, including challenging China's might in manufacturing. My recent discussions with Chinese executives have suggested that China is carefully considering opening up the single-child policy in a phased manner to avoid any huge birth spikes, and a key driver for opening up this policy is China's concern about being able to sustain its competitive advantage in manufacturing by having a larger working-age population. Population forecasts suggest that if the current one-child policy continues in China for another 20 years, then a child of today could, at the time he or she marries at the age of 20, face the task of taking care of as many as four parents and eight grandparents.

Generational political shift

A few months ago, I had the pleasure of enjoying the company of the ex-dean of my business school who is now a Lord in the British House of Lords (Lord Ken Woolmer). Ken recently invited me to join him for a traditional English cup of tea accompanied by cucumber sandwiches and scones with jam and clotted cream at the Palace of Westminster (House of Parliament), an experience I always treasure whenever I am lucky enough to get a Parliamentary invite. Ken has had a good political career with the Labour Party, and we started discussing my latest work on Mega Trends and growing interest in politics. During our discussions, Ken suggested a trend I should explore, which he termed 'Generational Political Shift'. He suggested I look into how generational political shift can impact a nation's politics and bring widespread change, and he referred to Tony Blair, who was one of the youngest Prime Ministers in the UK at the age of 43, as an example. It was an interesting idea and I further explored it when I met couple of months later with one of my friends, Pritviraj Sathe, a third-generation politician in India, who also studied in the business school with me in Leeds, UK.

With about 850 million of India's 1.39 billion citizens expected to be younger than 34 by 2020 (India will have the world's youngest population by 2020), and India on the cusp of a generational shift in politics with the fourth-generation member of the Gandhi family,

Rahul Gandhi, expected to take charge of India's biggest party, the Indian National Congress, sometime prior to 2020, it was indeed an interesting and revealing discussion. Prithvi confirmed that like his father, Rajiv Gandhi, who was India's youngest Prime Minister at the age of 40 and an architect of some major policy changes (Rajiv is widely acknowledged as the person who brought science and IT to India in the 1980s, which has led to the country's current status as a global software powerhouse), Rahul could also be a game changer. Similarly, Prithvi mentioned many other third- and fourth-generation politicians in India such as Jyotiraditya Scindia (born 1 January 1971), Sachin Pilot (born 7 September 1977), Agatha K. Sangma (born 24 July 1980 and presently the youngest Minister of State in the current Cabinet) and Jitendra Pratap Singh Prabhakar Bahadur (born 12 June 1971) who are now in their late 30s and early 40s, and already hold ministerial positions in India. What is interesting about these young, urban intellectual leaders, who were educated in some of the world's leading universities/business schools, is that – unlike their politician fathers/mothers – they have grown up with money. Therefore, they may be less open to the pressures of corruption and be strongly motivated to achieve and make their country great. When Prithvi mentioned that the Indian Youth Congress, which is headed by Rahul himself, has implemented the country's first-ever compulsory leadership training module for its office bearers, it did seem like a step in the right direction. Prithvi confirmed many other interesting facts which Rahul and his team are lining up to improve the standard of leadership in the Youth Congress, which suggests that the next generation of Indian politicians will have a very different set of principles and priorities compared to its predecessors.

I further dug into this trend and found very interesting facts worldwide, including in North Korea and China, which in particular will see President Hu Jintao, Premier Wen Jiabao and most members of the Politburo Standing Committee stepping down in the next year or two to make way for the country's fifth generation of leaders. Now the person most likely to take the lead in China, unlike in India, will not be a 40-year-old but rather Xi Jinping, the existing Vice President, who is currently 58. It is, therefore, possible that one of the world's biggest and fastest growing economies could also see some major ideological and structural changes in its political governance.

Now what could this generational political shift mean to the corporate world? Overall, this is good news for the businessman. Growth, innovation and leadership, a mantra used in the corporate world, will spread to political governance. There will be a great deal of importance placed upon professionalism and leadership development in the political world. Corruption in the developing world will decline as politicians become better educated and as intolerance of corruption increases among the society's youth, as seen in India recently. Democratic agendas could be pushed into nations which currently do not practice it, in some cases forcibly, as has recently been seen in Egypt and Libya. Nations which make this political shift will adopt modern business practices and a global outlook within the government. There will be increased privatisation of government assets, public–private partnerships for infrastructure development will boom, and government will outsource more business functions to private industry.

A word of caution may be in order. Political structures and powerful established interests of a socio-economic nature (even religious nature in some societies) do not change or tend to change at the same speed as the age structure of a society. Pressures from a more youthful society cause tensions with the existing political and established order. Youthful enthusiasm for change is rarely based on a thought-through and common agenda especially in the face of more conservative forces. What is possible in India may have a different path and a different pace to changes in China, Libya and Egypt. But the optimism of youth sees the potential for impact on generational shift in these and many other countries too in the years ahead.

For sure my wily old fox dean-cum-Lord is right: the world does stand on the cusp of a generational political shift this decade; and, combined with a young planet where 56% of the world's population is below 34, one can expect some major political changes by 2020.

REVERSE BRAIN DRAIN AND GLOBAL TALENT WARS

The twentieth century saw a peak in economic migration from the developing world to developed countries. In the twenty-first century, we will see not only a reverse brain drain whereby these first, second and third generation economic migrants will return to their home countries, but also witness well-educated people from the developed world move to countries like Brazil, India and China, seeking improved jobs and opportunities. We will see a lot more aggressive policies in retaining talent by nations and corporate world in the future.

I am an economic migrant myself, and I came to do my MBA at Leeds University Business School in the UK at the age of 25 with the key objective of finding better career prospects and a higher income. I must admit that my first preference was to go to the US, but the Americans did not give me a student visa. Their loss. Sixteen years later, I find that many of my classmates and friends who relocated to the US and Europe like me are attracted to jobs back in India. Many of them are returning to senior executive positions with jaw-dropping salaries and envious perks that even my very German wife finds attractive enough to make it worth the trumpets, horns and chaos of Indian streets.

The shortage in the supply of talent and the economic boom is attracting and bringing the best talent back to India, one of the first countries to witness this phenomenon. During a research project that I led in 2006 and 2009, we noticed that by 2015, there will be as many as two million BPO–KPO jobs for foreign nationals from China, Poland and the Philippines, with salaries on par with developed countries (in terms of purchasing power), and India will have a huge shortage of over 200,000 CXO positions that will be filled not only by return-ing Indians but also by Americans and Europeans looking for jobs. Already, Indian companies are recruiting Western executives to run their businesses locally in the country and plan their global expan-sion. In February 2010, India's most well-known car company and manufacturer of the world's cheapest car, Tata Motors, announced that Carl Peter Forster had been appointed as the group CEO with overall responsibility for Tata Motors globally, including the British Jaguar and Land Rover units. Before joining Tata, Carl Peter Forster was head of General Motors' European operations. Recently, Carl Peter resigned citing personal reasons, but still sits on the motor company's board. Similarly, many leading Indian companies in pharmaceuticals, bank-ing, finance, real estate and many other sectors are hiring foreign CEOs. There is even a huge demand for foreign pilots in India, and in 2011 there are about 1000 foreign pilots working for domestic airlines in India. Some of them are worrying as many are Russian pilots who hardly speak any English or Hindi.

In America's graduate business schools in 2010, India was one of the favourite destinations for MBA graduates to find jobs, and most were willing to work as interns to gain local market experience. Many of America's top business schools report an increase in the number of students who are interested in working overseas in emerging markets, such as India, China, Russia and Brazil. Roughly 25% of 2010 Wharton MBA graduates are now working abroad, compared with 16% a few years ago, and the trend no longer applies only to international MBA graduates. This goes to show that more future jobs will be created in the developing world, than in the developed countries.

Macro to micro implications

Hire educated global, working local

I sit on the advisory board of Leeds University business school, and the board has recently noticed a huge influx of Chinese students to both our graduate and undergraduate programmes. They have overtaken Indian students in the last seven to ten years. Thanks to the British government's new University fees structure, the school and possibly even the University would have struggled to maintain their high standards had it not been for the soaring flow of Asian students. The majority of these students want to return to their home countries and cite foreign degrees as a great enabler of even better jobs and salaries.

In my company, we have a research excellence centre in India, where we centralise many research functions. This is very common in the research and consulting world and practiced even by the likes of McKinsey. As my team in India covers the globe in terms of research, I initiated a policy of hiring Chennai-based students who are studying in our core markets like Germany, France and the US. (For some reason, the young generation in South India, especially Chennai, prefer not to work anywhere but Chennai. Yet people from the North, East or West India do not remain in Chennai. I have never understood why, but to reduce the churn rate, we created a guideline in the company that we will hire locals for local offices. It has worked well so far.) This policy has worked wonders for my team and has since been adopted by many other groups within the company. I have talented Chennai-based engineers on my team who obtained their Master's degree at some of the top German engineering schools, and after spending four years in Germany, they even speak German with a strong Swabian or Öcher Platt accent, which can fool any Frau or Herr in German when on the phone.

Recently, due to issues in finding qualified English-speaking Chinese nationals in our Beijing and Shanghai offices, I have initiated a similar exercise with business schools in the UK to hire Chinese students who will work and train with us for a few months there before relocating back to their home cities. These Chinese students prefer to work for a European headquartered company back in China as it is seen as much more prestigious for their career.

In many job fields in the developed world – such as research and development, medicine, engineering, analysis and nearly all jobs that require good scientific, analytical and quantitative analysis skills – there is a high influx of educated students from the developing world. The youth in the developed world are not interested in science or engineering, made obvious by the declining number of students in these courses at universities. In the US, three out of five doctoral students today are foreign nationals, compared to two in five in Master's programmes. As a result, it is much easier now than in the past to hire these students to return to their home market.

I strongly recommend organisations that are expanding in developing countries to source overseas students from their local universities and train them locally and then relocate them back to their home countries. You will find a much more motivated, dedicated and talented team.

Nations turn headhunters

India is not alone in facing this growing influx of foreigners and returners. Beijing is actually much more organised in getting its educated migrants back. In January 2009, the Chinese Communist Party become a headhunter and launched the Thousand Talents Program, offering top scientists grants of 1 million yuan (about $146,000), fat salaries, perks and generous lab funding to return to China for work. The goal was to address the biggest roadblock to China's aspirations of becoming a global force: address the acute shortage of professional research scientists. According to some of the scientists who have moved to China under this programme, the main allure was the opportunity to build a science programme from the ground up, especially given the funding slashes in the West, where most research and development houses are struggling for funds.

India and China are not the only countries facing this trend. Taiwan, South Korea and recently even Latin American countries like Mexico and Brazil are pulling their talent back. Interestingly, reasons differ. In Taiwan and South Korea, there is a strong cultural affinity and obligation to return, especially if you are the only child of the family.

Some countries, like Russia, still do not understand the impact of the Brain Drain. Ever since World War II, Russia has seen a steady trickle of its experienced scientists leaving the country, and the trickles became a flood after the Iron Curtain came down. This is seriously impacting the nation that was first to put a human into space. The Russians are now slowly beginning to realise their loss, which was confirmed by Prime Minister Vladimir Putin in September 2011 when he spoke of taking specific action and formulating policies to bring talent back and arrest the exodus.

Countries like the US have used their immigration policy very well and benefitted from 'Brain Gain'; about 50% of the Silicon Valley start-ups were founded by immigrants. On the other hand, countries like Germany have had a strict policy restricting Brain Gain, but they have still done well due to a strong organisational culture that supports innovation and engineering excellence. However, with countries like India, China and South Korea churning out more engineers and scientists, including developing stronger local academic and business schools, it is imperative in the future that Western nations develop immigration policies that nurture and restrict talent travel.

I would not be surprised if in the future, Western nations attempt to nail a permanent indefinite stay visa or green card to foreign nationals studying in their home country. And my recommendation to you is that if you are a second- or third-generation Indian, Korean, Brazilian, Turk or Chinese living abroad, you need to seriously consider opportunities for relocating back to your home nation for a few years. And if you are a Japanese, European or American, I suggest you start padding your CV with language and experience in working in Asian or Latin American business cultures.

MIDDLE BULGE: DOMINANCE OF THE MIDDLE CLASS

The world has been talking about the middle class for decades, and how it can transform the world. Well, now is the time for action.

This decade will see the emergence and growth of the world's middle class, which in turn will drive economic growth in the developing world and has the potential to take Europe out of its economic doldrums.

The definition of 'middle class' varies from region to region, and it was one hell of a nightmare for us here at Frost & Sullivan when we tried to pull the global data together. Even the UN does not have consistent global data to describe and compare the size of this middle bulge. Therefore, after days and weeks of collecting, collating and comparing the data, we came up with a definition that defined people with annual incomes roughly between $3,200 and $60,000 which varied for each developing country (depending on its economic growth and exchange rate). For sure, someone in this income bracket in the Europe or the US will fall below the poverty line, and therefore one could argue that they are not middle class. To be honest, I might agree with them, but for the sake of global comparison, this is the best figure. A figure of $6,000 in a developing world like India is equivalent to someone earning $35,000 in the US. So in relative terms, we are not that far away.

So if we analysed the total number of people in the world who will earn between $3,200 and $60,000 in 2020, you would be amazed to know that over 42% of the world population will fall in this middle bulge. India will have about 864 million people falling in the middle-class incomes, which can be segmented into three tiers, with the lowest tier starting at an income of $3,200 per annum. Chart 6.3 shows the middle class population for India in 2010 and 2020. As per a research conducted by McKinsey,[8] the Indian middle class' spending will help India climb from its position as the 12th-largest consumer market today to become the world's fifth-largest consumer market by 2025.

China's middle class will grow from 65 million in January 2005 to over 949 million by 2020, driven by continued strong economic growth. By 2020, the middle-class share in Russia should be 40–70% of a population of 140 million. Similarly, Brazil will have over 140 million individuals in the middle-class segment. In South Africa, we will see 'White flight, Black diamonds', a phrase used in the country to suggest that 'Whites' will leave the country and the rising black middle class will drive the region's economy.

This burgeoning global middle class, with its growing income, will transform the global consumer market in the next ten years, which is extremely good news for businesses. Lessons from research on spending patterns of the middle class suggests that apart from spending plentifully on essentials like groceries and beverages, they will spend lavishly on housing costs, transportation, health care, leisure goods and services, household goods and services, personal goods and services, and clothing and footwear, in that order. The car industry will benefit tremendously as annual car sales will go past 100 million cars per annum globally with over 50% of these sales happening in Asia and mainly in the small and compact car segment, bought by middle-class aspirants, some trading from pushbikes straight to cars (as was seen in China in last decade). The hospitality and retail industry, in particular, will benefit tremendously as we will see many first-timer holidays, flights to overseas destinations and theme parks. The middle class will consume everything, from smartphones and iPads to Coca-Cola and American Express.

The biggest opportunity for businesses is in developing affordable products and thinking out of the box with new business models.

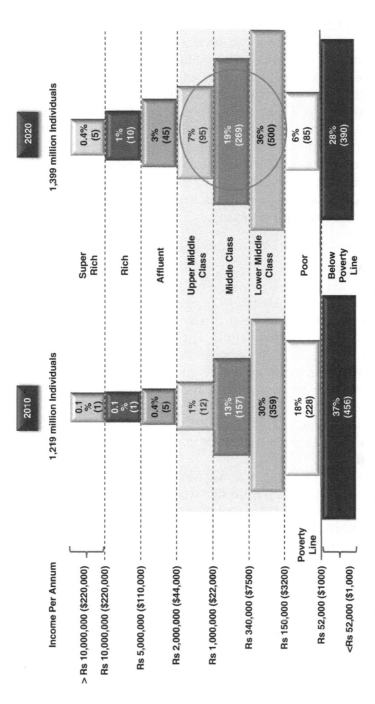

Chart 6.3 The middle bulge: Middle-class individuals to account for 62% of India's population (864 million) in 2020

Source: National Council for Applied Economic Research (NCAER), Frost & Sullivan Analysis.

Note: Figures in the brackets are millions of individuals. Poverty Line is based on Planning Commission's definition of poverty – Rs 4365 per month per household.

In Chapter 8, 'Business Model of the Decade – Value for Many',on business models of the future, this book discusses the 'Value for Many' business model that can be leveraged by businesses in developing innovative and affordable products and services. In a project that I led with Proctor & Gamble (P&G), during the brief that I was given, (directions for which came straight from the CEO's office), I was, asked how P&G can increase its products usage from five billion people daily on this planet to six billion. The answer was simple: position a new and existing portfolio of products to the new entrants into the middle class who will be first-time buyers of P&G's vast product portfolio.

This middle bulge will certainly be the most important and expanding class of the twenty-first century.

GIRL POWER

The role and power of women in the twenty-first century will be lot more evolved than it has been in the previous century. As women continue to break the glass ceiling, their empowerment in 2020 will reach new heights. One in three workers globally will be a woman. Not only will salaries of women be at par with or more than men in most countries, but women will also increasingly don the roles of CEOs and corporate heads in charge of business strategy and finance. Over 40% of the labour force in the US, India and Europe in 2020 will be women, and their representation in governments will be around 25% globally.

In some countries and regions, including Europe, we could see legislation forcing employers to place women in boardrooms to achieve 30% of the total board of directors. The European Commission is eager to emulate Norway, which has the highest female board representation through a quota legislation of 40%. Ten out of the top 17 countries in Europe have a quota or corporate governance code effective today. However, the number of women in global boardrooms is still sparse. Only 12.5% of FTSE 100 companies in the UK have women directors in the boardroom and only 11 of the top 500 American companies have women CEOs. This will all change very rapidly.

More women in jobs will have a serious impact upon society and culture. This will spur new family trends such as late marriages (which, particularly in countries like India, could have a huge impact on society and birth control), late pregnancies, stay-at-home fathers/

house husbands, one-child families and single parents. Already we see in the UK a ten-fold increase in the number of women aged 40 and over receiving fertility treatments.

An interesting debate I got into, which could be a game changer, is that we will see the launch of a wonder drug this decade which could delay women's menopause by five to ten years. This could lead to a fertility revolution, allowing women to wait longer to have a child and prolong their educations and careers. Currently biology works against them in having a full status equivalent to a man in employment, but this drug could help overcome certain career challenges in the early part of their professional lives.

In almost all professions, 'girl power' will grow significantly. Particularly, in the consumer industry, over 50% of customers are women and 90% of decision-makers are women. Even in a B2B market, women will increasingly feature in the buying group as influencers and decision-makers. As a business, one will need to increasingly accommodate this change and train staff accordingly. When running a workshop for a lighting company, where we worked on the impact of this Mega Trend on their business, a business development manager who worked in their public lighting sector told me how frequently he has to sell his solution to women decision-makers and influencers. He found he had to focus less on the technical and functional aspects of his product and more on the emotional, aesthetic and well-being features. With women, decision-making is a slightly longer sales cycle, but the process is a lot more thorough with an emphasis on checking the functionality of the product in a collaborative team environment.

I can relate to all this. I was involved a couple of years ago in a five-member committee which was conducting the final round of interviews for our new HR director. There were more women than men in the selection committee as well as in the short list of candidates. The dynamics of the group, observations and selection criteria regarding the women were an eye-opener for me. For a start, the women in the selection committee were much more harsh and unforgiving to female candidates than their male counterparts, and even their fashion sense, colour and choice of clothing, including the type/brand of handbag, was discussed. We blokes, on the other hand, hardly noticed. Even basic things like a warm and firm handshake were perceived to represent a particular behavioural characteristic. The candidate who was voted the highest by the women on the selection committee was someone who spent lot more time getting to know and listening to them, communicated clearly and directly, and who was the least pretentious and the most open minded.

Women will be a significant better half as a customer, as well as a colleague and co-worker, in the future workplace. Our personal and business working practices will need to adapt and change to accommodate that.

7

HEALTH, WELLNESS AND WELL-BEING

If you asked me what was the biggest Mega Trend of the last ten years I would say it is *sustainability and environment*. I predict health, wellness and well-being to be the most important factor of discussion and differentiation in this decade, with farther-reaching impact than *sustainability*. In fact, if we follow the logic of the Kondratieff Cycles, this is the next major cycle, stretching all the way to 2050 and beyond.

Globally, the flow of money supports the critical importance of this trend. Health care spending in the Western world is already, on average, between 10% and 15% of GDP today. In countries like the United States, it is as high as 17% of GDP, cresting over $2.5 trillion in recent years. In almost all countries worldwide, per capita health care spending is rising faster than per capita income, and if this trend continues, health care spending as a percentage of GDP will more or less double in the next 20 to 30 years. The US could be spending 20% of its GDP on health care before 2020, rising to 30% by 2050. These levels of health care spending are unsustainable, and something will have to give. This is why President Obama used so much of his political capital in his first few years in office to revamp health care – he and his team knew the current spend on health care in the US had to be modified dramatically to avoid the dire economic consequences facing any nation expending 20–30% of GDP towards health care while at the same time shouldering a massive debt burden.

In 2010, only about 8% (583 million) of the global population was aged above 65. By 2020 this will increase to around 10% (840 million). People aged above 65 utilise three to five times more health care services than younger people and 75% of people aged above 60 have one chronic condition, while over half have two or more chronic conditions (chronic diseases account for more than 60% of all health care spending). With one in six people in Western economies today living up to the age of 100, both these demographic data and the aforementioned unsustainable health economics data dictate a shift in spending – away from treating and towards predicting, diagnosing and monitoring.

I, therefore, expect a paradigm shift in the health care business model in this decade with the whole concept of health care shifting from an age-old model of treating symptoms towards a more holistic, preventative model of predicting, early diagnosing and ongoing monitoring. In the 2000s, around 75% of the government funds were spent on 'treatment' and only about 25% on diagnosis, prediction and monitoring. This trend will completely reverse with treatment share declining to around 40–5% by 2025 and share of monitoring, diagnosis and prediction growing threefold. With governments unable to sustain the spending, technical innovations and growing social awareness, the whole concept of health care will shift from 'find and fix it' and 'health care' to an emphasis on 'wellness and well-being'.

HEALTH, WELLNESS AND WELL-BEING REDEFINED AS THE MIND, BODY AND SOUL

I led a consumer study in 2007 that included focus groups and 3000 interviews across major European countries to define and understand the concept of health, wellness and well-being (HWW). Our findings showed that the three human cornerstones – the body, mind and soul – contribute to the human definition of HWW. Through our research we were able to break each of these cornerstones into further elements which are defined as shown in Chart 7.1.

Our research showed that humans relate to the 'body' with their sensory systems like sight, smell, touch and feel, etc. The 'mind' is all about mental health, mood, stress levels, attitude, security and safety. The interesting one was the 'soul' findings, which had resemblances to the 'self-actualisation' level in Maslow's hierarchy of needs pyramid. The respondents listed personal fulfilment, values and self-image/actualisation as factors which contribute to soul and to overall satisfaction with well-being. People buy certain products not because they find appeal in their basic attributes but because they appeal to their soul and portray an internal image of personal fulfilment or an external image of self-actualisation. An example is people in California

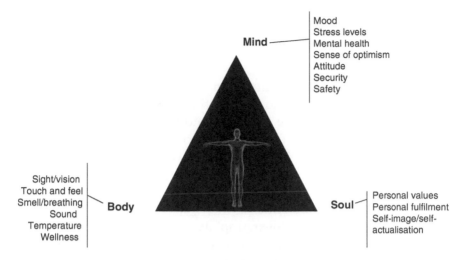

Chart 7.1 The three cornerstones – the body, mind and soul – contribute to the human definition of health, wellness and well-being

Photo credits: Dreamstime.
Source: Frost & Sullivan.

buying Toyota Prius hybrids when the vehicle was launched; their primary motivation was not to buy a car which saves the planet or saves fuel bills, but a car which portrays certain personal values and self-image.

This discovery was a Eureka moment for us as we had solved the conundrum of what defines wellness and well-being, something which many organisations even today struggle to define correctly. Most reach up to the first level, which constitutes the body, mind and soul, but are unable to fathom what makes them up individually. We then tested this theory against many industries and diverse products and it held up well. My recommendation to you, if you are making products/services which impact health care, is to focus on features and attributes of your products/services against the factors shown in Chart 7.1. Do the acid test on your products/services' ability to influence these factors, and if they positively influence over 70% of these factors with an average of 7 or above (on a scale of 1 to 10), you have a winning product/service. Then promote those values of your products/services which scored heavily and focus not on the health care part in your communication to your customers but on the wellness and well-being factors. You will then have a winning 'healthy' strategy.

113

FUTURE OF HEALTH, WELLNESS AND WELL-BEING

Power patients

Do you remember the last time you got sick and, either before or after the doctor's visit, did not Google the condition you thought you might have? Probably, like me and almost all others, it must have been more than ten years or more since you did not research the possible conditions you might have prior to your doctor appointment. Most patients are a doctor's nightmare today as 'doctor knows best' has been replaced by 'Google knows best'. In fact, Google has wisely recognised that they are either a 'first stop' location for health care search information, or a 'next stop' as a second opinion is sought online once the physician has delivered a diagnosis. We term the patients of today who arm themselves with reams of free, web-based information as 'power patients'.

A prime example of a power patient is the famed cyclist Lance Armstrong, winner of seven Tour de France jerseys. Raised in a single-parent home and educated only through high school, Lance embarked on his cycling career early. He was soon diagnosed with testicular cancer that had metastasised to his brain. As soon as he heard this diagnosis, he morphed into a power patient: devouring information on his condition, assessing various therapy paths and returning to his physician's office having already determined to demand surgical intervention at a specific care facility by a specific surgeon – since the balance impairing side effects of the more common radiation therapy would almost certainly destroy any hope of resurrecting his cycling career. We all know what happened after that.

However, the health care industry, after being subject to nuisance patients for over a decade, has now found an answer. They are empowering patients more, and actively equipping these motivated power patients to take charge of their own health.

Shift in health care services delivery to outside hospitals

In the future, there will be a huge shift in power from clinical staff to non-clinical homecare due to a shortage of trained staff and budgets. As much as three-fourths of health care provisions, in some countries, will be outside the hospital by the end of this decade. On an average, it costs about $620 to the health care system in USA when a patients walks into a hospital for consultation, and it is higher for older people. Governments can sustain this and therefore patients will need to take care of themselves.

Home health care will evolve from a sporadic practice today to a mainstream care-delivery model. Services like online consultations, in-home vital-sign monitoring and online disease management will increasingly gain momentum. Scandinavia is already at the forefront of remote/home monitoring where the test results are sent to the doctor directly without the patient needing to step out of home, and we will see different variations of this idea being adopted across rich and poor nations alike. You could even be given charge of maintaining and managing your own health records and life history. Moreover, if you live in a country which pays for your health care, like the UK, you might be given your own personal health budgets by the government to spend based on your personal preferences or situation. For example, if you suffer from chronic pain following removal of, say, a tumour, you could choose your personal health budget for extensive massage and hydrotherapy sessions to relieve chronic pain without the side effects of painkilling drugs, such as drowsiness and disorientation, while another patient could prefer to give that budget to his or her daughter to look after her last few months at home.

As a result, we will see certain homecare solutions becoming standard offerings. The self-service health kiosk promises to be an attractive solution in the future for homes as well as for use in offices for employees, public places like airports, and in hospitals to avoid queuing up before meeting a doctor. A health kiosk can do lot of basic functions which, in the past, would need a trip to the local hospital, such as accessing the patient's medical history; measuring weight, pulse and blood pressure; and running blood tests for checking basics like glucose and cholesterol levels. If required, kiosks may also direct patients to a hospital if the measures suggest a manual check-up that can also help in wellness and well-being management by monitoring one's health fitness with options like monitoring health statistics and showing progress against New Year's fitness resolutions. I am told these kiosks can be particularly beneficial in sexual health services, when placed in hospitals or university campuses to get Gen Z patients to have confidential check-ups or get condoms/the morning-after pill without subjecting them to a doctor's interrogation.

An interesting example of an innovative product for the future home or office is the automated external defibrillator (AED), a portable electronic device that can automatically diagnose and treat life-threatening cardiac arrest. At a price of around $1500, the sticker shock might give you a heart attack, but at least you can resurrect yourself.

At the same time we will see a shift in the healthcare delivery model with primary care settings (e.g. local general practitioner) coordinating our overall care. This is already the most cost-effective way of keeping patients outside the hospital for less important reasons. You can expect to see your GP more often in the future, where routine procedures may be conducted at the GP surgery/day care centres. This trend is likely to happen across the countries – irrespective of the degree of industrialisation or sophistication. For example, countries like Indonesia and China are spending billions of dollars building primary care hospitals and UK is restructuring the GP primary-care system.

Health care tourism

Just when the people are getting used to customer services being outsourced to Asia or Latin America, comes the next big trend: health care outsourcing aka medical tourism. Don't be surprised when, the next time you go to your doctor or insurance company in the US or Europe for a surgery, they suggest you take a medical holiday in Thailand and insist that while you are there you rest for a few extra days to enjoy some sun, sea and sand. And if you are a professional sportsman like Kobe Bryant (basketball) or Terrell Owens (American football), you might rather pop over to Europe or South Korea for stem cell therapy than risk another complicated conventional surgery in your home country.

Medical tourism started in the last decade and will see huge growth in the next ten years. The total global medical tourism industry is estimated at around $20 billion in 2010 and is expected to see healthy growth rates and competition as new regions and hospital chains fight for market share. Countries like Brazil (for plastic surgery), Mexico (for dentistry and plastic surgery), Costa Rica (one in five visitors is a medical tourist), India (for alternative medicine, bone marrow transplant, cardiac bypass, eye surgery and hip replacement), Singapore (organ transplants and experimental drug treatment) and Thailand (reconstructive surgery) are becoming hot destinations for medical tourists.

With approximately 30–50% lower cost, comparable infrastructure and better success rate of procedures, these medical tourism destinations will keep attracting more patients from the Western countries.

Increased sophistication of hospitals that remain

There will, in the future, be an increase in providing specialised care delivery around specific therapeutic areas and an increase in need care for a specific condition through focussed world-class specialist hospital facilities. It will need to balance economies of scale with selective procedures, drawing on advances in technology. It will need fewer beds, but it will definitely need more operating theatres and recovery areas. Already we are seeing the trends towards assembly line operations in specialist heart procedures and eye procedures in hospitals. For example, some hospitals in India routinely conduct hundreds of cataract surgeries in a day with almost 100% success (as against the usual five–15 operations per day in a routine hospital in the Western hemisphere), thereby bringing down the cost of surgery to the patient to as low as $25 for a cataract operation. The trend is likely to be adopted by these specialist hospitals across various parts of the world. The hospital of the future will therefore need to be extremely flexible, because the diseases it treats and the ways in which it treats them will be very unlike those in the present day.

Further, the hospital of future will be more integrated than ever. With the convergence of information technology and advanced imaging and monitoring techniques, the operating rooms will look more like a command station from *Star Trek* with a robot performing surgery on the patient.

Gene therapy: The dawn of personalised medicine

Fundamentally, it is understood that aging is something that is programmed in our genes. Outside of regular wear, abuse and, in some cases, neglect, the biggest reason for organ failure is diseases tied to our genes. Being able to understand which genes control what processes, and how they can be influenced, could go a long way to preventing breakdowns.

To give you an idea of how far science has advanced in a short time, take for example the ambitious Human Genome Project. The Human Genome Project was an initiative by researchers to sequence the entire human genome. Formally initiated in 1990 and requiring nearly $3 billion in funding, results of the groundbreaking study were presented in 2001 with 90% of the 23,000 genes in the human DNA sequenced.[1]

A genome sequence essentially is the equivalent of scientific fortune-telling. You could identify disorders before they present any symptoms, potentially understand how effective certain drugs might be in an individual and ultimately the Holy Grail would be to develop genomic therapeutics that could treat disorders.

In January 2012, barely a decade after the completion of the Human Genome Project, two major biotechnology firms announced the introduction of systems that could sequence an individual's genome in mere hours for a cost of $1000. Lowering the cost and time in which a test could be conducted makes sequencing available to the larger public. More importantly, it gives researchers the ability to study large sample sizes of individuals to understand if genetic similarities exist in those who have shown a greater ability to fight diseases and even aging.

As a friend told me recently

During my last annual blood test, the doctor did genetic analysis that uncovered why my paternal grandmother and two of her daughters had died from sudden, catastrophic strokes: a defect in one component of our cholesterol that leads to premature carotid atherosclerosis. I found it absolutely fascinating. I have the genetic structure my grandma and aunts did, so I had to start cardiac medicines, but hopefully the discovery will enable me to avoid their fate.

Rather than making decisions on inference and best guesses, the era of personalised medicine offers the opportunity to provide treatment that is optimised to the individual sooner.

Through that research, scientists now believe they have narrowed down the set of genes that control the aging process. Identification might have been the easy part; now that the genes have been identified, researchers face a more challenging question. How can those genes and the biological pathways they control be influenced or modified to reverse the aging process? In animal models gene therapy research has shown the ability to extend average lifespans by 20% or more.

The other implication of mapping the human genome has been the ability to compare the genetic changes in a diseased versus normal individual. With the ability to pinpoint the culprit genes responsible for diseases and conditions like cancer, psoriasis, rheumatoid arthritis, etc., scientists have been able to create a whole new class of drugs that act at the genetic level. Herceptin is a good example that has helped treat breast cancer patients by binding itself to defective HER2 proteins (that form the genes) and preventing them growing uncontrollably (this uncontrolled growth causes cancer). Just when we have been running out of options of treating various diseases and conditions using traditional chemical drugs, we can now expect much more emphasis on gene therapy in the future.

The field still has a long way to go before we see real-world treatments on the order discussed. Given how far the field has advanced in such a short period of time, it's not hard to imagine why so many are so excited for what might be on the horizon.

Tissue engineering: Custom body parts made to order

If you consider the body to be a system of mechanical parts, electrical wiring and controllers, the theory behind restoration is greatly simplified. If an organ system or part is faulty, you would replace it as you would in a car or home appliance in need of repair.

The field of tissue engineering and organ replacement opens the possibility for people to have replacement organs seeded with their own cells and grown in a lab.

Currently, organ transplants and replacement is only a last-resort option due to limitations of donor lists, concerns of rejection and a host of other factors that are highly unpredictable. Clinicians even prepare risk profiles involving a patient's long-term life expectancy, lifestyle habits and other qualitative decisions to determine if the patient is qualified to even be considered for the list.

Tissue-engineered organs would be from an individual's own DNA as there is then a lower chance of rejection, lower risk profile and no need for wait lists.

Clinicians have already shown that they can grow a wide number of organs, from lungs to ears, in a lab and successfully transplant them into a patient. Companies are even exploring how adipose-derived stem cells from an individual can be used in breast reconstruction, as opposed to artificial materials like saline and silicone.

The long-term goal is to develop more sophisticated organs like artificial pancreases or livers. The game-changing potential of these, if successful, would turn the current treatment paradigm on its head. Imagine a diabetes patient who, instead of complicated diagnostics, pumps and injectors, could simply replace his or her dead pancreas with a functioning one.

Cybernetics: Part man, part machine – the future of prosthetics

The 1970s classic American TV show *The Six Million Dollar Man* famously opens with the suggestion that we can build a bionic man who is better, stronger and faster than he was ever before. The show focuses on a man who was critically injured in an accident, at which point government researchers intervened to replace his body parts with cybernetic parts. It is a topic that has been revisited countless times in the cannon of literature and film since. The truth of the matter is that, while it might have been pure fantasy in the 1970s, scientists now are moving towards a point in the near future where they can truly say, 'We have the technology.'

A prosthetic device is essentially an artificial device that replaces a damaged part or organ of the human body. Initially, prosthetic devices were developed as a functional placeholder for lost limbs. Peg legs, glass eyes and hooks have been used in limb replacement as far back as 300 BC.

Those archaic options have given way in recent times to products with greater range of motion and vastly improved aesthetics. However, the dawn of a new era is on the horizon. A new class of products are being researched to explore prosthetics with the ability to collect, gather and act on information.

Simple mechanical prosthetics are giving way to sophisticated machined systems with unparalleled levels of user control. The first generation of devices had limitations that restricted them functionally, resulting in unreliable performance. They served more as a demonstration of concept than clinical value. Today, experiments have reached a stage where smart prosthetics are being integrated with the nervous system, whereby signals from the brain are tapped to communicate and coordinate with a resulting action.

Researchers at Duke University in North Carolina have done studies with primates whereby a rhesus monkey was able to manipulate a robotic joystick by simply thinking the action. Electrodes implanted in the monkey's brain were able to capture and translate the motor signals into action.

For individuals who have lost sight in their eyes due to disease or trauma, researchers were able to develop a prototype bionic eye that was capable of capturing images and sending the signal to the brain's visual cortex. While the patients could not see full images, they were able to recognise general shapes and movement.

This new era of prosthetic technologies is transitioning towards those that can more comprehensively mimic lost functions. Having to cope with the loss of organ function, limb or mobility is an incomprehensible compromise in quality of life. Bionic prosthetics are life-changing solutions that have the capability to revolutionise what is possible for those living with disability.

Era of immortality?

For humans, most research seems to indicate cognitive and physical decline begins in our mid-20s and continues to accelerate beyond that. Essentially the biological processes that allowed for growth and regeneration in our youth slow down and eventually stop, affecting our brain, muscles and organ systems. We call this self-destruct sequence 'aging'.

Over the course of human history and development, we have seen average life expectancy extend from 20 years in the Neolithic era to 28 years during ancient Rome and all the way up to 45 years by the 1800s. At the start of the 1900s, life expectancy on average was only about 50 years. However, due to some major advances in medicine, it jumped to 65 by 1950 and ultimately settled around its present-day range of 75 to 80 years for most developed nations. Given those advances and the potential for new medical breakthroughs, it is possible that one in six people alive today, in the developed world, will be centenarians and some of these supercentenarians.

Like the 80–20 rule, when it comes to life expectancy, two numbers to keep in mind are 80 and 120. The number 80 refers to what is considered the current expected average life expectancy, and 120 refers to the age of the oldest recorded human. The oldest woman recorded lived to the age of 122, and there are a number of currently living individuals who have reached 115. Are these people anomalies? Is it possible that improvements to the way health care is delivered can help others approach that age?

Paradigm-shifting biomedical advances in the twenty-first century, once imagined in film and literature, have elevated the concept of 'immortality' to a matter of when and not if. Immortality involves a complex combination of gene therapy techniques, tissue engineering and cybernetics used in concert to restore or replace failing organ systems.

While realistically extending life indefinitely might not ever be possible, over the next decade we likely are going to see significant progress made in extending healthy life expectancy.

Wonder and nature-changing drugs and treatments

Did you know that a majority of medicines only work for a small subset of the human population? Migraine and asthma drugs work in only about 50–60% of the patients and it gets worse with cancer drugs, where the chances of their working is one in four patients. However, this could change in the future with medicines and even diets tailored to individuals. We could see designer drugs, like diet pills, that can reduce weight without any side effects.

Many companies like Pfizer are already conducting clinical trials on weight reduction drugs, which can reduce one's appetite by behaving like a hormone called oxyntomodulin, which is created in our stomach when it is full. The company believes the drug can be expected to be available with a prescription in three years' time in the UK. Within the next few years, we could see wonder drugs that can cure various forms of cancer. We could see drugs that could delay woman's menopause by five to seven years, thereby manipulating not only the women's bodies, but also changing the dynamics of society, as women could delay children and prioritise careers in the early phases of their lives.

However, these designer drugs come with a designer label price too. Herceptin use is controversial because of its cost, as much as $100,000 per year per patient. Certain private insurance companies in the US and government health care systems in Canada, England and elsewhere have refused to pay for the drug – especially because the drug works only on 30–40% of patients with a specific genetic make-up. Yet again, the gene mapping is providing the solution and there has been an increased focus on using genetic tests to identify patients on whom these drugs can be used – thereby reducing the chances of administering expensive drugs to patients who may not be suitable for treatment. In the future, we can expect an increasing number of designer drugs with complimentary tests to be available for patients.

In particular, the cancer therapies market will see huge R&D investment with a large number of products under development (about 100 drugs for cancer, over 90 for breast cancer, about 70 for colorectal cancer, about 17 for leukaemia and 13 for lung cancer are currently in development).

There is talk of designer baby studios which could help create athletic, designer babies. And let us not forget stem cell treatment which could completely alter the health care landscape. One could argue how far one can take it.

MACRO TO MICRO

Nutraceutical (functional foods and beverages) and nutricosmetics market to have a makeover

A Frost & Sullivan study in 2009 evaluated the global demand for the food and beverages industry to be around $11.6 trillion in 2009 and expected to reach $15 trillion in 2014.[2] Despite huge growth in the industry, there is a significant shift globally. Consumers are increasingly concerned about the health effects of some of the ingredients that may contain pesticides, mercury, trans fats, growth hormones, genetically modified foods, antibiotics and high-fructose corn syrups. As a result we are seeing wellness and well-being solutions, such as functional food and beverages that help manage weight and improve health, being preferred over conventional foods and beverages.

Functional foods and beverages provide functions like energy enhancement, improving heart health and aiding digestion. Functional beverages differ from regular drinks such as water and soft drinks due to their formulation, which includes physiologically active ingredients such as vitamins and electrolytes, amino acids, essential fatty acids, probiotics, prebiotics and other substances which are naturally contained in fruits and vegetables such as anti-oxidants, phytosterols and dietary fibre. In most of the cases, the usage of these ingredients is supported by scientific evidence, which allows the manufacturers to make not only health claims but also structure/function claims from the Food and Drug Administration (FDA) on their products.

The functional beverage market can be segmented into three main categories:

1. Rehydration and nutrient-fortified: Sports drinks and enhanced water beverages
2. Energy enhancement: Energy drinks
3. Health improvement: Nutraceutical drinks

Given this growing need for enhanced health and wellness, the nutraceutical market has emerged. Nutraceuticals are defined as any food, or part thereof, which provides health benefits, including prevention or treatment of disease. This definition has now broadened to include functional ingredients such as vitamins, minerals, amino acids, fatty acids and probiotics. As a result, most food and beverage companies today, including ingredient suppliers, have a specific business unit devoted in one way or another on taking advantage of the health and wellness Mega Trend because they understand that this trend is a significant contributing factor to the overall global growth of the food and beverage industry.

The global nutraceutical market saw huge growth in the last decade, growing at an annual average growth rate (AAGR) of almost 15% as per Frost & Sullivan analysis, but the growth was mainly in the US prominently, and Europe (the US and EU combined were an $85 billion industry in 2010). The industry is expected to maintain comparable growth through 2020 due to the continued rise of the middle class in India, China and Brazil, the aging of the United States and Europe, and the increasing costs of curative health care solutions.

This industry is also recession proof, as was seen in 2010, when – in the middle of a deep recession, especially in the US (currently the US is the biggest market for nutraceuticals) – the global nutraceutical market actually experienced a surge in growth that became even stronger post-recession. It makes you wonder if the bankers were suddenly using their bonuses and loss of job to start having a healthy lifestyle. Unfortunately not, as the official reason is that the high cost of health care and the after-effects of the recession, especially in the developed world, drove consumers towards dietary supplements and functional food and beverages in a bid to remain healthy and avoid treatment costs.

This shift in the global demand for more healthy food and beverages will, in turn, provide opportunities for food-ingredient suppliers as the industry shifts away from promoting food product health claims that report it is a 'Reduced Bad' alternative (such as 'Reduced Fat', 'Reduced Salt', 'Low Sugar', 'No Cholesterol') to promoting its food product as being a healthier alternative due to its inclusion of a given additive ('added goods'). For example, dairy product offerings are increasingly being promoted as being fortified with probiotics or omega-3 DHA. In fact, global fortified dairy product sales growth continues to outpace that of reduced-fat dairy products at an accelerating rate today.

Not only are we going to see a healthy change in the food and beverage industry, but the concept of wellness will also spread to the personal care industry. The increasing focus on personal care and general health is driving demand for functional foods and, consequently, the market for specific functional products. Personal care products are also being driven by the need for wellness, which goes beyond general health and more towards personal grooming.

Nutricosmetics is a perfect example where health and wellness merge to offer the 'feel good' factor for humans. Nutricosmetics are products which, when ingested, have an effect on skin, nails and hair such as anti-aging, skin lightening, sun care, nail fortification and hair repair. The increasing aging population continues to drive a healthy demand for nutricosmetics products, especially those for sun care and anti-aging.

On the other hand, the concern for skin lightening, coupled with rising awareness of the links between food consumption and enhanced beauty and health, has made consumers in emerging markets open to embrace more beauty food products. Nutricosmetics tend to be high-end personal care products because of the complexity of processing involved in ingredient purification and formulation. Nevertheless, strong GDP growth and higher discretionary spending by a wealthier middle class in Asia Pacific and Latin America on such consumer items will boost sales.

The global nutricosmetics market is already a multibillion-dollar business that is expected to exhibit double-digit growth by 2020. Anti-aging, which is the largest segment, is forecast to experience the fastest growth, followed by the skin lightening and hair care sectors.

The nutriceutical and nutricosmetics market growth is leading to acquisitions, collaborations and even repositioning of industries. Within the nutraceuticals market, we are seeing traditional chemicals and materials companies picking up pace in acquiring specialists to help their transition to become 'health care' companies. Examples include DSM's acquisition of Martek Biosciences and DuPont's acquisition of Danisco. Between the food industry and cosmetic companies, from 2007 to 2010, 131 acquisitions were done, mainly by European companies acquiring US-based organisations. This was somewhat of a record as by far the largest number of acquisitions carried out by companies from a single region, within an industry, during this period.

The future of this market will see a huge number of new product launches, customisation of the products to market segments and even regional cultures with market consolidation, including cross-industry partnerships, within this industry as it becomes truly global.

CASE STUDY: BRAND DIFFERENTIATION USING HEALTH, WELLNESS AND WELL-BEING

Let us look at how health, wellness and well-being will, in the future, become an important element of product and brand differentiation even in products and industries far removed from it today.

In a branding and positioning study I led in the automotive industry, we tried to determine what factors car companies use to differentiate their brands. We narrowed them down to seven key factors, which were:

1. Quality and reliability: The Japanese were particularly good at this and used it to enter the US market.
2. Safety: Car companies like Volvo and Mercedes use this factor to differentiate themselves.
3. Design and styling: French car companies, like Renault and Peugeot in particular, use this factor to give their vehicles unique style and curves.
4. Cost of ownership: Very important for volume car manufacturers like Hyundai.
5. Environment: A very important factor today, both from legislation as well as customer point of view, for all car companies.
6. Comfort and convenience, as seen from a plethora of new features like heated seats, car ergonomics, etc.
7. Driving experience, which is related to steering feel, vehicle agility and roll during turning.

Most car companies have a very well-established process which they use to focus on two or three of these seven key factors for positioning their vehicle brands. For each factor, they evaluate whether they want to be 'best-in-class (BIC)', 'among the leader' or 'a follower'. Those factors which strengthen their brand values are normally bracketed in the 'BIC' box (e.g. Volvo on safety, BMW on driving dynamics). Whenever a car company develops a new car model, it uses certain vehicular features or technologies to help strengthen its BIC brand position. For example, when Volvo launched its first sports utility vehicle (SUV) the XC90, they came up with the first-ever SUV which had roll-over protection to maintain their BIC position in safety. It was a clever move in those days, as there was a huge hue and cry over Ford Explorers tumbling at high speeds. Volvo as a car company is always one of the first to come up with new features and technologies in safety, as was evidenced recently when it premiered the world's first vehicle with emergency brake assist, which stops the car even if you don't brake when it is in the vicinity of an obstacle.

Over time the importance of these factors changes, as has been evidenced recently with BMW's, which was once the 'world's ultimate driving machine', new label 'efficient dynamics'. As you can see here with its slogans, BMW has evolved over time from being a brand which was positioned solely on the 'fun of driving' to 'fun and responsible' driving.

I strongly believe the next big factor for competitiveness and brand/product differentiation for car companies will be 'health, wellness and well-being'. This factor will evolve from the current focus on environment. We already see huge evidence of this factor in modern cars. As seen in Chart 7.1, all sub factors of mind, body and soul can be related to the car.

The 'body' is all about our sensory systems, and cars can contribute to all of these like sight/vision, temperature, and touch and feel. Similarly, a car can influence your 'mind' – for example, it can lower your stress levels, attitude and security if caught in a traffic jam as seen recently by improvements in comfort and convenience functions like automatic traffic guidance systems and individual climate control systems. With respect to 'soul', it is highly evident as people buy cars to portray a self-image as seen with Hollywood stars buying Toyota Priuses or electric Teslas (over 50% of buyers of Toyota Prius hybrids buy them to showcase their personal image).

So don't be surprised if your next car comes loaded with health, wellness and well-being features like a steering wheel which changes colours based on your mood (can be very practical to judge the frame of mind of your wife/girlfriend), oxygen-level conditioner and humidifier (can be handy for driving in polluted Megacities of the developing world), swirling chairs for easy access and exit (especially for older people), health-conditioning monitors and alcohol/dizziness vehicle lock features.

Hamburger tax: A state-based well-being system

'Governments cannot legislate morality, but can tax sin': this is about to come true for the food and beverage industry as junk food taxes are starting to gain weight globally.

By the end of this decade, we can expect the majority of the countries in every continent across the world to be following the example set by Hungary, Denmark and Taiwan in taxing unhealthy foods.

Consider all your favourite indulgences – McDonald's burgers, fizzy drinks, chocolates, crisps, sweets, ice creams, Indian curries, to name a few costing up to 20% more. Governments have realised that, by raising taxes on cigarettes, they have reduced consumption, controlled smoking-related illnesses and, at the same time, generated much-needed tax revenue. This strategy will now be applied to unhealthy foods.

Hungary and Denmark were among the first countries in the world to introduce the so-called fat tax (also known as the hamburger or sin tax) which, in Denmark, is imposed on foods containing more than 2.3% saturated fat. Interestingly, recently in Buenos Aires, the capital of Argentina, salt shakers were removed from dining tables unless diners specifically asked for them. This was done because it is estimated that 3.7 million people in Buenos Aires have hypertension and that the average Argentinean consumes 13 grams of salt a day, which is 8 grams more than the recommended level.

Countries like Britain, where one in four people are obese, will be unable to ignore this issue, and if left unchecked it can double the number of obese people in the country within the next 15 to 20 years. All foods which are classified as high-calorie, high-fat or high-sugar foods could be targeted by the junk food tax. At the same time, governments which face high obesity health care bills will organise funding programmes like gym memberships for citizens, obesity reduction benefits like vouchers for buying specific type of low-calorie foods and calorie counters printed in restaurant menus. The cost of health insurance or contributions will also increase, with premiums going up for non-healthy patients.

Like it or not, eating that quarter pounder with a jumbo chocolate thick shake at McDonald's will not only be expensive in the future but will also weigh heavily on your conscience while the government builds up its coffers. None of us will argue that there is anything sweet about these government tactics.

Changing dynamics in the pharmaceuticals market with drug patents falling off the cliff

The pharmaceuticals industry and leading branded market players are expected to have a tough time in the coming decade, as can be seen with the trend within the US market. Revenues in the US pharmaceutical market are projected to grow very gradually from $309 billion in 2010 to $358 billion in 2015 as per Frost & Sullivan analysts. The small-molecule, oral dosage pharmaceuticals market is in jeopardy as a huge number of patents are due to expire during 2011–16 as shown in Chart 7.2.

Drugs such as Lipitor, which is the biggest money-generator for Pfizer (also the makers of Viagra) and has sales in excess of $10 billion a year, will soon lose its patent protection.

At the same time, as the small-molecule pharmaceutical market is falling, the biomolecular drugs (biologics) market, which consists of vaccines, allergenics, gene therapy, etc. that are used as therapeutics to treat diseases will witness huge growth from an industry valued at $88 billion to over $173 billion by 2015 in the US alone.

Someone's loss is another's gain, and as a result the generic drug manufacturers, especially from Asian countries, are benefiting from the growing number of off-patent drugs. In particular Indian pharmaceutical companies, aided by India's past legislative policies on patents will benefit immensely and will see doubling of revenues in the next ten years. Ranbaxy was recently given approval in December 2011 to launch generic Lipitor in the US. If you have not done so yet, it is worth putting Indian pharmaceutical stocks in your watch list.

This may not be good news for the industry, but it is good news for consumers as the drugs will get much cheaper, most by as much as 50% from today's prices, when they come off patent.

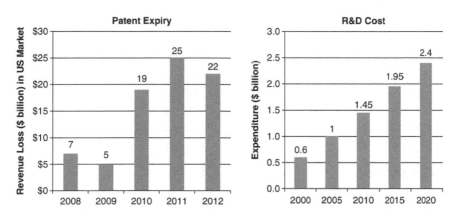

Chart 7.2 **Revenue loss from patent expiry and increased R&D costs are a concern for biopharmaceutical companies in the US**

Source: Frost & Sullivan.

Increasingly, new drug launches now have to cross the additional hurdle for approval in a given country –where the state regulatory will have increasingly stringent requirements to show economic benefit of the new drugs over the currently available treatments. These economic benefits will be measured in terms of decreased cost of hospitalisation or cost of management of side effects. Good examples are the National Institute of Clinical Excellence in the UK and Drug Related Group (DRG) in Germany where they have a system that rewards only real innovations in health care based on strong empirical evidence.

There will be increasingly a strong 'return on investment' approach by health care authorities. Tough days for pharma industry ahead.

The medical home of the future

Similar to companies that offer services to set up one's entertainment room with the latest gadgets and advances in home media, we could see the rise of medical home experts that customise one's home with the latest home health technologies ideally suited for that individual. Whether patients suffer from diabetes, emphysema, arthritis, congestive heart failure or some other condition, there are assistive tools that could aid them in their daily lives and ensure they keep up with their daily monitoring and treatment regimen activities.

A room could be devoted in one's house to various home tests that might range from basic biometric monitoring to more advanced diagnostic tests. Basic biometrics might involve heart rate, blood pressure, weight and other commonly tracked health metrics. For diabetes patients, the paraphernalia would include their testing strips and readers. More advanced diagnostic tools might involve urine or blood analysis to potentially identify developing issues. The information gathered could potentially feed into an online system where a caregiver could track patients' disease state daily, ensure compliance with their treatment regimen and even on occasion provide web-based consultation regarding any questions or concerns.

Robo-doctors

The applications of robots in health care will witness astonishing growth, as has been found in several studies done by Frost & Sullivan analysts. In particular, robot-assisted surgery (RAS) will witness significant growth with the industry growing from a mere

$495 million in 2007 to an industry worth $2.8 billion by 2014. Of this projected $2.8 billion revenue generated in the RAS market by 2014, over 75% of the market is expected to originate from the United States, with Europe just now starting to catch up with and appreciate the potential of this technology. RAS involves a robot that boosts the accuracy and dexterity of medical procedures, making them less invasive and, therefore, reducing recovery times, decreasing risks and boosting success rates.

Companies in this business are expected to see explosive growth with fantastic margins. A particularly good example of a company making fortunes in this industry is Intuitive Surgical, Inc. (ISRG), the developers of the da Vinci surgical system. The company, founded in 1995, went for an IPO in 2000 and has grown to be a $1.41 billion company in 2010, with sales up 34% from 2009. It expects 2011 figures to represent around 25% growth. By mid-2001, the company had sold only about 58 of its patented da Vinci systems. As of 30 September 2011, its installed base of machines was 2031 da Vinci® systems with three in four of its machines fitted in the US. With the company cultivating the market internationally, and the installed base of these machines growing, ISRG's revenues will see a sustainable growth rate of 25% or more annually, both for new sales as well as servicing of the existing fleet of machines, despite new competition entering the market. Interestingly, ISRG was one of the top five with most valuable stocks in the US during 2011.

I can see other niche early-stage companies, including robotic manufacturers external to the health care industry, exploring and entering this market with more private equity funds flowing into the industry. Emerging companies in this field include Armstrong Healthcare Ltd.; Hitachi Ltd.; Integrated Surgical Systems, Inc.; MicroDexterity Systems, Inc.; Richard Wolf Medical Instruments Corporation; Ross-Hime Designs, Inc.; Sinters SA; Terumo Medical Corporation; Toshiba, Inc.; Prosurgics Limited; Medsys; EndoControl and Mazor Surgical Technologies, although some of these companies' products are still a few years away from regulatory approval.

Size matters: Nanotechnology in health care applications

Imagine, in the future, going to the doctor to get treatment for a persistent fever. Instead of giving you a pill or a shot, the doctor refers you to a special medical team which implants a tiny robot into your bloodstream. The robot detects the cause of your fever, travels to the appropriate system and provides a dose of medication directly to the infected area, and within no time you are back on your feet. Surprisingly, we're not that far off from seeing devices like this actually used in medical procedures. They're called nanorobots and engineering teams around the world are working to design them for the treatment of diseases ranging from haemophilia to brain cancer. Nanotechnology experts propose to build machines made of molecules, atom by atom, with great precision. In the future, nanorobot technologies could be used for targeted drug delivery, cell repair or even surgery using micromanipulation tools.

Nanotechnology in health care holds huge promise in the coming decade. It will move, albeit slowly, from the R&D stage to the growth phase, but this decade will see some quantum leaps in discoveries and new inventions in this field. Two key premises are driving interest in this technology.

1. Sickness in humans is caused largely by damage at the molecular and cellular level.
2. Current surgical tools are too large in comparison to the body cells being treated.

The greatest advantage of nanotechnology is the size of the nanoparticles themselves. Being one millionth of a meter, nanoparticles are as small as atoms and molecules, which makes them perfect for passing through the membranes and delivering drugs to the infected cells, thereby arresting the cellular process more effectively than conventional drugs. As a result, nanotechnology will be used in five main applications in health care.

The most prominent application of nanotechnology is targeted drug delivery with two in five organisations worldwide currently focussing on this application. Owing to their size, it is possible for nanoparticles to pass biological membranes and cross the blood/brain barrier effectively. They can, therefore, support the provision of targeted deliveries for cancer, as well as neurological diseases such as Alzheimer's and Parkinson's, and administering treatment against debilitating diseases. Current conventional methods of cancer treatment typically involve chemotherapy – which, although effective, tends to wear out the normal as well as abnormal cells at the same time, thereby resulting in some strong side effects. In the case of neurological disorders, treatments are directed towards select neurological molecules and their binding capacities to their respective receptors. However, the effect of these drugs is temporary and the arrest of neuronal degeneration is not absolute. A key reason attributed to the limited activity of modern-day drugs on neurological disorders is because of the difficulty of getting imaging and therapeutic agents across the blood/brain barrier. The presence of the blood/brain barrier safeguards the brain from being assailed by harmful pathogens. This beneficial barrier is, however, the major obstacle for treating neurological disorders. The limited and minute size of nanoparticles holds promise for ferrying such agents across the barrier.

Other promising applications of nanotechnology are therapeutics – which, although currently a niche, include medical materials and implants, diagnostics and analytical tools, and instruments. The use of nanotechnology in implant dentistry is already very popular, as seen from the growing market share of European brands like 'Nanotie' (from Biomet 3i), 'OsseoSpeed' (from Astra Tech) and 'SLActive' (Straumann). Nanotechnology-based dental implants help in decreasing healing time and improving osseointegration.

Market projections suggest that, by 2020, nanotechnology will consist of 15–20% of the pharmaceuticals, diagnostics and medical devices market, thereby making this a more than $100 billion industry by 2016–17. There are around 400 companies in this market today globally, with over two-thirds of these being nano start-ups from university or research lab spin-offs that focus on a particular nanotechnology or application. Most of these will be gobbled up by bigger players in the next few years once they prove they have a feasible and commercially scalable product. The rest of the industry is made up of major tier 1 and tier 2 pharma and medical device manufacturers that are attracted by the potential of this market.

The market today is dominated by European and North American companies with Asian markets now starting to realise this industry's potential. European companies are clear market leaders in this space compared to their American counterparts, which is quite surprising given that the US leads in biotech research. Therefore, investors should focus their investments on the European or the burgeoning Asian industries, both of which are heavily funded by the government. In particular, those interested in quick returns should invest in companies which have expertise in the drug delivery space as this industry will grow tenfold within this decade. If you are an adventurous investor and like to take risks and high returns, aim for the players in the therapeutics industry, as it is currently a niche but has high growth potential. The medical materials and implants, diagnostics and analytical tools, and instruments market is fairly developed and is currently the biggest revenue generator within this industry.

The Holy Grail in the medical industry will be when biotech and nanotech merge to create 'binano tech'.

Globalisation is globalising health care

'Be global, think local' has been a management mantra in business schools for a couple of decades now. It somehow did not reach the health care industry. It did not need to with the developed world, primarily US, having such a huge share of the pie. However, with the increase in health care demand in Asia and the developing world, the health care business model is changing. Some key changes that we will see are

- Pharmaceutical and technology R&D migrates to Asia.
- Affordable and low-cost products being reversed in deployment from low-cost countries to high-cost regions.
- Global governance structures, like WHO, will become more and more important in formulating international health policies. International agencies will increasingly collaborate on regulations and we will see some levels of harmonisation of health policies.
- Social networks will play an important role with global communities of people sharing common experiences being formed and increasingly targeted by companies.
- Diseases will have no boundaries.
- Medical tourism will be a global industry.
- There'll be virtual doctors and hospitals.
- Every health care company will be global.

Moore's Law applied to medical technology

When I went for my first MRI scan, I was amazed at the size of the MRI scanner. A room of the size of roughly 10 metres by 10 metres housed the machine, its accessories and the workstation. On top, I thought the machine was rather loud and bulky. And I almost fell off the machine when the operator told me these machines can cost anywhere between $1 million to $2.5 million depending upon the size and model. I wondered if the health care industry had ever heard of Moore's Law. To my astonishment, when I did the research for this book, I was told by experts that my wish is now coming true.

Gordon Moore, Intel's co-founder, released a fairly seminal paper in 1965 wherein he outlined his theory on the pace of development for computing hardware. The concept now known as Moore's Law has proven to be a fairly accurate predictor of integrated chip development, and is still used today in setting long-term guidance for involved tech firms. Devices are able to improve processing speed and performance while simultaneously lowering costs for production. Personal electronic devices like mobile phones, TVs, laptops and tablet PCs are often outmoded in 12 months.

While regulatory and other barriers prevent medical technology markets from churning new products at similar rates, advances in computing are no doubt enabling new devices that are more efficient and have greater functionality with reduced power requirements. One has to only look at the transition of pacemakers over time to understand the magnitude of engineering that has gone into improving device function and capabilities. The first pacemakers contained only two transistors, and were the size of a hockey puck. Today devices are approximately the size of a silver dollar, and have multiprocessors that can simultaneously capture and adjust treatment in fractions of seconds.

The future of medical equipment and devices suggests a halving in price over the next ten years, much more powerful devices/equipment with doubling of functionality and much smaller weight-to-size ratio. Every specialist will be a target for a medical equipment to help with his or her job. Most medical equipment in the future will be portable, connected to the Internet with Wi-Fi and will look like iPads. Even Gordon Moore would be proud.

Low-cost medical equipment

Currently there exist significant disparities in health care delivery for patients in one part of the world versus the other. Despite accounting for a little less than 12% of the global population, the US, Japan and Western Europe account for well over 80% of the world's consumption of medical device technologies.

In most consumer markets, there are fairly distinct tiers of products: luxury, specialty, mid-tier and low-cost options. Manufacturers even specialise their products in various regions to conform to the buying habits and preferences of the local market.

When it comes to medical technologies, for the most part companies make only one class of products: best of class. That emphasis is partially dictated by the safety and regulatory burden placed on medical products and supplies. Those products are then pushed straight through to foreign markets with limited attention towards any region-specific needs assessment.

Take, for example, a country like India, with a vibrant economy, growing middle class and escalating incidence of chronic diseases. A little over 75% of national health care spend in India comes from out-of-pocket expenses. In the US only 12% is out-of-pocket, and the rest is addressed through government and private insurance providers. Factoring in who is paying for the equipment greatly affects adoption.

Companies have begun to rethink their approach to addressing the needs of markets like India. Similar to what the automobile industry discovered, many medical technology companies are now taking a 'built in, built for' approach. With regional manufacturing, designers are now able to develop products ranging from diagnostic and monitoring equipment to rescue ventilators at a third of the cost in other markets. One of the companies that have been at the forefront of customising and designing products in their regions of use has been General Electric. They now have dedicated manufacturing and design teams solely focused on the Indian market and that gather feedback on usage requirements unique to care settings there. Through that initiative, they have designed CT scanners and ultraportable patient monitoring equipment that sells for a third of the cost of higher-end systems in other markets. Manufacturing in local regions also allows GE to be more reactive to demand and reduce supply chain costs. Despite only representing a fraction of GE Healthcare's nearly $20 billion global revenues, there is a strong belief that the innovations happening in India can be carried to other emerging markets that face similar challenges in their health care systems.

GE is not the only major multinational medical device company looking at innovating lower cost solutions to bridge the divide between need and access to care. Siemens is doing the same. It recently developed a Fetal Heart Monitor, an idea conceived in India, which costs far less than the $4000 or so as it uses microphones instead of the expensive ultrasound technology. It will not be long before some of these low-cost equipment developed in emerging markets like India and China are sold in developed markets.

Another significant technological development has been in enabling technologies that allow for greater mobility and ease of use.

Technology now exists that can convert one's smartphone into a hand-held ultrasound scanner or EKG reader. Being able to convert one's existing laptop or smartphone into a multifunctional device limits the amount of spending required on capital equipment and allows for access to any patient regardless of location. Taking it a step further, electronic records and images that can be easily transmitted reduce the burden of needing to have a specialist on-site to provide a diagnosis.

Medical technology companies could look at this disparity from three perspectives. One, that there is a tremendous unaddressed opportunity for growth in emerging markets, if they get their product pricing right. The other perspective is that their current solutions just are too cost-prohibitive to be considered in these markets. Thirdly, if they don't develop low-cost devices or equipment, they will soon face profitability erosion from companies who can.

Health care industry shakeout

The first half of the Y2K decade saw tremendous strides in product development on all fronts in the health care industry. Equipment manufacturers were developing more and more powerful scanners, hospitals had the cash to splash out on state-of-the-art equipment and clinicians loved their new toys. Stock markets were booming and customers were happy to utilise services via fancy health insurance deals or pay out of pocket. However, in the corridors of power at the national level, financial planners and economists were doing the math and somehow the numbers were not making sense. Health care spending at 15% of GDP and predictions on the quantum of dollars needed to provide care to a burgeoning elderly population did not look sustainable.

The middle of the decade also saw some suppliers in this industry start to feel the pain of saturation and the commoditisation of some of their products and solutions. Growth rates started to dip and some regulatory agencies started to tighten the noose. Free flowing reimbursement clearances for new medical procedures were starting to be questioned and expensive drugs were being taken off the prescription lists. While there was a sense of ownership at the hospital level to improve efficiencies and resource use, the payers for these services also started to exert their influence on curbing free spending in health care. The biggest blow came about in 2008–9 when stock markets crashed – lending was restricted, dollars kept aside for R&D were frozen and, more importantly, health care capital asset acquisition and replacement ground to a near standstill. This was a wakeup call for many a multinational health care conglomerate. Some were hurt really badly; others had a more resilient business model that allowed them to absorb much of the shock. The industry changed in a big way.

The future looks rough and challenging with drug patents falling off the cliff and wellness and well-being becoming more important than treatment. Most industry experts predict that about ten to 15 tier 1 companies will be left by 2020–25 and only 25 to 30 tier 2 companies will prosper globally. The industry will see more consolidation. Forward-looking companies like Novartis and Aventis are more likely to survive as they are more adaptable to change because they are getting into new businesses and business models like tele-health. Pharma companies will make more profit from health supplements than from selling antibiotics, and will be in the business of health management rather than making pills. Companies are moving from core product sales to creating additional service revenue opportunities. Due to the decrease in hardware costs and hence margins, additional value-added services are the way to go to retain customers. Bayer has partnered with Medtronic to offer glucose-monitoring solutions along with its insulin pump device. These systems are now being integrated into Ford vehicles.

Device companies seem to be generally on the right track. They are moving into the service model. Siemens Medical, for example, has tied up with a Spanish regional health authority to maintain equipment services for the next 15 years in a multi-million-dollar contract. Device manufacturers will, in the future, offer more of this type of service to hospitals and to communities that leverage social media.

One could see some types of hospital staff, like nurses, working more frequently outside than inside hospitals, as companies will hire specialists even in functions like sales. Tele-health services (covered in Chapter 10, 'Connectivity and Convergence') will provide opportunities for new entrants like mobile operators and Silicon Valley IT powerhouses. Watch out for these information and communication technology companies as they launch a multitude of customer apps and develop virtual and connected hospitals.

One other notable example is the shift away from product sales to service delivery in the medical consumable industry. Hospitals are used to procuring large volumes of consumables as per their consumption patterns. They are then responsible to dispose or process the items for reuse, which takes up considerable resources. An innovative company in Europe is promoting the concept of 'pay per use' for consumables, in return taking responsibility for the disposal/incineration or processing for reuse. Both stakeholders thus win through this value-added service.

All types of service industry will benefit. The training and education industry will, in particular, benefit the most. New rules in safety and health standards for hospitality, retail and health care facilities provide opportunity for software companies to license online and blended training modules.

Entrepreneurs will find opportunity in the vast industry value chain with new business models. There will even be a big recycling industry, not just for hospital waste but also for medical devices and implants. For example, an Indian company plans to buy used pacemakers in the US, recondition them and sell them at cheaper prices in the developing world. 'If you are not bold enough to donate your organs, at least you can be charitable enough to donate your used pacemaker' will be the marketing motto of these recyclers.

Even the franchising business model, which is so well practised in the hotel industry, will spread to hospitals, as the premise behind it is quite similar. Private hospitals and clinic businesses in South Asia is notable with Apollo Hospitals, Max Healthcare and others using such business practices. Several American health care organisations are also lending know-how and best practices to private hospitals being set up in Turkey and the Middle East. Other examples also include companies using their strong brand name to distribute medical consumables after rebranding.

Almost every other Tom, Dick and Harry company will be a health, wellness and well-being provider. Even your local supermarket, if it has not already done so, will become a one-stop shop for everything from in-store blood tests to blood pressure checks and providing Viagra and other pharmaceuticals over the counter. Your local gym will not just provide a running machine, but also offer, alongside the existing spa, private health care services like dentistry, screening, physiotherapy, pharmacy and complementary therapies. A good example of an organisation already doing this is Nuffield Health in the UK. The company, through clever acquisition of Cannon gyms and careful planning, has combined fitness and gyms, hospitals, health clinics, diagnostic units and a range of medical treatments into one complete health care service. While you are at work, you can pop out for a run and a quick doctor's check-up in the afternoon, all within the same premises. So what do all these changes in health, wellness and well-being mean to you as a person and an employer? Well, as an individual, for a start, trust no one but yourself to pay for your own health care as there is a good chance you will live beyond the age of 90 and will need a lot of self-care. Be prepared to be a DIY patient. Second, start becoming accustomed to eHealth and technology. Thirdly, and most importantly, focus on wellness, well-being and prevention more than on cure.

As an employer, it is important you start adding wellness and well-being benefits to your employment package to lure good talent. Employers in the future will increasingly sponsor their employees' well-being and create an office environment that promotes and incentivises healthy living. Companies will encourage outdoor meetings, replacing junk food in vending machines with healthy alternatives, friendly reminders suggesting the stairs instead of the elevators, offering free health screenings for individuals and their families, and many other measures like providing healthy canteens, the hope being that their employees will as a result be healthier, happier and more productive.

8

BUSINESS MODEL OF THE
DECADE – VALUE FOR MANY

There is an interesting correlation between battles and business models. Just as invention of a new weapon has meant competitive advantages in the battlefield and victory for nations, new and sustainable business models can guarantee success for corporations in an increasingly competitive world. And just as warfare can be broken broadly into five generations – linear (Napoleonic column formation), trenches and mass sieges (World War I and World War II), blitzkrieg (highly mobile form of infantry and armour working in combined arms teams), guerrilla/insurgency (Vietnam, Afghanistan and Iraq) and now cyber warfare – one can also roughly break business models into five similar generations: conventional (Industrial Revolution era), convenience (McDonald's), magnitude (hypermarkets and Walmart), dot-com (eBay, Amazon.com, Netflix) and now Web 2.0 (apps). Take notice of the convergence that is taking place in the fifth generation.

Interestingly, in both warfare and business models, technology, innovation and entrepreneurship (read as bravery in warfare) play an important role in an entity's success. But the important question is: how significant is the role of technological superiority in the overall determination of victory? Very important; but it is not a guarantee of success, as we have seen in recent military conflicts in which the US has been involved, such as Vietnam, Afghanistan and Iraq. Despite having an armoury of sophisticated weapons, the US was unsuccessful in its missions in these countries. Similarly, in business models, technology is playing an increasingly important role today but is not a guarantee of success. A good business model needs to be backed up with a good product and clever positioning. However, technology is enabling the development of new, wonderful and innovative business models, some of which are discussed in this chapter. A key benefit of technology today is its ability to reach a large number of customers, almost the whole world, with minimal cost.

During our research on Mega Trends, we spent considerable time trying to understand new business models and mapping out business models of the future. As a matter of fact, we have plans to do a full-fledged book on this fascinating topic. We found examples of some unique, inventive and groundbreaking ideas but, in the end, we narrowed down to one business model that we believe will rule the world. We called this business model 'value for many', not 'Value for Money'. We borrowed the term 'value for many' from R. A. Mashelkar's TED talk on the same theme which was very inspiring.

Before we build evidence of why this value for many business model is the most important business model of this decade, let us first have a look at some of the unique business models which we will see increasingly being followed in our universe.

BUSINESS MODELS OF THE FUTURE

Following are some selective examples of unique business models which will become prominent in our world.

Customisation and personalisation

Before I describe this business model, it is first important to define and differentiate the two distinct terms of which it consists, as they are often misunderstood to be the same.

Customisation means developing a product or service tailored to individuals' needs and preferences. Examples of customisation could be you buying a car with yellow wheels, pink doors, green roof and purple interiors (why would anyone have such horrible taste in colours?). Nike is a good example of a company which sells customised shoes. One can go onto its website and develop a tailored shoe in one's own choice of colours and also place one's name on it – all for a neat $200 plus, whereas the same shoe without customisation would costs one-fifth of the price. My children's au pair, who bought a pair of customised Nike shoes with her name on it, absolutely loves them and would not buy any shoe off the shelf now. I, however, would not pay that kind of money for a running shoe, and would never ever want my name on a shoe. Similarly, Makeyourownjeans.com is another example of a company that customises jeans to its customers' tastes. So if you wanted your jeans to hang lower than anyone else's bottom, almost to your knees, they can do it for you.

Personalisation is where you take an existing product and help the customer adapt it to their taste by changing some features or characteristics. Microsoft could be complimented as one of the first companies who came up with this strategy with MS Windows, which allowed computer users to have a personalised screen saver and wallpaper. An example in the car industry is the issuance of two different keys for husband and wife, where car settings like the side mirrors, steering wheel height, climate control, music and other internal electronic gimmicks will automatically reset themselves depending upon settings programmed into the key that is inserted.

Future value creation will reside in how companies allow customers to customise or personalise the products and services for their consumption. In the rush to achieve cost benefits from mass production, companies have compartmentalised every customer into six or ten distinct customer segments. The premise is that every customer is inherently unique, given a choice of distinct preferences. Amazon.com is one good examples of a personalised experience where the company learns about customer interests and adapts to their needs. It pushes recommendations to customers based on their previous buying history of books and other products.

Is the customisation business model expensive? Not really. One can use the Internet to reach customers and connect orders directly to suppliers/factories in China, who are guided by a flexible manufacturing system to develop made-to-order products and have them shipped at a relatively low cost to customers for a sweet premium. Again, personalisation is about using digital technology to provide options.

In most cases, customisation leads to new revenues with healthy profits, but personalisation is more important for differentiation and retaining customers. However, one needs to be careful to not get sandwiched between the two. BMW tried that by offering a bit of both so when you bought their car you could choose literally millions of options – from metallic paints (costs the car companies a handful of dollars but they charge customers around $400) to alloy wheels, sporty suspension, different engine configurations – and design your own car filled with gadgets. It seemed a great idea at the start as customers were spending 15–20% more than the cost of the vehicle (compared to 2–5% as the industry standard) but it was a nightmare to manage as it threw their strategy of economies of scale out of the window, resulting in their cars being much more expensive to produce compared to the likes of Audi and Volkswagen, who were using economies of scale to reduce costs. Since then BMW and many other car companies like Mercedes customise specific packages: for example, a sports package which combines alloy wheels with a sporty suspension.

We are in the early stages of seeing the traditional brick and mortar companies capitalise on this trend. By the end of this decade it will be safe to assume that, by leveraging the Internet as a medium, every brick and mortar company will be offering a very customised and/or personalised experience of purchase and consumption to consumers.

Co-creation

Co-creation is a business strategy that works more like a business forum and is born out of enterprise social software. It involves the coming together of different elements of the value chain to mutually benefit each segment – right from idea generation, resource allocation, revenue generation, implementation and delivery of the product or service. This mutually creates new types of capabilities, interaction and learning experiences and creates an open space for innovation, research and development, production planning and even customer feedback and satisfaction.

The business model is best explained with an example. Quirky is an industrial design company headquartered in New York. Its entire co-creation business model is web-based. It allows collaboration among different segments of the value chain. This is how it works. An inventor submits an idea for product development at the rate of $10. An idea is picked on a weekly basis and voted upon. Factors such as uniqueness, capability and capacity of manufacturing are considered. The chosen one will be passed on to the design, marketing and branding team of Quirky. This entire network is crowd-sourced.

After manufacture of the product, revenues from sales are shared with the entire spectrum in the value chain. Of the total revenue, 30% will go to the idea generator. Another 30% is allocated to the product designer and another 30% to the company who made the design possible; and the rest of the profits are distributed proportionally across other segments. This value for many business models not only brings 'value' to a larger community outside the design and manufacturing company, but it allows invention to be made more possible and generated ideas more probable to implement. What more?

The unique selling point of this model is that the very products are designed by the consumers themselves and, with pre-design voting and product acceptance ratings, it ensures success.

Pay as you go

One business model with which we are very familiar in the mobile phone industry is that of renting cell phones through a flexible pay-as-you-use model. One can top-up one's mobile phone with as much as $10 in the developed world, not to mention as low as 10 cents in countries like India. This pay-as-you-go concept is now being increasingly applied to all forms of assets.

Thales rents its Unmanned Aerial Vehicles (UAVs) in Afghanistan to the Allied militaries using a pay-by-the-hour model. It not only owns the UAVs, it also operates them on battleground for them.

With the motorists a model gaining popularity is pay-as-you-drive (PAYD) or its successor called pay-as-how-you-drive (PAHD) vehicle insurance, concept developed to link the insurance policy and the premium with the driver's risk and driving behaviour, rather than on the traditional method based on just demographics, age and type of vehicle/neighbourhood. In seven of the major European countries, there are expected to be over 1.5 million drivers using this usage-based insurance model from just around 100,000 in 2007, with Italy taking a lead.[1]

Similarly we are seeing new pay-as-you-go models in the energy sector, where this model is deployed to allow consumers to control their energy costs for gas and electricity consumption. Other examples where this model is being used is in road pricing, broadband and even gym memberships – pay as you run.

This model is spreading from the consumer to B2B market, driven by the shift in the strategy of organisations to focus on their core competencies. Companies prefer not to not acquire assets but to lease them for their needs, thus keeping their balance sheets light and having the flexibility to scale based on business needs. This has been one of the primary drivers of the cloud computing business proposition in the information and communication technology (ICT) industry. It is a win-win business model as it ensures greater utilisation of resources. The same trend also applies to us in our personal lives. We acquire a lot of assets which we use for a very limited extent of its complete capability. An example is the car. We use it less than 10% of the time during the day, and we generally use only one seat, but we like to buy big cars with five seats and four doors.

The pervasiveness of the Internet, and the push to a service-based world, will ensure this business model will become more common-place in our everyday lives through offerings from insurance, automotive and durable consumer goods manufacturers, energy and, of course, the telecom world.

Collaborative buying

The concept of collaborative buying is not new. However, what is new in this decade is the innovative ways of deploying the collaborative buying strategy – leveraging on the Internet, mobile phone technology and, of course, social media.

Traditionally, the roots of group buying can be traced back to China and not to Groupon. Tuángòu is a practise where a group of people bargain together with a retailer to decrease prices. This group of people are usually friends or complete strangers (who connect online) and have previously decided to purchase the same product or a service on a predetermined date. The group will 'mob' the store on that date and bargain with the retailer to lower the price. The newly agreed lower price will be applicable to the entire group. As of 2011, there were 5877 Tuángòu websites operating in China – which roughly accounts for around 42 million Chinese consumers contributing 20 billion RMB in sales in that year.[2]

So, with the advent of the Internet, collaborative buying today can be defined as 'a mutually beneficial online shopping strategy for busi-nesses and consumers that harnesses the "collective buying power of a group" to attain massive discounts by leveraging the popularity of social media'.

The model of collaborative buying is quite simple. The advertise-ment for a discounted offer is normally offered online. When a minimum number of consumers sign up for the same offer, the deal is confirmed.

This business model has a three-way benefit. The consumers benefit from a hefty price cut. Businesses benefit from a whole new crowd of customers – with the minimum guaranteed number. The group-buying website benefits from the commission it receives from the business.

The first move of group-buying sites was to leverage mobile apps and social media (e.g. Groupon apps). The next innovative move from group-buying sites was to geographically segment their customers by cities. Sites like Groupon began to offer deals by cities and even by sub-city levels: for example, South London deals. These made the deals more local, exclusive and convenient for customers. The third move, which is still being tried and tested in pilot cities in the United States, is to provide location-based offers to customers via GPS (e.g. Groupon Now!).

Now lets look more into the success story of Groupon and its collaborative buying business model a little more in depth. From selling its first deal for a pizza outlet located in the first floor of its own building, Chicago-based Groupon has now spread its global footprint in 500 markets in 44 countries. Since its inception, Groupon has made the headlines for being a leader in the daily deals market with 142.9 million subscribers and $1.6 billion in revenue in 2011.

The business model of Groupon is quite straightforward. A business decides to promote its business on Groupon's website. Registered consumers pay the heavily discounted price through the group-buying site. To illustrate, a customer pays $40 for a deal worth $80. The deal is heavily promoted through the Internet, including social networking platforms. If the minimum number of consumers signs up, then the deal is on. The heavy discount is applicable for the entire group. Groupon retains up to 50% of the returns (e.g. $20 of a $40 sale) and the businesses benefit from a large group of consumers.

Since its inception, Groupon has helped many businesses get rid of unused inventory and reach out to untapped customers. But none were more sensational than the GAP deal which offered $50 worth of GAP accessories and apparel at the rate of $25. This daily deal saw sales of 441,000 Groupons worth $11 million. Of course, GAP had to share the $11 million revenue generated with Groupon, which remains an undisclosed amount to this day.

It came as no surprise when Groupon was finally valued at $12.7 billion in November 2011 with a float of 35 million shares at the rate of $20 each. When they made their IPO at NASDAQ, the price of shares skyrocketed to $29.52 each.

Groupon's challenge is that it is not alone anymore.

The one-off business model

Fancy an unforgettable experience like aerobatic stunt flying, or a one-night weekend escape in a castle as a prince and princess, served by Michelin five-star gourmet chefs and entertained by courtiers; or, even better, a space flight circling the earth. All of this is more or less doable today or will be even easier in the future as we see entrepreneur companies launching one-off experience business model shops like the company called 'Red Letter Days'. Soon they will be facing competition from even the likes of Tesco and Walmart, which will soon offer similar services.

Look out for increase in those T-shirts which read, 'Been there, done it, sent my mum a T-shirt'.

Sharing – what is yours is mine

Car sharing as a concept has really taken off. From less than one million members globally in 2010, Frost & Sullivan expects over 30 million members worldwide by 2020. The concept is now evolving to peer-to-peer sharing, whereas in which a private individual leases a vehicle to a car sharing operator (e.g. Relayrides). Who would have thought ten years ago that we possessive humans will share the second most expensive asset in our lives – the car.[3]

An Internet company called Patientslikeme.com is another example of a similar business model. This company shares people's medical records. By offering a free service, PatientsLikeMe attracts thousands of patients to share their experiences, symptoms and challenges. Then with their permission, PatientsLikeMe gathers data that is resold to third parties (pharmaceutical, medical devices companies, etc.).

Sharing is a business model which is really taking off, driven largely by Generations Y and Z who prefer to share than own and believe that humans need to be social. Rightly so! Why buy a car when I only drive it less than 5% of the time on average in a day?

This thinking has led to many innovative business models and we can expect many more such entrepreneurial business models emerging in the future.

Free-premium (Freemium)

Free-premium (Freemium) is a business model which has existed in the software world for over two decades now, but is now finding more widespread acceptance thanks to the generosity of the Internet, where all information and services can be shared by the click of a button.

Freemium refers to a product or service which is provided at no cost, but for which a premium product/service is available which, for a fee, includes advanced features, benefits or functionality.

Spotify[4] is a good example of this business model which blossoms on sharing music and offering freemium services. The basic music-streaming service is free, with advertising revenues covering the base costs. However, once you get addicted to the free package, the business model thrives on you shifting to the premium services which cost about £9.99 a month in the UK. Premium services include advanced features and benefits like gift cards, offline mode (where you can listen to music even when not connected to the Internet), ability to take your music abroad, no advertising, enhanced sound quality and many other similar benefits.

Community-based business models

Thanks to Facebook (FB) and other social networking sites, one can expect a huge jump in community-based business models. None other than FB themselves will lead this business model. A possible example of this could be people with a similar form of rare illness, globally coming together on FB to develop a sub-community. This sub-community can then be targeted by specialist firms to market products in the guise of managing and maintaining that site and members.

Pay or sell with a tweet

A powerful marketing tool exists where, as an alternative to paying with cash, users buy products through providing publicity or doing some basic chores. Size matters in this case, as the larger the magnitude of your network, the bigger the payment.

The model is best described with the workings of Paywithatweet. com.[5] This is how it works. People sell and buy the product through the value of their social network. The seller first advertises the product and creates a 'pay button'. People who view the website click on the 'Pay with a Tweet' button and post about the product, after which they can download a file – whether a song from an album, an article from a magazine, a teaser from a book or even a presentation from a thesis. When someone clicks on the button, all followers and friends will soon 'view the tweet' and the product soon becomes famous throughout the social network.

The release of Innovative Thunder's book titled *Oh My God What Happened and What Should I Do* launched the start of Paywithatweet. com in the summer of 2010. Three days later there were 13,000 downloads of the book becoming the third-highest trending topic globally and, to date, there are over 170,000 downloads of the book.

VALUE FOR MANY – THE BUSINESS MODEL OF THE DECADE

Almost half the world, more than three billion people, lives on less than $2.50 a day. With globalisation, the rise of the middle class and Internet penetration to increase to five billion, it has become important for companies to 'make one, sell many', more than ever before.

The 'make one, sell many' concept implies produce and sell the same product or service to the masses in developing as well as developed countries or pull the market globally using a platform like the Internet. It also implies leveraging the licensing model to franchise the brand, something Proctor & Gamble, which touches lives of four billion people with its products everyday successfully, does.

By the previous definition, even most of the business models covered in the earlier part of the chapter can be classified as value-for-many (VFM) business models. Groupon's collaborative business model is nothing but a VFM business model. It is leveraging the Internet to connect buyers and it buys goods en masse to get the discounts. Even crowdsourcing, a popular mass collaboration fad these days where tasks are farmed out to the masses, is nothing but a VFM business model. The sharing business model of car or medical-records sharing is a VFM business model. It will only work if it has a high number of members or users. Even FB is a value for many business models – its platform is connecting 850 million users which, for sure, is reflected in its valuation at the stock exchange.

The most interesting feature of the VFM business model is that it drives innovation across a whole spectrum of industries right from low-cost flights to low-cost affordable health care products. Forward-thinking companies are the ones who envision the need to re-engineer their existing R&D and design process to create cost and social innovation and embrace and replicate successful strategies in different regions. The last decade saw the adoption of many 'low-cost product' strategies coming into play. The $2,500 Tata Nano car, $100 XO laptop, $35 mobile phones in India and $1 pregnancy kits are some examples of low-cost products that provide basic features of the erstwhile sophisticated and expensive versions. This strategy makes goods affordable that were previously deemed inaccessible to the bottom of the income pyramid. What companies need to address to stay at the top of innovation is to maintain the tightrope balance between cost and quality. Once businesses nail that, they will have implemented a successful VFM model.

Siemens is one such company that has not only adopted this strategy but is also planning to open six more new factories in India to manufacture low-cost, innovative products. Titled SMART for 'simple, maintenance-friendly, affordable, reliable and timely to market', these products saw a 100% growth in Siemens' 'low-cost, high-innovation engineering solutions' during 2010–11, contributing to 10% of new orders. Siemens sees this low-cost market size for India to have a potential of around €21 billion, with the bottom of the income pyramid accounting for 70% of the market.

Another forward-thinking company, GE Healthcare, rolled out portable electrocardiogram (ECG) machines worth Rs 25,000, called MACi, for rural India. These machines lowered the cost for each ECG by 50–70%, bringing the price per ECG to as low as Rs 9. Each ECG system boasts of a three-hour battery charge and the ability to generate 500 ECGs per month – which is equivalent to a month's operation in an Indian rural village. Today, GE Healthcare has a team of 1200 scientists and engineers who are specifically focussed on launching innovative products and solutions for the Indian market. It has already pumped around $50 million into its Indian R&D laboratories to create around ten products a year for India. And the phenomenon does not stop here. Other examples of VFM include:

- Aravind Eye Care Hospital, which charges an average cost of $25 per cataract operation compared to costs of $3000 to $4000 in the West, has applied the business model common in the automotive industry to health care to achieve this amazing and profitable business. Eye surgery is conducted as an assembly line operation with standardisation of equipment, staff and training across the surgery chain. It keeps its surgical equipment in operation 24 hours a day, which reduces the cost per surgery. Doctors focus only on performing surgery, and nurses handle pre-op and post-op care, which increases doctor productivity.
- Grameen Bank's provision of microfinance earned it a Nobel Prize and the Medal of Freedom from President Obama in 2009. Grameen

Bank is a microfinance organisation and community development bank founded in Bangladesh that provides small loans to poor and needy people without requiring collateral. A key target customer for the bank is women, who they believe can be trusted more than the men to take the loan seriously with lower risk of default. On 10 December 2006, Mosammat Taslima Begum, who used her first 16 Euro ($20) loan from the bank in 1992 to buy a goat and subsequently became a successful entrepreneur and one of the elected board members of the bank, accepted the Nobel Prize on behalf of Grameen Bank's investors and borrowers at the awards ceremony held at Oslo City Hall. Grameen Bank is the only business corporation to have ever won a Nobel Prize.

- E-Choupal is an initiative of ITC Limited, a large multi-business conglomerate in India, to link directly with rural farmers via the Internet for procurement of agricultural and aquaculture products like soybeans, wheat, coffee and prawns.

- Godrej's 'Chotukool',a refrigerator worth Rs 3,700 ($69) is for the rural Indian consumer. The name is innovative too, as it suggests a 'cute', 'small' and 'cool' fridge. The fridge is available in two capacities: 30 litres and 43 litres, weighing 7.2 kg and 8.9 kg respectively. The fridge was designed specifically for the food-buying needs and consumption habits of rural and low-income households, which earn $5 a day. It, for example, does not have a freezer compartment as these customers do not necessarily stock ice cream or eat frozen food, preferring to cook fresh every time. As most of these households don't have a consistent power supply, this fridge can run on batteries and it does not have a compressor. Not surprisingly, the consumer goods conglomerate Godrej & Boyce Ltd., who created this product, now plans to create a 'Chotu' portfolio of low-cost products. In the pipeline are 'ChotuWash', a low-cost washing machine, and a low-cost water purifier.

- A friend of mine buys wine through an online company which has a crowd-buying concept for wines. It gives its users a small selection of wines to choose from, buys it in container loads directly from the vineyards and ships it straight to its customers, eliminating the wholesaler and the retailer.

A disruptive VFM business model can be seen in the newspaper business in the developed world. In the autumn of 1833, New Yorkers were in for a surprise when they woke up one morning to find their favourite daily newspaper, *The Sun*, offered for one penny.

The publication sold like hotcakes, with sales reaching 15,000 copies per day within the next two years. A new business model in the newspaper industry was born. Today, the same business model has been adopted globally across various newspaper publishing offices – some of them even offer their publications for free. The profits gained through advertising revenues are more than sufficient to keep the price low and circulation high. *Metro UK*, which is a free newspaper, distributes 1.3 million copies to more than 3.5 million readers every morning. A commuter's favourite in UK urban cities, *Metro* is cleverly designed to provide reading material for at least 27 minutes, which is the average commuting time for Londoners. This is an advertiser's dream, because this translates to more than 20 minutes of undivided marketing attention.

The *Evening Standard* came up with the same business model and started selling its evening version (*Metro* is a morning version) free in the UK. Within months of adopting the VFM business model, the 180-year-old newspaper boasted an average net circulation of 610,226 for February 2010, a record compared to its highest figure of 256,229 recorded in September of 2009 when it was a paid newspaper. In February 2012, it overtook mainstream newspapers like *The Guardian* with its circulation figures.

It is often misunderstood that VFM is a business model for poor nations and masses. Not true. Ford Motor Company's survival strategy during the recession in 2009 was to make limited number of models on global platforms and sell the same vehicles in all markets of the world.

This VFM model can also be applied to licensing and franchising. Scott Adams, who created 'Dilbert', says that he became a cartoonist because he liked the idea of being paid multiple times for the same work. He draws a comic strip and is paid by the newspapers that run

---

CASE STUDY: FORD – THE NEW VALUE FOR THE BLUE OVAL

It was 2009. The global automotive industry was reeling under the impact of the economic downturn and kept a low profile. Its participants were scouting for best practices to avoid losses and stay alive. The severity of the recession was felt most strongly in North America with key passenger car manufacturers opting to slash jobs, close plants, sell brands, file Chapter 11 bankruptcy and even take bailouts from the federal government to stay alive. One company from Detroit,

Michigan stuck to the basics and drew inspiration from its century-old historic past. Experts in the industry now understand that Ford Motor Company did the right things to avoid bankruptcy and shelved a bailout to save the Blue Oval brand. Its strategy not only won the hearts of its brand-savvy customers, but also paved a path for others to follow. This strategy was built on value for many – build the same cars and models in all parts of the world with market customisation and personalisation.

About 100 years ago, Ford invented the business model of value for many in the motor industry by mass-producing its Model T on a conveyor belt assembly line. Its business model was disruptive. It replaced the horse, which in those days was the fastest mode of mobility, with a car.

Ford did well for about 90 years and then lost its way. However, it repeated history with its new strategy of 'One Ford' in 2009. At the heart of the strategy was a roadmap of deploying a global vehicle platform and realigning its entire vehicle manufacturing DNA globally. Ford, under the leadership of its new CEO, Alan Mulally, standardised the right models and then intro-duced the same models in the right markets worldwide – be it North America, Europe or the Asia Pacific – while weighing the pros and cons of its partners (presence of right vendor and component base), its plants (proximity to production locations) and markets (current core and future expansion) while keeping launch price and timing also optimum. The products were tailored to the market demand – smaller, lightweight and fuel efficient with attractive electronic gimmicks.

As a result of the value-for-many platform strategy, Ford Group in 2010 had only 14 platforms spinning off nearly 50 models to the tune of 5.1 million units of vehicle production. This is at least two times better than the 27 different platforms that produced more than 90 different models in 2007. Micro-factors indicate that, in two out of three key indices, Ford outperformed even the feats achieved by key competitors like Volkswagen and Hyundai, which came close. For instance, in the average vehicle production per platform in 2010, Ford was number one with 0.36 million units of production per platform while the industry average was around 0.24 million units per platform. Similarly, it ranked number two among the 12 average models per platform in 2010 with 3.57 models per platform, while the industry average was 2.65 models per platform.

Ford's adoption of its universal platform strategy saw the emergence of a strong Global C and Global B platforms targeting 'Focus-sized' and 'Fiesta-sized' car models retooled from its specific plants and scaled up for volumes. While North America is expected to witness increased model production from Global C, followed by Global mid-sized platforms, Europe is expected to strongly support its Global C followed by Global B platforms, targeting the C and B segment of vehicles, respectively. The strongest growth market – Asia Pacific – is expected to support with Global B followed by Global C platforms and the B and C segment of vehicles. These B and C platforms, considered to be core platforms, are expected to contribute to nearly 60% of the 7.5 million units targeted by Ford in 2020 in comparison to half of the 5.1 million units sold in 2010.

Common suppliers and standardised component sharing across these platforms to the tune of 60% are expected to reduce differences between regions and keep them closely knit. With millions of dollars at stake, Ford clearly understands that platform strategy in this value-for-many business model could bring in more than 60% reduction in engineering-related costs, along with more than 40% investment costs, and still target increased production as well as sustainable growth.

The success of that strategy reflects in the company's share price, which has gone up from lows of under $2 in February 2009 to peaks of $18 per share in mid-2011. The company has since had straight six quarters of growth and profitability.

it. He is paid again when the strip is collected with others into a book or run in a calendar. Adams has since licensed his characters and drawings for use on products, including notepads, magnets, clothing, mouse pads, plush toys, an animated television show and, in his words, any product that will hold a label.

So what are the key ingredients for success of this business model? Some are listed next:

1. Think about what common denominator your customers have that you can leverage: for example, Internet or mobile phones (just wait for mobile banking to take off).

155

2. Define the universe (potential customer base) for your product and develop a disruptive, out-of-the-box model: for example, the *Metro* newspaper. Why ask customers to pay for newspapers when the advertising business model is based on pay per subscriber? The more the subscribers, the more the advertising money.
3. Sell the same product/services with minimum customisation in global markets: for example, Ford with its vehicle platform strategy.
4. Leverage connectivity and global platforms like the Internet: about five billion people in this planet will have access to the Internet. Connect the buyers online.
5. Globalisation is harmonising tastes; exploit it.
6. Sell VFM from day one. Scale the business from day one.

Value for many – 'make one, sell many' – will be the defining strategy of global businesses by 2020. This means mass standardisation with local (and individual) customisation/personalisation, cutting out the middleman and developing new universal marketing programmes, and, most importantly, leveraging a mass platform like the Internet and mobile phone (Web 2.0).

9

CONNECTIVITY AND CONVERGENCE

Multi-touch screen, biometrics, iris recognition, personalised advertising, insect robots, 3D video, e-papers and surface browsing: when Steven Spielberg featured these futuristic technologies in his 2002 sci-fi movie 'Minority Report', little did we know that he was mind-bogglingly spot-on as to the possibility of these being plausible technologies in our everyday lives by 2020. Developments in connectivity and convergence will allow us not only to enjoy these cutting-edge technologies with their manifold ground-breaking applications but will also allow us to play and control devices and data by mid-air gestural movements and with holographic immersive technology – in a similar way to what Tom Cruise did in the movie.

So, in 2020, be prepared to welcome an era of connectivity and convergence – an era that will allow us to complete tasks at the blink of an eye and the touch of a finger. Here we will see not only mind-bogglingly creative and converging products and gizmos in our very homes, but we will also see the walls of major industries such as technology, health care, transport and energy simply crashing down before us to create a seamless and intelligent life for us.

In this era you will see, globally, by 2020, 80 billion connected devices, nine billion mobile phones, five billion Internet users, five connected devices for every individual, ten connected devices for every household and 500 devices with unique digital IDs (Internet of things) per square kilometre. Global data traffic will, undoubtedly, reach gargantuan proportions, driven by growth in online video, social media, and download/upload of digital imagery and on-demand gaming.

CONVERGENCE OF PRODUCTS, TECHNOLOGIES AND INDUSTRIES

Connectivity and convergence, today, are two technically inclined but very distinct Mega Trends that cannot be more intertwined with each other. Connectivity is one Mega Trend that has perhaps had one of the steepest evolutionary curves this decade as well as, perhaps, the one Mega Trend that is taken the most for granted. It has given us the power to communicate, respond, interact and broadcast information anytime, anywhere – giving us a mobile life and bestowing every one of us with a unique digital citizenship.

For the purpose of this book, convergence is defined as the integration of current products, technologies and industries that will lead to the emergence of new, innovative and unique products, technologies and industries in the future. These newly converged products will either have a combination of features or a unique feature distinct from their parent form.

Convergence can be broadly categorised into three types:

1. Convergence of products (e.g. computer + phone = smartphone)
2. Convergence of technologies (e.g. building technologies + automation = intelligent home automation)
3. Convergence of industries (e.g. space + energy = space-based solar power)

CONVERGING GIZMOS: ONE PRODUCT, MANY APPLICATIONS

The evolution of machines or devices has seen continuous metamorphosis over the past decade. We have seen the continuous morphing of machines into products and then into gizmos and, perhaps, as justly predicted by Bruce Sterling in his book titled *Shaping Things*,[1] we will soon see the advent of 'spimes' (devices with RFID + ambient connectivity + GPS etc.) and 'biots' (biologically engineered devices) in this decade as well.

Today, converging gizmos are offspring of two or more consumer products – making them baroquely multifunctional and highly convenient. The mobile phone, today, has more computing capability than all of NASA in the late 1960s. We are dependent on our mobile phones for on-demand email checks, texting, social networking, Internet browsing, navigational support and of course for making calls – all applications that were, at one time, offered by different devices.

The striking feature of ambient connectivity is the way it has changed our personal lives, communication styles, working patterns, mobility choices, day-to-day activities and even personal decisions and relationships. This has inadvertently impacted business, industries, business models, markets and even marketing channels in the past decade. Coupled with the expected mammoth growth of online data consumption, the need to inherently integrate several applications into one product and the desire for a faster and speedier life, we will soon see the birth of highly innovative consumer products, some of which will change the very pace of life along with the decisions and choices we make. If this is the power of connectivity that we hold in our hands today, imagine what connectivity and convergence can do to our future lives and our future world.

NEW PRODUCT AVATARS: MAKE WAY FOR 'PHONCIERGE' AND 'I'M WATCH'

The mobile phone, today, has transformed itself from its archaic functionality of making mere calls to assuming the digital responsibilities of a wallet, a ticket, a map, an organiser, a browser and, at times, even a trip advisor or an on-demand entertainer. In the future, we will see all of these functions being integrated – empowering the phone to act as a concierge, a secretary, a banker, a grocer and even, perhaps, an accountant who assists our daily routines by making 'independent' yet accurate decisions such as personalising text messages, answering and screening calls, making grocery orders and even ordering flowers for our friends on their birthdays on our behalf. This new phone avatar would be pre-programmed and attuned to the user's preferences, contacts, food habits and favourite geo-locations and would respond and react intelligently without the need of or with minimal human intervention.

In the near future, we will see a lot more similarly designed converging and intelligent products such as the 3D smart television (no need for glasses), Internet-enabled microwave, intelligent alarm systems and even digital picture frames that can download photos automatically from your Facebook profile. Wearable computing will soon take off with wristwatch computers taking on the role of smartphones, watches and hubs for music and video downloads. The Italian company, Blue Sky, launched a similar smart Android wristwatch called the 'I'm Watch' in early 2012. This watch will play the roles of image viewer, media player, microphone plus speaker, cloud host, apps store and, of course, support online browsing and Internet – and, most importantly, will also tell time.

This digital fabrication and integration will not only engulf existing consumer electronic devices, but will also engulf items that are mere objects today, such as a photo frame, a table top or even the very walls of your house.

FUTURE CONNECTED HOME: INTELLIGENTLY CONNECTED DEVICES

Let us beam ourselves into the future to understand how our digital homes might look like.

In 2025, a typical evening at home after work would be as follows. Retina scanners would check your entry into your premises. You will be greeted at the front door by virtual artificial intelligence (AI) technology that can detect your mood, and respond intelligently to your entertainment requirements for the evening. This AI has been working in conjunction with your 'phoncierge' the whole day – answering/screening calls and making independent decisions that it is pre-programmed for. Internet nodes will be integrated into everything – paper, food items, microwaves, furniture, security systems – allowing machines not only to intelligently communicate and work independently, but also to enable remote monitoring from the phone, car, office PC or any other mobile device.

All these consumer devices will not only be web-enabled but will also work on haptics and voice recognition technology. Connectivity with the in-house refrigerator – which houses 'digitally tagged' food products – enables prior planning of suitable menus for dinner. A digital menu with options is displayed on the touch-screen kitchen table top.[2] Holographic technology will have been introduced as well, which means you can have your favourite celebrity chef 'virtually' guiding your cooking preparations for dinner.

Security systems and child monitoring devices, in connectivity with an interactive house map, would indicate the whereabouts of other family members. For ambient surroundings, temperature and sensors would detect the 'mood' of the inhabitants and accordingly calibrate the lighting and digitally customise the environment. Home entertainment would be completely 3D, with wholly immersive holodecks creating an all-round sensory experience.

All devices can play on-demand music and video content which is saved on the phone, tablet devices, PC and car, and shared anywhere, leveraging the power of the connected cloud. Digital wallpapers would enable interactivity, gaming and other communication options on the walls of every room – thereby changing the desktop interfaces that we have today into full room-sized displays. And for the fashion-minded people, even the very mirrors in the room will be interactive – where they can recognise RFID-tagged garments and give fashion advice – a concept that will be heavily adopted in future retail stores as well.

This connected home communication can be extended to various scenarios such as an entire building that is fully connected with its occupants, with cars, and even perhaps leading to intelligent infrastructure for an entire city as well. There is no end to the scale for ambient intelligent connectivity in our personal lives.

MACRO TO MICRO

Now to drive home the point of macro implications of connectivity and convergence, let's beam ourselves again to the year 2020 and see how our lives will be governed by the rules of this convergence game.

Data deluge: Say hello to the zettabyte era

A key aspect of ambient connectivity is the volume of data traffic that is expected to swell within the digital universe in 2020. Coupled with the additional onslaught of future technologies and innovative web-enabled consumer products, we will soon see data traffic, particularly global IP traffic, reach the exclusive 'zettabyte' club (or 1000 exabytes) by 2015, recording around 4.8 zettabytes per annum according to CISCO.[3] A whopping total of over 60% of the content of this IP traffic will be in the form of video (mobile video, Internet TV, PC) signifying that it would take approximately five years to view the one million minutes of video content that will cross IP networks in one second in the year 2015.[4] This data deluge, or 'infobesity', as I would like to call it, has led to the much hyped concept of cloud computing. Cloud computing, as we know, is a result of infrastructure convergence – an integration of servers, software, storage and networking platforms. Data has now moved from our own desktops to massive remote server farms that allow us to access either our personal or business cloud anytime, anywhere and through any device. Web companies like Google and Facebook that deal with gigantic volumes of data per second have started to build their own centralised server farms. Google has around 15 server farms globally. It came as no surprise when Facebook, with its 800 million users, decided to build a server farm in Lulea on the Arctic Circle to house its computer servers in October 2011. This $760 million server farm, which will cost around £45 million per year in its energy supply, will be, thankfully, powered by renewable energy.

For companies using the cloud, these server farms mean one simple thing – a huge reduction in computing costs, especially capital expenses like buying servers, software and equipment. Therefore, cloud-computing companies like EMC will be the game changers in the connectivity world. A pay-as-you-go model will be commonplace. For example, a start-up gaming company can have anything from six users to 100,000 users, thanks to the cloud. Access to the cloud will mean access to infinite resources.

Morgan Stanley has stated that the workload handled by the cloud would increase by 50% every year for the next three years. Today, one can even rent a cloud from companies like Amazon or Microsoft. Amazon's Elastic Compute Cloud, for example, costs around $0.02–$0.03 per hour or $14.40–$21.60 per month for the smallest Micro 'instance' (virtual server or machine). For higher memory or CPU 'instances', storage costs around $2.48 per hour. This allows companies to run their in-house software and store company data in the rented cloud instead of managing their own private in-house servers.

Data integration also has micro implications. Infobesity, cloud computing, business analytics and social media are creating data-driven strategies across every segment in the value chain. Businesses are now rediscovering revenue streams and new business models from avenues that were previously never imagined. The zettabyte era, with its immense magnitude and amplitude, will throw open opportunities in data storage, data processing, data collaboration, data exchange and even data spaces which, in turn, will create new business models, new departmental enclaves, new organisational models, disruptions in value chain and investment in digital infrastructure. This will open up new partnerships with competitors and suppliers and create new corporate ecosystems.

Knowledge on effective leverage of in-house data is now creating a new competitive differentiator between companies – and the likes of Google, Microsoft and Facebook are no longer the only obvious competitors. For example, Groupon's recent acquisition of Hyperpublic, a location-based database company, was a strategic move to complete its ecosystem in the daily deals business with mobile phone technology. By acquiring Hyperpublic, Groupon has just opened up a sea of opportunities – those that involve smart ways of monetising silos of location-based data. This new strategic possibility will soon change Groupon from a mere group-buying website into a customised service that all websites and app developers can soon promote.

The power of data has unbridled potential for innovative opportunities across every segment in the value chain. Consider, for instance, the insurance industry, which is no longer merely product driven. Today the tech-savvy customer is more mobile, intelligent and has a plethora of information at his or her disposal through technology. He or she will soon expect to access the entire insurance process – selling, applying, renewing, etc. – through technology and, even more surprisingly, through the mobile phone if possible. Now, if we add on the more interesting digital layer of data analytics, we will open a whole new world of opportunities for different players. TomTom, the SAT NAV (or 'SAT NAG' as I call it) manufacturer, has now liaised with insurance company Motaquote to introduce a new product called the TomTom Pro 310, which allows safe drivers to take advantage of cheaper premiums. This device not only warns drivers during late braking or sharp cornering but it also (along with a tracking unit) monitors driving habits and displays them on the dashboard. If one's driving habits are reckless, one's premium for the 'Fair Pay Insurance' service would be higher. This is a testimony to the potential of the unique convergence of telematics, insurance and navigation.

Some of the data analytics that can be gathered on humans today can be described as 'intrusive, exciting and quite revealing'.

Implications for work culture: Collaborative and connected workplace with each employee a CEO

Digital and physical media not only impacts our leisure time but also impacts our work culture – meetings, sales, service, the works.

Paperless meeting rooms with touch-screen tables, holographic keyboards and mood lighting with sensors will be devices used in the office of the future. Emergent communication technologies such as teleconferencing, videoconferencing and others will see team members being digitally distributed in different countries. Combined with 3D technology, we will soon see the day when our colleagues across the world are digitally beamed next to us through holographic technology.

As a result, the connected corporate world will witness a shift from traditional managerial style of single manager/subordinates to collective and connected leadership, empowering each employee to see and review decisions and policies through connectivity and task-tracking tools. This has encouraged, or rather given rise to, transparency and has revolutionised productivity management, leading to 'Info-Democracy' which makes 'each employee a CEO'.

Social analytics, too, will come into play in the office environment. IT – savvy 'hyperconnected employees' – will soon use corporate collaborative tools such as wikis and blogs, video, VoIP and social networking interfaces to communicate with their colleagues at work – eliminating the need, in some cases, for a hierarchical style of management and thereby making the organisational structure flat.

New working styles such as work from home, flexible working or self-employment, coffee shop–office hybrids and rental office spaces (like Regus) will skyrocket as the need to be physically present at work will diminish.

Implications for new business models: It's all about convergence

Connectivity has, perhaps, made the most impact on new business models. These business models are inherently born out of converging gizmos, applications and even from the converging of industries. We have digital strategies today that are wholly designed based on connected devices. Some of the business models are highlighted further, and some are discussed in Chapter 8, 'Business Model of the Decade – Value for Many'.

M commerce: The black gold of the digital era

With the advent of mobile phone technology, companies are increasingly getting cognizant that it could be the sole means of getting through a consumer in the future. M commerce will be a dominant form of e-commerce, accounting for $119 billion in 2015 (around

100 times more than the 2009 number of $1.2 billion), making it the black gold of the digital era.[5]

We should soon see different types of convergence here: physical with mobile cash; separate utility providers into a single service provider; physical, location-based with augmented reality services leading to highly pioneering and extremely innovative business models; not to mention new forms of digital advertising, some of which are apparent even today.

Tesco, a grocery retailer from UK who opened shop in South Korea, has figured out a cool new way of tapping into the waiting time of tech-savvy commuters in the subway stations of Seoul, South Korea to improve their bottom line. It installed virtual stores – which are nothing but illuminated LED screens of their groceries – with QR codes. Commuters can scan the products they wish to purchase with their smartphones and Tesco will deliver it to their homes. This innovative strategy, although it meant not opening any stores, led – not surprisingly – to a 135% increase in sales within the first two months of its launch. Not to be left behind, Yihaodian, one of China's largest grocery retail stores, adopted the same strategy in Shanghai, China in 2011 with the hope of reproducing Tesco's success.

The very model of banking, for example, has metamorphosed with M-payments, M-loan services, SMS consultation, M-investment support and M-marketing coming into the picture. Services such as loan payments, savings accounts and transfer of money will be wholly managed through the cloud. According to PricewaterhouseCoopers (PwC), by 2015, mobile banking will emerge as the most preferred banking channel overtaking traditional channels such as branch banking, driven by a strong demand for digital banking solutions and consumers' preference for convenient methods of banking.[6] According to Frost & Sullivan, M-banking is expected to grow to as high as 6.4 billion mobile banking users in 2020 (300 million in 2011). In some countries in Africa, Frost & Sullivan expects mobile banking to account for 70% of total banking transactions. Additionally, India is expected to see 250 million mobile banking users with nearly 30% of the country's banking transactions being done via mobile phone in 2020.

As banks are learning to get more innovative with their business models, they are soon beginning to learn that they are not the sole players in the financial space. Payment engines such as PayPal, Zynga, Amazon and Google are intruding into this sector. Banks will soon need to start collaborating with IT players to create their own ecosystem of digital banking.

The potential size of this partnership/ecosystem is immense and largely untapped. BNP Paribas, the French Banking Group and Orange did just that last year. They collaborated to form one of the first mobile banks in France, with innovative M-banking and M-payment services. BNP Paribas also included Near Field Communication (NFC) payments and banking through tablet PCs. Commuters in Nice, France, can already use NFC to ride a bus without the need to buy physical tickets.

Location-based personalised advertising

Another apparent implication of connectivity and convergence that we will see is advertising industry dynamics and expenditures.

Global advertising expenditure totalled $430 billion in 2011, with Internet advertising accounting for approximately 20% of the total.[7] Online advertising will increase by 12.8% in 2012 and reach approximately $117.5 billion in 2016, thereby accounting for 21% of a whopping $560 billion total spend in 2016.[7] The undisputed winner of online advertising has been Google, which accounts for 44% of the total Internet advertising expenditure.[8] The acquisitions of YouTube and DoubleClick have significantly bolstered this growth over the past year. Image-rich ad content such as videos, especially in social media platforms, will increase to $28–35 billion in 2016, accounting for a larger piece of the online advertising pie.[9] BRIC countries will drive future ad spend growth as access to Internet grows in these countries. In 2011, China saw online ad spending of $8.1 billion narrowly overtake print media spend of $7.1 billion.[10]

Online 'customised' advertising will gain traction this decade, with consumers being segmented by behaviours and buying habits. Multichannel advertising, especially with the rise of web-enabled devices such as online TV, will soon increase its touch-points with consumers. This will throw open opportunities for companies dealing with web analytics packages, analytical tools and data metrics as businesses will soon have the power of integrating silos of data, which will yield clearer metrics on potential consumers.

New trends that we can expect in advertising will entail augmented reality, location-based advertising, 'hyper-niching' of consumers (focusing on the micro audience), social media adverts and video displays. Advertising can even change based on how people tweet or respond to the message. So in the future, you and your friends can expect to see completely different advertisements on your respective online TV sets, even if you are viewing the same channel at the same time.

The ads you will see in the future will be the advertisements you 'want' to see.

Mega-connectivity platforms of the decade

We are likely to see the emergence of three mega platforms – namely, Google, Apple and Facebook, which will dominate the Internet ecosystem for the next five to seven years. We will see a frenzy of acquisition by these three firms as they build services and applications on these platforms. It was envisaged that companies like Sony, Samsung, Panasonic and Philips would have a potential strong play in the 'Internet of things'. However, these companies have not shown any strategic partnerships or fully understood and harnessed the power of connectivity. The reigning champions of the connectivity world, with the greatest amplitude of innovations, are still the three Mega connectivity players. We should, however, not rule out Microsoft. While it has not been at the forefront of innovation in the last decade, it has excelled at competitive strategy. As the market matures, it is quite possible that Microsoft may resurge as a possible fourth player in this market.

Convergence of industries

Mobile phone technology has provided unparalleled connectivity and convergence across industries. Mobile phone technology, today, has pervaded every aspect of our lives, from browsing to music downloads, from shopping to banking, from trip planning to finance advice. This is nothing but a whole-scale convergence of IT, telecom, banking, retail, finance and even global positioning systems – ably powered by mobile technology platforms and being made available to consumers through the incredible world of apps. But information, communication and media are not the only industries that will see convergence in the coming decade.

Chart 9.1 shows the convergence of products, technologies and industries for different sectors.

Connected health care

A look into our 'homes of the future' would reveal numerous converging products – those that allow us to experience, interact and play with data and other users within those data spaces – while sitting

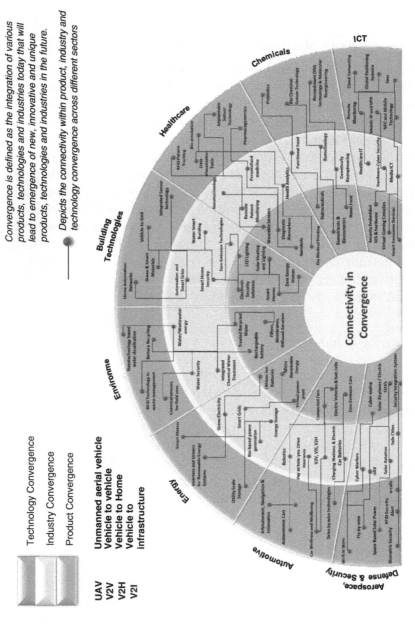

Convergence is defined as the integration of various products, technologies and industries today that will lead to emergence of new, innovative and unique products, technologies and industries in the future.

● Depicts the connectivity within product, industry and technology convergence across different sectors

Technology Convergence
Industry Convergence
Product Convergence

UAV   Unmanned aerial vehicle
V2V   Vehicle to vehicle
V2H   Vehicle to Home
V2I   Vehicle to infrastructure

Chart 9.1 Convergence of products, technologies and industries for different sectors

Note: Convergence is defined as the integration of various products, technologies and industries today that will lead to the emergence of new, innovative and unique products, technologies and industries in the future.

anywhere in the world. This means our future home will not only be intelligent and smart, but will also boast of converging gizmos and applications that connect us virtually to our office, car, local hospital, local grocery store, local bank and even products and people in the local network. Home automation will be heavily converged with robotics, artificial intelligence, energy, health care, sensors and telecom industries – as well as the Internet – to have a fully intelligent, smart, green, connected structure that will operate on voice recognition.

Building management and control systems will have inherently converged with security applications and biometrics, leading to more sophisticated access control, identity management and theft detection systems.

A peep into your local hospital in 2020 will see a whole lot of convergence between the health and IT sector. Tracking systems will have integrated with other digital technologies, such as RFID tagging, to trace patients in a hospital, check inventory and monitor delivery of medical services across the city. The mobile phone will be used more as a tool or a mode of collaborating with different doctors, patients and even hospitals. On a macro scale, geographical visual software of outbreaks and health incidents (such as HealthMap), connecting distant hospitals through satellite, virtual self-help groups and disaster management technologies (e.g. InSTEDD's GeoChat) will change the very dynamics of the health care industry and will help experts to understand the incidence of occurrences and accordingly deploy methods to keep them at bay.

Governments, too, are becoming cognizant of the inevitable health and IT marriage and are pushing initiatives towards this trend. For example, as part of the American Recovery and Reinvestment Act (ARRA) of 2009, legislation was introduced to motivate health care providers to accelerate adoption of electronic health records (EHRs). Full integration of EHRs across the US health care system theoretically would reduce medical and billing errors, cut the cost of patient care and improve long-term health outcomes. By 2014, 95% of hospitals in the United States are expected to have some kind of EHR system deployed. Europe is more advanced in EHR deployment since the establishment of the European Institute for Health Records, or the EuroRec Institute, in 2002. As of 2011, 23 EU countries have decided to spend on an interoperability project costing €36 million from 2008 to 2013 that involves cross-border sharing of EHR information (patient summaries and e-prescriptions) across different EU languages. This is possible, thanks to the trend of cloud computing. The power of crunching and integrating these silos of data are endless. Researchers can now monitor health patterns of population, the spread of infectious diseases and even seasonal variations based on location. Diagnosis will move from traditional treatment to predictive and preventive – bringing down the health care costs of many countries.

Many companies are rapidly moving in the e-health space. StatDoc is an e-health-based virtual house call that connects patients to virtual physicians on demand, online and 24×7. By leveraging the Internet with EHRs, StatDoc offers e-diagnosis and e-treatment through certified professionals. By seamlessly integrating medical groups, physicians and patient networks, StatDoc is extremely popular for minor medical conditions that can be diagnosed virtually and immediately.

Health care via mobile phone, popularly known as M-health, is now boding well for health care delivery, particularly for developing nations. This will involve the convergence of mobile platform developers, medical and life science players, wireless network operators, and app developers to provide necessary infrastructure and technology for each user. Chart 9.2 shows the convergence of key players to form the mHealth apps ecosystem.

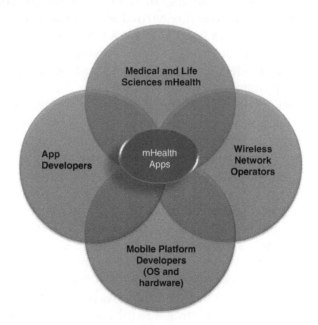

Chart 9.2 **Convergence of players in the mHealth apps ecosystem**
Source: Frost & Sullivan.

Some mobile phone operators are even providing financing for health care services. For example, Safaricom in Kenya is using its mobile banking platform, M-Pesa, to store, transfer and distribute banking credits to villagers. Although not launched particularly to cater to health care needs, this system has proved extremely beneficial for health care financing, particularly for immunisation of children in villages. This mobile banking service, which is deemed to be the largest in the world with its 13 million active customers, is cleverly leveraging on the same platform that it uses for banking services to provide on-demand health care financing as well.[11]

Further convergence of technologies in health care this decade has brought in concepts of wellness and telemedicine and extended decentralised health care services through remote monitoring, new drug delivery systems, virtual surgeries and monitoring, and virtual hospitals – creating innovative opportunities across all segments in the value chain and unquestionably saving lives.

In the sector of personal health care, remote diagnostics and diagnose-it-yourself gizmos will skyrocket. Your own home will have products such as low-cost mobile phone eye testing, a portable microscope that can stream results into smartphones or tablet PCs, digital cameras that can detect cancer, web-based stethoscopes, intelligent body monitors, self-diagnosis tools, handheld clinics, SMS consultation and apps such as 'eMedonline' that alert patients of medication schedules. These applications and products will allow us to avail the services of a health care clinic without leaving the comforts of our home.

Wellness and well-being will be the order of the day in 2020. Wellness concepts would pervade into technology, health care and energy, making every environment – be it the car, home or office completely ergonomic. Performance statistics and biometrics data in convergence with mobile phone apps will lead to the development of various innovative 'wellness' products and applications such as bike-powered phone chargers, motion sensor products such as Fitbit that monitor activity levels, and other nutrition and fitness routine apps. Today, apps such as Adidas miCoach and arcade-style gyms are some innovative concepts and applications are leveraging on the wellness and well-being concept.

Not to leave gaming scenarios out of the health care picture, we have wearable technology devices such as Switch2Health (S2H) that rewards you with points based on your fitness levels and allows you to redeem accumulated points for promotions and prizes. Didgets that can be plugged into Nintendo DS systems check glucose levels of gamers and reward them with virtual currency for new skills in games.[12] For more information on health care and wellness trends, refer to Chapter 7, 'Health, Wellness and Wellbeing'.

Connected car, connected mobility

A look at the inside of your car in 2020 will be a bit of a surprise. It no longer serves you as a mere vehicle, but will have the potential to be your office, your home, your entertainment hub – giving you a fully connected mobile experience while sitting behind the wheel. Microsoft expects the car to be the third-most connected device after the mobile phone and the tablet PC in the future. Rightly so, the automotive industry will fully converge with IT, energy, sensors, satellite systems and telecom bringing in to implement concepts such as the connected car, autonomous driving, apps store, EV charging stations and even Facebook on wheels.

The first approach towards the connected car is personalisation of content. BMW, with its ConnectedDrive vision, is working on something similar, where a near field communication key, after identifying the driver, will allow the driver to access contents (music, news, etc.) which they were accessing earlier while at home. Additionally the mood-based playlist will ensure that the user is listening to his or her favourite genre of music.

Starting from entry into the car, near-field technology will be made available on smartphones which act as a virtual key, which will prove to be extremely useful to start a car, particularly when users misplace their keys. Once inside, users will be greeted by a personal voice assistant and their phone will be wirelessly paired with the car's infotainment system. The intelligent system will import all the data and the personal voice assistant reminders will alert drivers of the important meetings scheduled for the day, as well as read out the texts, tweets and emails with the ability to reply to them in a natural voice.

Car companies will also develop automotive app stores which will offer certified applications for in-vehicle use similar to what we have today with smartphone apps.

Connected cars of the future will use applications which make use of augmented reality to aid in presenting content in a very interactive manner to users. While the debate goes on about the pros and cons of smart apps in cars, it eventually comes down to how the user interacts with the car and vice versa. So it's the in-vehicle user interface which decides how much freedom lies in the hands of users.

Mercedes Benz's Dice concept is a perfect example of how augmented reality, coupled with voice interface, could ease the workload. Toyota's window to the world is a groundbreaking technology which shows how a simple window could be used as a display and a means to transmit information.

The car's navigation system, which would have historic data about all the journeys, would recommend the best route, which would save fuel and enable the driver to reach his or her destination quickly. The enhanced local points of interest search would give local listings such as restaurants, gas stations and other necessities on demand. The navigation system would be intuitive enough to offer situation-based routes (if it's a weekend, the navigation system would give an option of a beach-facing route with lots of restaurants on the way).

On the entertainment side, apart from the social networking and radio apps, users would be allowed to play games, watch movies and even browse the Internet when the car is not in motion. Dual-view displays would be used to fulfil the entertainment needs of passengers. Geo tagging and mapping would allow tracking of friends and navigation systems would lead the user to the respective place. The passenger seat windows would be used as a personal interactive media place with personalised content access even for the passengers.

Smartphones would be used to control the alarm sensors, temperature, door lock/unlock, ambient lighting and start/stop ignition, and would get updates about vehicle diagnostics. Users would be able to seamlessly transmit data from central display to cluster with the swipe of a finger. This will help display content in front of drivers' eyes. The car's dynamic instrument cluster will guide users to achieve the best fuel efficiency by providing details about the pressure on the gas pedal, an accurate reading on driving speed, optimised gear shifts and steering angles. Based on inputs from environment, driving patterns and face/position detection sensors, the system would keep tabs on drivers' health. An example here would be a system that will raise the windows on detection of pollen content in the air to avoid allergies.

Autonomous driving will have kicked off by 2020 with the artificial intelligence, mechatronics, and navigation and satellite systems industries heavily converging inside the car. So don't be surprised if your car has the capacity of the Batmobile – to be driverless – in 2020!

All this is possible in the car and beyond. The challenge for car companies is how to make money from all these gimmicks. Additionally, convergence will be inherent and all-pervasive in the future of transport systems. Ambient intelligence will be the norm of transport infrastructure with prime cities having a serious advantage of integrated mobility that not only pertains to functions of real-time information, mobile ticketing, contactless payment and vehicle-to-infrastructure integration but also includes integration of the bigger picture of transport infrastructure, such as convergence with satellite systems, safety and signalling systems, mobile technology platforms, banking services, reservation systems and traffic modelling platforms creating new business models and partnerships among telecom operators, banks and transport authorities.

Convergence in energy, manufacturing and growth of biometrics

The energy sector will be seeing some interesting convergences. Sustainability and renewable energy will be the order of the day, with the energy sector seamlessly integrating with building materials, IT products and even the space industry. Smart grids will be the 'Internet for Electricity', converging the realms of energy and IT even further than what we see today. Smart grids have seen the coming together of efficient building systems, the Internet, smart end-user devices, renewables such as Photo Voltaics, plug-in hybrid cars, distributed generation and storage, advanced metering infrastructure, dynamic controls, home automation networks, data management, utility communications and building energy management systems, thereby converging the industries of energy and infrastructure, automotive, automation, and control and IT.

Another radical convergence of industry that is wholly based on pioneering technology is the marriage of space and energy – or, as popular industry jargon would have it, space-based solar power (SBSP) – which is capturing atmospheric solar power for Earth's consumption. Although the first pilot satellite will not be launched until 2030, SBSP could become an alternative means of satisfying Earth's energy demands, thanks to the pioneering efforts of various agencies such as Japan Aerospace Exploration Agency, or JAXA, and NASA.

Within the manufacturing sector an important convergence that has taken place this decade is that of manufacturing and IT. The factory floor in 2020 will have made an evolutionary leap with the majority of assembly lines becoming fully mechanised. Today, Honda, ABB and Mitsubishi have not only learned and adopted robotic technology in some of their factories, but have also paved the way for new forms of modern manufacturing. Manufacturing today is no longer labour intensive. It is intelligent, super-fast, IT-inclined and devoid of defects. Machines building machines will not only step up factory productivity – they will, sadly, lead to a decline in manufacturing jobs in the future.

Biometrics is another interesting industry that is seeing integrated multifaceted solutions and is finding applications beyond mere entry to buildings. According to Frost & Sullivan, the civil biometric market (used for civil applications), currently estimated at $1.42 billion, will increase to $4.66 billion by 2016. Advancements in 3D face technology, renewed interest in the form of upgrades and growing interest from applications outside of e-documents, such as public surveillance, will attract new venture capital investments. Face recognition technology is now currently being deployed for security purposes in public places such as banks, public gatherings and even casinos.

The future of biometrics, however, is not about conventional fingerprint and face recognition technology. The future of biometrics will be based on identification of behavioural and physical characteristics like electro-physical signals, typing speed and even typing style. The major evolutionary leap in these technologies will be that they are non-intrusive in nature and they do not require any command from the user. For example, voice recognition requires the user to speak. But in the future, biometrics will be proactive rather than reactive. Users will not have to give any sort of command (e.g.mind reading and thermal tracking).

In the future, thanks to biometrics, we will no longer need to check if we have the keys to our car/house or our wallet with us each time we step outside – our fingers and eyes will suffice.

Implications of connectivity and convergence on personal lives

Digital citizenship: Identity 3.0

Connectivity has had many implications on personal lives. Converging gizmos have not only affected lifestyle choices but have also changed the very pace of life. This 'ubiquitous computing' has inadvertently bestowed on each of us a unique digital citizenship – an 'Identity 3.0' – that gives each person the individualism, the knowledge-sharing preferences, the ability to 'socialise everyday routines' and the option of accessing all of these perks of that digital citizenship while we are 'on the go'. Coupled with location planning and mood sourcing capabilities, these digital citizenships have inadvertently created a new form of class distinction – the divide between the plugged-in versus the unplugged – making the plugged-in more digitally empowered than the unplugged.

Another benefit of digital citizenship in the recent years has been the deployment of e-governance programs by governments globally. E-governance includes a host of e-programs and functions that can be broadly classified into three – Government to Government (G2G), Government to Citizens (G2C) and Government to Businesses (G2B). G2G services are meant for administrative purposes; G2C is used as a platform to provide public services; and G2B is a tool to engage with businesses and entities. An interesting example of an e-governance program is the Indian government's adoption of online tools to optimise the usage of Bangalore city's public transportation system. Through online tools, the government has managed to record traffic densities and track offenders easily, thereby streamlining their revenue monitoring and ticket collections verticals.

This digital citizenship is not exclusive to citizens. In the future, every product will have a physicality or a purpose – a unique ID – that connected devices can pick up, identify and inform users of their uses and content. Google Goggles does just that. Google Goggles is one such revolutionary application that allows you to take a picture of your surroundings, such as a product, and use image recognition technology to produce search results.

Everything social: Digitalise my life and garden

In the past, an everyday routine such as collecting laundry, or grocery shopping was a single boring action. Today, thanks to connectivity, every activity in our daily life can be made a social event. Even a mundane activity such as shopping can be made into a collaborative and networked event and, with the additional help of location-based advertising and augmented reality, the activity itself can be a social encounter that can be recorded on social media platforms. Additionally, Gen Y, with their need for instant gratification and ambient connectivity – not to mention personalised solutions – has led to the development of on-demand video, live video streaming and personalised phone apps. 'Connect Me Now', 'Entertain Me Now' and 'Every Service Needs to be Social' have now become an actual reality.

Docomo, the Japanese-based mobile operator, has released a product called the 'Garden Sensor' which digitalises routine hobbies such as gardening. This stick is inserted into the soil and records moisture and sunlight levels. The data is then sent to Docomo (through the cloud) where consultants will communicate expert advice via phone, text or email on proper care for the plants or vegetation. It is an extremely simple business model that leverages sensors, cloud computing and mobile phone technology, which increases touch-points with Docomo and its customers.

Even social meet-ups, gatherings and events, particularly collaborative and networked events riding high on ubiquitous computing and digital empowerment, would be the vogue in the future. These events require a whole deal of synchronisation, which will be made possible through ambient connectivity. 'Flash mobs' are now taking the world by storm through heavy propagation by viral emails, connectivity and social media platforms.

The Fox TV show, *Mobbed*, is one such reality show that is built on the flash mob model and is hugely popular in the United States. This live music group spectacle is made possible through connectivity of hidden cameras and other devices, making special moments in life a digitally televised and highly synchronised event. Other popular collaborative events are networked running events – such as Nike Web Nationals and Cross Nationals – that connect communities.

Augmented reality

Converging gizmos and the resultant maze of connectivity will enable cool and new ways of technology development, some of it with radical impacts on personal life. We have discussed earlier concepts of converging gizmos, such as haptic technology and touch-screen interfaces, impacting everyday technologies in the future. As established in Chapter 6, 'Social Trends that will Model our Future Society', geo socialisation will be the next level of social networking, riding high on location-based contexts and existing social media platforms. Other concepts such as augmented reality and virtual worlds, which are today apparent in the gaming industry, will soon knock on our doors through many other applications. Location-based content will be further enhanced by concepts such as augmented reality thereby making some of our current mobile and computer applications seem extremely Jurassic.

Imagine a world where 'EVERYTHING' is interactive. In 2020, if you are walking down Fifth Avenue in Manhattan, New York, you will be able to see digital data augment your immediate surroundings. All you need is a computer or a mobile phone screen with a camera or, more surprisingly, maybe a bionic lens. This screen would superimpose information such as restaurant reviews, user profiles, product information while shopping or even real estate information of listed properties in your surroundings.

Augmented reality (AR) is one technological development that will see the apparent yet invisible and seamless blending of real-life surroundings and digital data. It is defined as a real-time augmented view of the environment through digital data such as text, sound, graphics, video and navigation systems that increase users' interactivity with the local environment. This extends business and mobility options, social interactions and experiences, which has implications on personal lives, businesses and even day-to-day activities. The first augmented reality browser, LAYAR, has thrown open diverse options and ideas that can have rippling repercussions on personal life, the business sector and even day-to-day activities.

Between 27 and 29 October 2011, Debenhams, a UK-based retail store, adopted an ingenious marketing strategy that made several UK shoppers exalt the praises of AR. It launched its pop-up virtual stores in various cultural locations across the UK, such as Trafalgar Square in London. Potential shoppers were then invited to visit these places with their iPhone or iPad to witness party dresses virtually pop up in their AR screen hiding behind the National Gallery or peeping from Lord Nelson's back. The customers could then take a picture of how the dress would look on them, order the item if they liked it and even post their picture on Facebook or Twitter to get real-time feedback. Chart 9.3 gives us an idea on some of the daily activities that will be 'augmented' through the use of AR.

For more information on augmented social networking, please refer to Chapter 6, 'Social Trends that will Model our Future Society'.

Virtual world: Welcome to your second life

At the extreme end of the spectrum of AR, we will find the concept of virtual world. Already rampant in the gaming world, these interactive 3D environments will literally enable us to lead second lives in the future. The key difference between AR and the virtual world is that the virtual world will have nothing to do with your immediate real-life surroundings and will have the capacity to 'beam you virtually' anywhere and anytime – bridging the distances between people, communities and industrial applications. This could mean that, in the future, students could have a 3D experience of a field trip to different countries or to the bottom of the ocean while sitting in any classroom in the world.

Social Networking   **Restaurant Reviews**   **Shopping**

Watching Sports   **Real Estate News**   **Driving**

Chart 9.3 **Augmented reality impacting different personal experiences**
Photo credits: Dreamstime, Wikitude, Buuuk, Tagwhat, The London Group.
Source: Frost & Sullivan.

Virtual Shopping allowing customers to try products without leaving their homes   **Virtual Surgeries and Medical Training**   **Virtual Business Conferences**

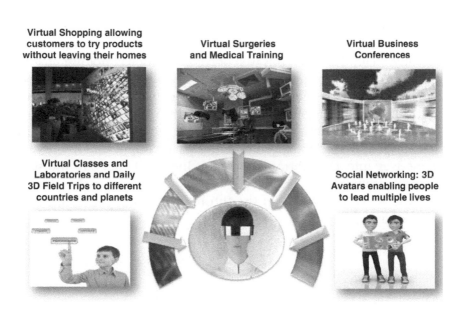

Virtual Classes and Laboratories and Daily 3D Field Trips to different countries and planets   **Social Networking: 3D Avatars enabling people to lead multiple lives**

Chart 9.4 **Virtual world 2020: 3D simulated environment for interaction and experience impacting personal mobility**
Photo credits: Dreamstime.
Source: Frost & Sullivan.

Business conferences can be attended virtually and even social networking will soon become '3D and avatarical'. Surgeries will be done virtually and shopping will also become wholly immersive. Another evolutionary leap in terms of applications is the use of the virtual world for military training. HMDs (head-mounted displays) would simulate an accurate 3D visual of various battle terrains, allowing for almost life-like training in military manoeuvres. This makes the training safer, more controlled and a great deal less expensive than actual training in the field.

Chart 9.4 shows us how virtual worlds can change our interaction and experiences, thereby affecting personal mobility in the future.

CONCLUSION

Connectivity has given humans the power to shape opportunities, devices and experiences in the future in the palm of their hands. The point of it all is that connectivity gives a digital sense to our everyday lives – it saves time, increases personal and business options, and introduces scores of innovative and multiple applications and choices while bringing people and communities together – every day and every minute. Connectivity has been taken for granted and will be taken for granted in the future. Every consumer is looking for the next killer app and every company is hoping to launch that one app that will unlock more opportunities in the value chain. However, this web of connectivity will not just change our business world; it will radically change the way we move and interact in our personal lives – creating an invisible network among people that has the potential to create a 'borderless world' in the future.

Mark Weiser, the father of ubiquitous computing, once stated, 'The most profound technologies are those that disappear. They weave themselves into the fabric of everyday life until they are indistinguishable from it.'

Maybe we will see a day in the future where 'being disconnected' will be a paid luxury.

10

FROM PLANES TO TRAINS – THE ERA OF HIGH-SPEED RAIL

If I had told my aunt ten years ago about a train that floats in air because of giant magnets under it, she would have thought one of two things: one, I had lost my marbles or, two, I never had any marbles to start with. Now that same aunt is talking about how wonderful the Maglev was on her trip to China last year. The Maglev (Magnetic Levitation) train has the highest recorded speed of 581 km/h, which was achieved in Japan during a test run, about 6 km/h faster than its nearest rival, the conventional French TGV.[1] With the top speed of these trains just 25% less than the average speed of the commercial airplane (about 800 kmph), high-speed rail is capable of nearly matching total travel times over short and medium distances. And Maglev trains, like planes, fly (to the airline enthusiasts: fine! They float; but they are darn good at it).

'Rail has always been around!' you might exclaim, so why is it a Mega Trend? Yes, rail has been around for nearly 200 years now, but it is fairly recent if you look at the larger scale of things (the last ten years compared to the 200 years since industrialisation) that will take us back to the future. Two important developments and courses in time have led us to this very important third event where man is forced to think, realise and act upon his decisions of the past.

The first development was the impact of the automobile. The automobile was an immediate success as it offered the benefits of personal space, freedom and ease to the passenger. In less than 20 years since the first production model was introduced, automobiles became the dominant mode of transport.

The second development was the birth and rise of a new business model in the airline industry: the low cost carriers (LCC). To compete with the pricing offered by the LCCs, full-service airlines reduced prices, services and profit margins. The last 15 years have seen immense growth and innovation within the airline industry. Passenger numbers increased from 900 million in 1985 to peaks of 2.4 billion in the last decade, driven by low-cost airlines that offered tickets, on average, 30% cheaper. Paper tickets are disappearing fast; check-in is now commonly done online, at a self-service kiosk or via mobile phones. On-demand in-flight entertainment has replaced video on demand, and we now see Internet connectivity at 30,000 feet.[2] There are now over 16,000 airlines globally. Airlines grew in size of fleet and liability, but not in profits and accountability. Perhaps a result of too many airlines and the heavy baggage of public sector, today some of the world's most prominent airlines worldwide are shutting shop due to spiralling costs and unprofitability.

The third event, which is the future, and a Mega mobility trend, is high-speed rail. In the future, high-speed rail will connect not only cities, states or countries, but also continents. One could, about 15 to 20 years from now, travel seamlessly from London, UK to Beijing, China and even have a detour into the Gulf countries using the global rail network. In the next ten years, I predict huge increases globally in high-speed rail and in the vast white space opportunities it brings with it. All regions of the world, including the Middle East and the laggard United States, will implement high-speed rail in the coming decade.

MEET THE JETSONS AROUND THE WORLD

'Remember the Jetsons?' George Jetson often took the tube (literally) to work. It's not too far in the future for a family living in Birmingham, UK to take a high-speed train and have a holiday in Continental Europe, as far as Eastern and Central Europe. China in 2012 has 6980 km of operational HSR tracks compared to zero kilometres of HSR tracks in 2000. By 2020, the Chinese ministry aims to complete 25,000 km of track which will connect all major cities. Some of these lines are passenger designated lines (PDLs), while others are capable of carrying freight as well: high-speed logistics, as they call it. The total cost of Chinese HSR ambitions is billed at around $300 billion when completed.[3] A British cricket mate of mine wrote to me the other day when he had to visit his Chinese in-laws in Manchuria (from Beijing). He did not have great things to say about the trip and meeting the in-laws (which we can all understand), although he did compare Manchuria to Sheffield (perhaps in reference to the steel industry there and joint hate for politicians) and comment on the HSRnetwork, 'What was nine hours on an overnight train on the Friday became little more than three on the way home on Tuesday. I am a fan of these Chinese bullet trains'.

Hopefully we can replicate his experience in the future in Europe, too. Europe already has an extensive HSR network (Figure 10.1). Interestingly, in Europe, it is not the rich countries like Germany and France who are the forefront of HSR but the Southern European countries struggling with debt, like Spain. Spain is expected to build 2827 km of new HSR by 2015. Another 1000 km is likely to be added by 2018.[4] Spain has become successful in exporting its HSR technologies to the outside world. Phase 2 of the Haramain High-Speed Rail Project in Saudi Arabia (450 km, connecting Mecca and Medina) was awarded to a Saudi-Spanish consortium.[5] HSR has wide socio-economic benefits and can be a vital source of income for countries that operate HSR networks as well as those that provide related technologies.

Chart 10.1 shows the high-speed rail network in Europe.

The British, despite being inventors of the modern railway, are only now finally starting to catch up on HSR. The department of transportation of the United Kingdom recently gave a green light for the first phase of the HS2 project that plans to link London with Birmingham, costing a total of $27.4 billion. The second phase of the project splits the line into two, giving it a 'Y shape', as the route to Leeds and Manchester. The entire HS2 project is expected to cost $47.3 billion for the 335 km stretch.[6]

The French were the original European proponents of HSR and their commitment is expected to continue through 2020. Germany has plans of about 670 km of new lines with target operations by 2025. One of the most anticipated developments in European HSR is the Lyon-Turin line that will connect the French TGV and Italian TAV high-speed networks (construction is expected to start in 2013 with a total project cost of $2.95 billion).[7]

Shockingly, the world's most influential country, which has a legacy of making rail billionaires from the days of the gold rush in California, lags behind the world. What is defined as high-speed rail in the US (speeds of 120 kmph) is considered the speed of a bull-drawn (rail) cart in China. It is a little sad to see that the richest country in the world operates only one high-speed line, as per real definition of HSR, capable of travelling at a speed of 240 km/h (the Acela express from Boston to Washington). Investment in HSR has seen

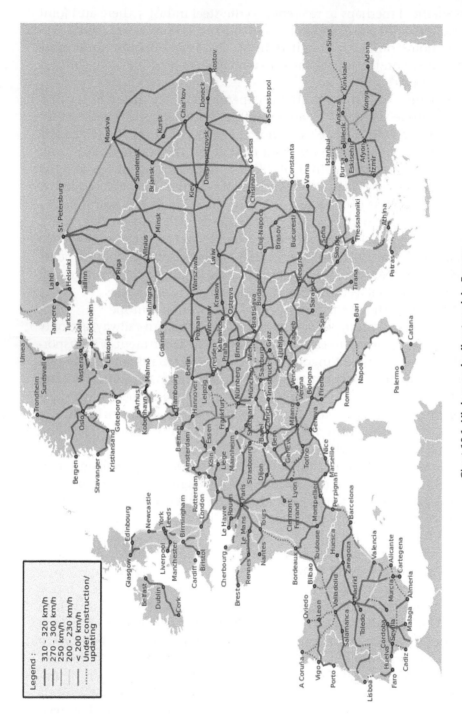

Chart 10.1 **High-speed rail network in Europe**

Source: Wikimedia commons, Akwa (FlyAkwa), Bernese media and BIL.

stiff opposition from Republicans in the USA. In 2009, under the Obama administration, the Federal Railroad Administration of the USA released its plan of developing high-speed rail through ten designated high-speed corridors. With state governor Rick Scott formally rejecting funding for the Florida HSR project, all hopes now rest on the California HSR proposal. The line would serve major cities including San Jose, Fresno, Bakersfield, Palmdale, Anaheim, Irvine, Riverside, San Francisco, Los Angeles, Sacramento and San Diego. The network is planned to be completed in two phases, with construction of the first line connecting San Francisco and Anaheim expected to start soon at a total cost of $65 billion ($98 billion adjusted to inflation).[8] This is expected to be the biggest-ever infrastructure project in the USA, making people reminesce about the California gold rush.

Mexico, USA's neighbour, is more ambitious and has HSR aspirations that aim at connecting Mexico City to Guadalajara with trains travelling at 300 km/h, cutting travel time to just two hours as compared to seven hours by road. At a cost of $25 billion, it will be the first true HSR in the Western Hemisphere when it opens in 2015.[9] Argentina was supposed to have started construction on its HSR project in 2008, but it is currently on hold due to financial reasons. Consultation on Brazilian HSR plans is expected to be finalised in March 2012. The initial bidding, which took place in 2011, has been rescheduled as the government finalises the local consortium to partner with foreign technology providers. The first phase is planned to connect Rio de Janeiro and Sao Paulo (518 km), costing $18.5 billion, and it is expected to serve an annual capacity of 33 million passengers from 2016.[10] Having been to that part of the world, it definitely needs more investment in public transport, especially with the upcoming Olympics and Football World Cup.

THE 2020 TRANS-SIBERIAN RAIL LINK: THE NEW ROUTE 66

It is actually possible today to travel by rail from London to Beijing via Moscow. A high level of enthusiasm for train rides is recommended, as the trip can be more than a handful (keeping in mind Murphy's Law or that baby on board). You can do it using the Trans-Siberian rail link. It will take two days to Moscow from London and then an additional five or seven days, depending upon the route you decide to take to Beijing.

The Trans-Siberian Railway, built over 120 hundred years ago, is the longest network of railways in the world connecting Moscow with the Russian Far East and all the way to the Sea of Japan. It is a double track electrified line, about 10,000 km long, theoretically capable of carrying up to 100 million tonnes of cargo per year There are branch lines to China through Mongolia and Manchuria, with service continuing to North Korea. The Trans-Siberian Railway and, in the future, the road link will connect continents – Europe with Asia, UK to China and all the way to Korea and Japan. It will have some major implications to the logistics and transportation industry, to the industrialisation and development of urbanisation in Russia and to tourism.

Moscow to Vladivostok is a major freight artery that offers a fully developed container service with average journey time (Vladivostok to Moscow) of ten days as compared to 28 days by sea. Currently, for containers to come from China to Europe by sea, it takes between 35 to 40 days to travel, and that is if they don't get hijacked by Somalian pirates. In the future, with the development and linking of networks across the European Union, Russia, China, Middle East, Indian subcontinent and Korea, containers from China can reach European shores in half the time it takes through containers, about 15 to 20 days. The Trans-Siberian Railway has been included in the projects which are being developed by the UNECE (Economic Commission for Europe), the UNESCAP (Economic and Social Commission for Asia and the Pacific) and Organization for Cooperation of Railways (OSJD/OSZD) as one of the priority routes linking Europe and Asia. Somali pirates, be disappointed and file for immigration to Siberia.

The Trans-Siberian Railway is set to become one of the most important transportation corridors between Europe and the Asia Pacific. There is large-scale investment of $330 million planned to upgrade and modernise facilities on the route, creating a multimodal, multipurpose and modern terminal network. This is expected to provide a robust logistics and warehousing network with a wide range of services. It is a priority route on projects developed by the UNECE and the UNESCAP.

Russia already has three operational HSR lines. The Sapsan HSR has been extremely successful with an occupancy rate of 84%, generating annual revenues in excess of $270 million with profits estimated to be more than $80 million.[11] Russia is set to prioritise the expansion of HSR through 2030 to grow by almost 17 times and reach the 10,000 km mark of the total HSR network size.[12]

The similar Trans-Siberian road link construction was fully completed in 2010 when more than 2000 km of road was incorporated into the road network connecting Western Russia with Eastern. However, it is currently not used as a transit route due to several reasons: rail transport is still more convenient and is cheaper when we talk about long-route transport (e.g. China–Western Russia), and road infrastructure is still poor (about 500 km of the 2000 km worth of road was constructed over 40 years ago). If the Russian government's future plans to focus on improving road conditions through continuous reconstruction are successful, we could see mega-trucks, 60 tonners, similar to what we see in the US, plying the roads of Europe and China using the Trans-Siberian road link. This could lead to an opportunity for truck manufacturers in Europe to develop and market 25-metre mega-trucks weighing up to 60 tonnes.

An interesting macro to micro impact of the Trans-Siberian rail and road link will be in the urbanisation and industrialisation of Russia. As we saw in the past, cities have traditionally grown around waterfronts as they provide an excellent mode of transport for goods. Similarly we will see heavy modernisation of the cities on the Trans-Siberian rail and road link. Cities like Novonikolaevsk, barely a small village before the creation of the railroad, have now become Novosibirsk, a thriving economy centre and at present the third-largest city in Russia. Other cities, like Tomsk, were larger before the advent of the Trans-Siberian Railroad but, with the railway bypassing it, were left behind. As the Trans-Siberian rail and road links develop, they will open up huge opportunities for trade and tourism making it the new Route 66. I personally can't wait to travel the route by rail or road and take a detour to the silk route. I can't wait to stop on my way to take in the sights and sounds of cities like Novosibirsk, Yekaterinburg, Krasnoyarsk, Irkutsk and Khabarovsk.

THE CHINESE RAIL JUGGERNAUT

High-speed rail has historically been developed to connect cities within countries. It is increasingly now becoming an important international mode of travel. Thalys is an international high-speed rail operator in Europe connecting Paris, Brussels, Essen, Cologne and Amsterdam with a fleet of 26 class trains built by Alstom. The Eurostar is now a preferred mode of transport between London and Paris.

This technology is not always successful in connecting countries, especially with old infrastructure. Interoperability between European nations is hampered by different signalling systems, electrification

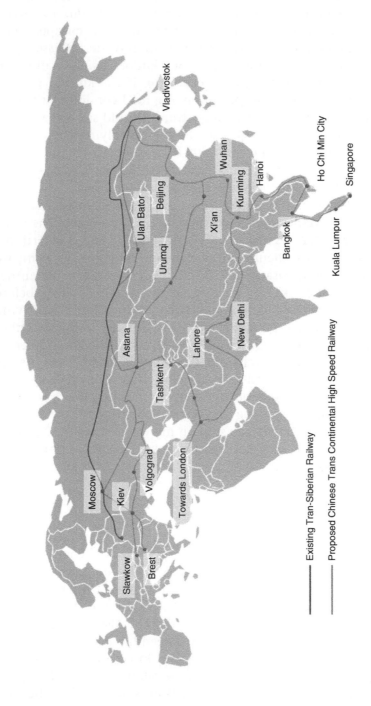

Chart 10.2 The Chinese vision to expand high-speed rail within Europe and Asia

Source: Frost & Sullivan.

188

systems and different gauges (the width of the railway track). In Europe alone there are 19 different operational signalling systems. This is a major barrier to interoperability and the reason why all new freight and high-speed rail lines in the EU are required to use European Train Control Systems (ETCS). The ETCS has become the textbook standard for all new signalling systems around the world.

However, what Europe has achieved or planned is miniscule, very miniscule, compared to the Chinese vision of HSR. China has laid out a plan to extend its HSR network to London as well as to Singapore through Laos, Vietnam and Malaysia (Figure 10.2). Construction of the Lanzhou–Urumqi High-Speed Railway (length 1776 km) is expected to reach completion by 2014 and will be instrumental in its aspirations to connect to Western Europe. China is in talks with 17 countries to lay HSR tracks within its own capital for the exchange of natural resources from participating countries. Once implemented, the networks will establish rail's dominance in the freight modal share between Asia and Europe.

CASE STUDY: CHINESE RAIL INDUSTRY, THE GLOBAL HIGH-SPEED JUGGERNAUT

In ten years, Chinese railways have achieved the unthinkable. It's like watching the climax of an episode of *24* (the TV series starring Kiefer Sutherland) where you tell yourself: 'Oh wait! Did that really happen in *one* day?'

Chinese rail has risen from an obscure, dark, damp decadent position to one of leadership and prominence that is spotlighted by trains that travel as fast as the eye can see. All behold the future leaders of the global rail industry: China.

It is natural that the expansion of railways leads to renewed interest and new orders for rolling stock. Generally, rolling-stock providers bid for and win contracts to supply a fixed number of units with options for more units (depending on the satisfaction of the operator). Things work a little differently in China. There are two major rolling-stock manufacturers: China Northern Railways (CNR) and China Southern Railways (CSR), which are the result of the consolidation of various companies. Both organisations are entirely capable of producing locomotives (electric and diesel), passenger railcars/multiple units and freight wagons as well as providing complete maintenance for rolling stock

189

through various sub-companies and divisions.

The divisions that are of most interest are the research companies under CNR and CSR (e.g. the CNR Dalian research company and the CSR Zhuzhou research company). Before China orders any rolling stock based on a newer technology platform (e.g. diesel locomotives with AC traction), completely indigenous designs are first constructed. Extensive testing and analysis follows. China becomes familiar with the platform and evaluates shortfalls in its design. Only after the testing is complete are orders for new rolling stock placed. Generally, nationalised railway operators place bulk orders. When China places an order, its terms and conditions include the inflexible rule of technology transfer, whereby the rolling stock provider transfers design details to China. With the technology-transfer condition, China fills information gaps in its indigenous programme, learns from its mistakes and makes a clean room design of an entirely new model of rolling stock that meets and satisfies requirements. All future orders to meet Chinese requirements are of the new and improved indigenous design (e.g. China acquired technology from Bombardier, Siemens, Mitsubishi, etc., in previous metro railcar orders. Now the majority of future orders are expected to be the locally designed Chinese Model A or Model B metro railcars).

Initially, China also used to place bulk orders for rolling stock. However, a new pattern has emerged where the foreign participant sells one unit that is assembled in its home factory with technology transfer. The remaining units of the order are manufactured in CNR, CSR or joint venture factories. Joint venture factories allow foreign presences to manufacture in China (share control between the foreign participant and CNR or CSR). All designs belong to the People's Republic of China and it is amazing to see design platforms being shared between competing CNR and CSR companies. Even factories that generally specialise in a particular rolling stock often cater to different segments to meet demand.

As Chinese high-speed rail plans and ambitions have already been analysed in the chapter, let's discuss a little about the mainline locomotive and metro rolling stock segments in China.

There are many different models of locomotives operating in China, like the Dongfeng 4. First, the locomotive power requirement in China has increased significantly. Thirty years ago, locomotive power ranged within 1800 to 4000 kW. In the last ten years, locomotives have broken into the 10,000 kW power segment. The lowest-powered locomotive acquired recently generates 3650 kW of power. Second, the majority of the market is middle aged (between ten and 30 years of age).[13] As the fleet ages, the Chinese rolling-stock market will provide enormous opportunity to the service, spares and maintenance industries. Third, the majority of Chinese shunter/switcher fleet has over 30 years of active service. There will be a strong future requirement for new low-powered locomotives to perform shunter/switcher duties. Finally, the small bubbles represent prototypes and are always followed by massive orders. This can be a flag for future potential orders.

Metro systems have many lines that connect different parts of urban areas. Each line has a dedicated fleet that serves it. In 2011, there were 13 cities with 65 operational metro lines, 20 lines under construction and 40 lines planned. By 2030, the Chinese metro and light rail market is expected to see phenomenal growth as there are 17 more cities that are planning metro systems.[13]

One can safely and surely say that China has gone 'metro-crazy' in the last ten years. A total of 2020 km of metro line length was constructed for 63 metro projects in the last ten years. That's borderline compulsive obsession. The Chinese are building longer line lengths as well. Twenty-five years ago, the maximum line length was 42 km. The maximum line length in the last ten years has crossed the 60 km mark. The fleet size serving each metro line has also increased, with over 150 railcars serving newer lines.

China went from a total mainline rail network size of 58,656 km in 2000 to a whopping 91,000 km in 2010. China prioritises economic and social development through five-year plans (the plans have been referred to as guidelines since 2006). The first five-year plan was in motion from 1953 to 1957. The railways have received significant priority since the 11th five-year guideline as rail is seen as an important contributor towards Chinese GDP.[13]

TABLE 10.1 **Growth and progress in rail in China between 2000 and 2010**

	2000	2010
Total number of steam locomotives in active service	601	0
Total number of electric locomotives in active service	3516	6486
Total number of high-speed trains in active service	0	204
Total length of the rail network (in km)	58,656	91,000
Total length of electrified network (in km)	14,864	42,000
Total length of high-speed network (in km)	0	6980

Source: Frost & Sullivan.

Table 10.1 shows the growth and progress in rail in China.

The Chinese government is currently making efforts on increasing growth and development in western and central China. The length of the network is expected to reach 120,000 km (with a high-speed network length exceeding 25,000 km) by 2020.[13] China is set to enter the public-private partnership (PPP) market by investing, constructing, supplying material, operating and finally transferring railway systems to the rest of the world. Chinese rolling-stock factories will produce the rolling stock and the Chinese ministry of railways will use its strong project management capabilities to manage projects. Chinese rolling stock will compete worldwide for orders, as well as competitively, as China has the advantage of low pricing. The China development bank loaned $10 billion to Argentina in 2010 to upgrade and improve urban transit systems in Buenos Aires and Cordoba.[14] China is forecasted to provide funding for many major projects around the world. With Chinese investments, it can be expected that Chinese railway companies will provide infrastructure and rolling stock.

When Kawasaki transferred the Japanese Shinkansen (bullet train) high-speed train technology to CSR Sifang, China in 2004, they were surprised when the locally made CRH2C was launched within two years (looks like the Shinkansen but all technology involved was developed by CSR Sifang). Kawasaki is no longer working with CSR.

Finally, Chinese railway will expand presence internationally as passenger service operators and, most importantly, as freight managing companies. China will soon open up network capacity for container traffic from the production centres in China to all major cities in Asia and Europe. The transcontinental and Siberian rail network gives Chinese rail logistics the unsurpassed advantage of reaching central Europe in less time than container ships. Chinese railways will be equal to the combined sizes of Deutsche Bahn, DB Schenker, SNCF, Keolis and many other Asian companies in the not-so-distant future. Forget the Chinese dragon – watch out for their high-speed rail juggernaut.

SELLING SAND TO THE ARABS

Five out of the top ten countries with the cheapest petrol prices at the pump station in the world are from the Middle East –Saudi Arabia, Bahrain, Kuwait, Qatar and Oman. With a litre of petrol costing $0.35 in Oman, one can drive a 6.1 litre, V8, Jeep Grand Cherokee to pick up local groceries every time. A can of Coke at the grocery will be more expensive than a litre of petrol.

Very much understandably, the oil-rich Middle East has thus neglected rail due to low gasoline prices and subsidised rates on automobiles due to trade agreements, although there was one significant rail link in the past, the Hejaz railway, which brought pilgrims from Damascus in Syria to Medina, a holy city in Saudi Arabia. The railway was damaged in the World War I and operations were never restored. During the latter part of the twentieth century, several nations in the Middle East expanded their rail transport networks significantly. But, unfortunately, none of the Gulf Cooperation Council (GCC) nations embraced railways as an important mode of transport, either for passenger or cargo movement. All this is about to change as rail projects worth more than $100 billion are currently being developed in the GCC.

Saudi Arabia has two railway lines for freight and passenger transport, respectively, between the capital city of Riyadh and the coastal city of Dammam on the Persian Gulf. With a total investment of $10 billion, the Haramain High-Speed Rail Project in Saudi Arabia is going to be the region's first HSR network. It will connect the holy cities of Mecca and Medina, serving a forecasted ten million pilgrims annually. It is expected to be 450 km long on completion with an operating speed of 320 km/h on its completion in 2014. The project is being developed by a Saudi-Spanish Consortium, Talgo, which will provide 35 trains. Renfe and ADIF will operate the line for 12 years.[15]

Nations in the GCC are becoming serious about rail. The Etihad railway project from the United Arab Emirates (UAE) aims to connect major cities with a network length of 1200 km. The first phase of the project is a 270 km dedicated freight line from Ruwais to the Shah Gas field scheduled to open in 2014. The signalling and tel-ecom contract, worth $1.28 billion was awarded to Ansaldo STS.[16] Electro-Motive Diesel (EMD) is supplying seven locomotives[17] and the CSR Corporation from China will be supplying 240 wagons to carry granulated sulphur.[18] A HSR line is planned between Dubai and Abu Dhabi. Two out of four lines in the Dubai metropolitan region are already operational; the other two are under construction. Abu Dhabi is planning for a tram network spanning 340 km to serve its city.

The most ambitious project in the Gulf Peninsula is the development of a regional railway network linking each of the member states of the GCC, to be known as the GCC Railway Network. When completed in 2017, the network is expected to change the face of transport and logistics in the region. It will offer remarkable efficiency in transporta-tion, apart from furthering the vision of a closely integrated regional community. However, to enable integration across nations, the six member states would need to have national rail networks. Driven by this agenda, each GCC government has launched various long-range and urban rail projects in its nation. Saudi Arabia, the UAE, Oman and Qatar have all launched projects in rail, and will bring the people of these countries much closer together as a result.

MACRO TO MICRO IMPLICATIONS OF HIGH-SPEED RAIL

High-speed rail is a cutting-edge technology, and its vast ecosystem and infrastructure needs provide diverse business growth opportunities.

The latest-generation traction motors, derived from wind power technology, allow for the generation of electricity when the train brakes. LED lighting lowers operating costs, life cycle costs, cooling requirements and carbon footprints. Computational fluid dynamics has transformed the bulky vented undercarriage air-conditioning system to a sleek overhead profile with strategic placement of blowers that allows for the dynamic circulation of air. Information technology has been integrated into every domain of the rail environment. Fare collection, passenger information, train scheduling, maintenance management and systems monitoring are all computer controlled.

Expansion of rail networks involves the stimulus of many different industries. Consumption of steel, copper and cement are key indicators of this industry's growth. Copper is used in the catenary systems for providing rolling stock with electricity. High-speed operators around the world are favouring and utilising copper magnesium alloys for HSR catenaries. Approximately ten tonnes of copper are required for every kilometre of dual-track catenary system. There is a driving demand for premium catenary alloys such as copper-silver (CuAg) and copper-magnesium (CuMg), although Asian countries prefer aluminium catenary wires. Growing traffic volumes are forcing network managers to opt for better-performing copper alloys such as CuAg to reduce maintenance and life cycle costs, improving network standards.[19] The UK thieves seems to really like the rail copper, and these days prefer stealing copper over robbing banks these days, so much that they steal cables to floss their teeth with. The number of cable thefts in the North Eastern region in UK alone totalled 1,184 in 2010.

China is the world's leading producer of steel, producing 683.3 million tonnes in 2011 (45.8% of the world's total production).[20] Construction of railway infrastructure in China is expected to increase the demand for steel by eight million tonnes every year. The 1,318 km Beijing–Shanghai HSR line is estimated to have required 300,000 tonnes of steel with more than 130,000 engineers and workers at work. As of 2011, a total of 17,166 km of HSR networks were operational, 8,838 km are under construction and 16,318 km are planned. Frost & Sullivan rail analysts estimate a total steel requirement of 2.1 million tonnes and an excess of 90,000 tonnes of copper for all the HSR projects under construction around the world. Enough demand to make the steel world's largest companies like ArcelorMittal serious about this opportunity to have a dedicated business focus on this sector. ArcelorMittal claims it can supply individual bars up to 90 metres long, tailored for this market, to create a competitive differentiation edge for itself over its competitors. When UK's Transport Secretary Justine Greening announced the government's $50 billion high-speed rail link, it was good news for Corus Steel, now called Tata Steel. It will help Tata Steel keep manufacturing going in its Scunthorpe steel plant. Similarly, in 2011, Tata Steel won a substantial contract to provide steel for the French HSR rail network.

Construction of a rail infrastructure starts a chain reaction that drives demand across the value chains. Companies like JCB, Komatsu, Caterpillar and Volvo see spikes in orders for off-highway, earthmoving and construction equipment. Construction tooling, spare parts and service providers also see higher volumes of business. So big is the opportunity that these equipment manufacturers are already scouting for mergers and acquisitions. Caterpillar, the big construction equipment giant, has spent over $2 billion in acquisitions in this market, its most recent purchase being of Electro-Motive Diesel for $820 million in cash from private equity fund owners.[21] Caterpillar's key reason for paying the premium is to take that business global, and is already making inroads into key lucrative rail markets like Brazil. Caterpillar's purchases have spiked interest from other construction equipment manufacturers to get into the rail business.

With HSR will come a lot of peripheral spending in the future, like new inland container depots, warehouses, sheds and intermodal traffic freight hubs, which can help move containers from trains to trucks and vice versa. The increase in volume of freight traffic will push demand in the locomotive market. Contrary to common belief, the increase in electrification will not make the diesel locomotive obsolete. A total of 10,682 diesel locomotives are expected to be delivered between 2010 and 2020 (in Germany, France, Italy, Spain and the UK). The 560 kW–2000 kW power range is expected to grow by 54%. There is strong demand for diesel locomotives in excess of 2000 kW. Vossloh has been extremely successful with its G2000 locomotives establishing diesel presence in the plus-2000kW category for the first time in 60 years in France.[22]

Information technology (IT) is an integral part of the twenty-first century rail network. It offers services such as condition monitoring, security, surveillance, data handling, ticketing, passenger information systems and much more to the rail environment. IT services are often outsourced to other countries, creating high technology jobs in several global locations. The enterprise resource planning (ERP) project for the Indian Railways alone is valued to be over $1 billion.[23]

Industries that are involved in construction safety (signs, helmets, etc.) are getting mobilised. Even farmers supplying fabric and raw materials are benefitting. Rail industry is boosting trade in the form of imports of material or technology which bring with it dialogue and social interaction. KA-CHING!

HIGH-SPEED LOGISTICS

Rail freight, the world over, travels much slower in speed than passenger rail applications. This is due to the higher load on the locomotive as well as on the rails. Passenger services are, in many countries, subsidised by freight operations. Traditional thinking is that using conventional lines for both passenger and freight causes delays and congestion and that separation of passenger and freight allows for a higher efficiency and greater revenue generation. This might be true in countries like India, where the network has a high utilisation rate, but not in many developed countries, as most often the high-speed tracks remain un-utilised at night.

The development of an HSR line has two major implications on freight transport. Firstly, it allows the conventional line to be exclusively used for freight. Secondly, freight can be transported on high-speed tracks, albeit at slightly slower speeds, during off-peak hours which will vastly reduce the travel time for goods and in the future become the important source of transporting perishable goods, like flowers from Holland to UK.

A look at the commodity types transported by rail in Europe in 2010 shows that 97% of the current goods transported by rail fall under the low-value and heavyweight category. The lightweight goods, though a smaller percentage, are significant contributors to the rail revenue. This category, primarily a niche for airfreight, is the one which will be attracted to high-speed rail, should it prove reliable. This means companies like FedEx, which runs the world's biggest fleet of airplanes for transporting freight, take notice.

That the low-weight and high-value goods are ideal for high-speed rail is proved by the successful network maintained by the La Poste trains run by SNCF. The 270 kmph trains that carry mail (less than 2 kg) and parcels (less than 20 kg) successfully across Europe make one hopeful. Interestingly, the percentage of revenue generated by mail transport in Europe reduced from 58% in 2003 to 52% in 2010. The parcel express showed an increase from 18% to 23% in the same time period, showing the positive effects of e-commerce on high-speed rail.

A fully dedicated high-speed freight rail is not in the cards with most governments. In Europe, apart from La Poste run by SNCF and the ambitious project taken up by EuroCarex, the idea of a dedicated high-speed rail to carry as much as 12,000 tonnes of cargo at more than 200 kmph is balked at. It is seen as dirty transport on clean rail lines. Interestingly, China is an undisputed pioneer in high-speed network construction, but only for passengers. Though serious about its commitment to increase rail freight revenue, it only plans to do so by shifting passengers to high-speed rail and freeing the conventional (read slower) rail tracks.

I believe this will all change soon, as the politicians and lobbyists (against HSR) will push for governments to rethink the business case of spending taxpayers' money, and open the HSR lines to increased freight mobility to recoup the capital investments. If La Poste's jump in parcel revenue is any indication, e-commerce websites are going to eye the passenger high-speed rail network growth with speculation and interest to move their goods at speed to their customers.

OLD COMPETITORS, NEW BATTLES

The railway industry is packing heat. The first decade of the twenty-first century has seen renewed interest in all forms of rail transportation. Cities upgraded aging tram networks to modern light rail systems and built new metro systems. The modal shift of freight to rail has become the number one priority for many transportation departments around the world. Construction of new rail projects is expected to be developed by PPP between the government and the technology provider. Funding is expected to arise from government bonds. Funding will be backed by government bonds from the respective native country for foreign participants.

As competition increases, companies are expected to form consortiums with shared interest. It is already regular practice for competing rail companies to bid together and develop the project together. The Bombardier-Alstom consortium is going to supply the city of Montreal with 468 new metro cars starting from 2013 at a cost of $1.2 billion. It is expected that Bombardier's share is $742 million and Alstom's share is $493 million.[24]

Another anticipated development is the open access to high-speed lines, allowing for private operators to offer services. Nuovo Trasporto Viaggiatori (NGV), an Italian company, is Europe's first private operator of 300 km/h high-speed trains. NGV aims to compete with the Italian state operator Trenitalia. What is most interesting is that the SNCF (French state railway) has a 20% stake in NGV. SNCF has successfully capitalised its experience in managing fleet and infrastructure, establishing itself as a strong private operator under the brand of Keolis (majority owned by SNCF). Keolis has presence in UK, Denmark, Sweden France, Belgium, Germany and Netherlands as well as in countries across the Atlantic (USA and Canada) with an annual turnover of $5.4 billion. Deutsche Bahn (DB) is another state operator that has successfully entered the private operator market outside its home market. DB now has presence in UK and in many other European countries. The AlRail service offered by DB allows passengers to check in at the ICE high-speed train station and directly board the airplane without having to carry baggage themselves.

Letting technology pass by can cause a large loss in revenue. Track maintenance and project management firms from countries with HSR experience are now bidding for work in other countries. Consultation projects alone run up to several million US dollars. Systra offers consultation for the tender process of the high-speed rail project in Mexico. Who owns Systra? SNCF and RATP (Paris metro) own the majority. Similarly, it is likely that China will fund, develop and operate high-speed rail systems in Argentina.

A lot of new participants are entering or strengthening their presence in the rail industry. Caterpillar recently bought EMD through Progress Rail, giving it exceptional presence in almost all the heavy equipment requirements of the mining industry. Caterpillar is rapidly expanding its presence in the rail industry to become a substantial player, putting fear in the likes of GE Rail with its aggressive strategy. GE, with its 67% share in the Brazilian locomotive market, is now worried about Caterpillar's intentions.[25] It knows that Caterpillar is a fierce competitor that is battle hardened with heavy equipment wars with Japanese players like Komatsu. Caterpillar first forayed into this market when it first supplied engines for two EMD locomotives. It acquired Progress Rail, a railroad equipment company, in 2006. In 2007 it acquired companies that expanded its strength in railroad equipment remanufacturing and signalling. In 2010, Caterpillar acquired four companies that serve the rail industry, with one of them being EMD itself, a customer and now a subsidiary. Caterpillar's strategy shows exceptional planning executed with clinical precision to compete with well-established companies like Siemens, GE and Bombardier.

Similarly hydraulic transmission and turbo-machinery experts, Voith recently launched two families of diesel hydraulic locomotives – called the Gravita and Maxima – ready to meet the demands of the European freight market and provide competition to Vossloh. Prime defence integrators like Finmeccinica Group, Thales and many others are bringing their leadership in IT, security, telemetry, telematics and centralised intelligent control centres to the rail industry. Selex (a leading defence contractor in the field of surveillance, air traffic control and communication systems) in a consortium with Ansaldo was awarded a GSM-R signalling contract worth $328 million in Libya.[26] In times of austerity and reduced defence funding, the rail environment provides ample opportunity for defence industry giants.

The $50 billion high-speed project from London to Birmingham is UK's biggest-ever rail infrastructure project in over a century and will create 9,000 construction jobs. Just what the ailing economy needs. Most such HSR projects worldwide will be written in the Guinness Book of world's largest infrastructure projects. The California HSR project, which could be over $100 billion when completed, could be the country's biggest-ever infrastructure project too. Similarly, India, with its $100 billion Delhi–Mumbai Industrial Corridor (DMIC) project, will invest a substantial amount of that budget in building separate freight and passenger rail networks.[27] With this kind of Mega spending on budgets, this 200-year-old rail industry deserves to be a Mega Trend even in the twenty-first century.

The high-speed rail industry sure is packing heat.

11

NEW BATTLEFIELDS: SPACE JAM AND CYBER WARFARE

In my work in analysing Mega Trends, I made three simple, but interesting and important, discoveries. The first one is that Mega Trends are significant forces of change; and, since these are forces, they are – my second discovery – subject to Sir Isaac Newton's laws of motion. In context to the application of Newton's laws to this chapter, my third discovery relates to Newton's third law in which Mega Trends are connected and intertwined, which suggests 'synergetic' opportunities between them. An impact of one Mega Trend can have an equal and opposite reaction to another Mega Trend.

Let us apply this theory to Space Jam and Cyber Warfare, two Mega Trends that are intricately linked and have an equal and opposite effect.

SPACE JAM

Outer space will be a seriously contested, congested and clogged place in the future. Aman Pannu, a space analyst at Frost & Sullivan, predicts that, in this decade, there will be around 1200 satellites launched cumulatively (between 2010 and 2020).[1] In comparison to the total number of satellites launched over the last ten years, this indicates a growth of about 25% over the next ten years. A combination of new navigation satellite networks, along with R&D programmes across various mass categories from micro to heavy satellites, and the ever increasing list of new space-faring nations continue to drive demand within this market. However, it is the trend of engaging commercial satellite platforms in dual applications – including that of the military – that is motivating many entrepreneurs to explore potential opportunities within this 'space'. Chart 11.1 gives

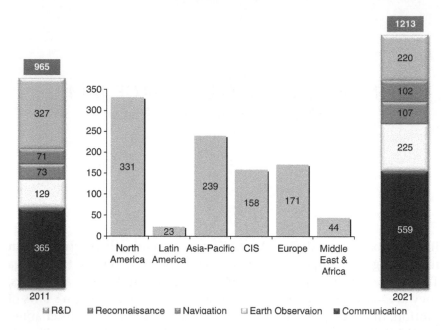

Chart 11.1 **Breakdown of new satellite launches by application and region (global), 2011–21**

Source: Frost & Sullivan.

the breakdown of new satellite launches by application and region from 2011 to 2021.

The traffic jam in low earth orbit, between 800 and 1000 km above our heads, is worse than the M25, the orbital ring road in London, on a Monday morning. NASA estimates that there are now more than 500,000 pieces of space junk, along with nearly 1000 active satellites orbiting the earth. And with countries like the US, China and Russia practicing shooting satellites down, that debris is only getting worse and more spread out. For many years, especially more so recently, experts have been talking about the threat of space debris to the active (and let's not forget very critical) space infrastructure. So it was not exactly a 'shock' when, in February 2009, the defunct Russian military satellite Cosmos 2251 collided with the American commercial satellite Iridium-33. Rather, many industry participants responded with 'surprise': they had always been aware of the potential risk but never acknowledged the imminent threat. I would not be surprised to hear of similar space collisions in this coming decade, so bad is the congestion.

RACE FOR SPACE

We all know and have read about the space race during the Cold War era between the Russians and Americans. There are even several conspiracy theories that the Americans never ever set foot on the moon and that half a billion TV viewers who heard the first words uttered by Neil Armstrong on the moon – 'That's one small step for man, one giant leap for mankind' – were actually hearing them relayed from a Hollywood studio and not the moon's surface. Even if the conspiracy theories are true, the fact is that huge progress was made by the Russians and American space agencies in this space race. However, this space race will be lot more crowded and contested in the next ten years, and more interesting beyond.

In beginning of 2011, the United States' NAVSTAR Global Positioning System (GPS) was the only fully operational GNSS (Global Navigation Satellite System, the correct term for describing all the navigational satellite constellations in orbit; GPS only refers to the US NAVSTAR constellation), which some of us vehicle drivers can relate to through our in-car SAT NAV devices like Garmin and TomTom which have replaced the old maps (and the wife; thus, they are often termed 'SAT NAG' systems). In October 2011, the Russian GLONASS system joined the American NAVSTAR system as the only two fully operational GNSS systems in the world. By end of this decade, we will have close to five, if not more, GNSS systems, with the Europeans finally getting their act together with the highly controversial Galileo positioning system, scheduled to be operational in 2014 and fully completed by 2019–20. Soon to follow will be China with its BeiDou-2 GNSS system, while Japan is already plotting the course for its own regional navigation satellite system, called Quasi-Zenith Satellite system (QZSS) and India is developing its GAGAN (means sky in Hindi).

The European Union (EU) is developing Galileo, which promises to be the most sophisticated, advanced and precise GNSS ever available to date. It is the first ever GNSS built primarily for civilian applications and the only GNSS system which will be fully under civilian control. Unlike the GLONASS and GPS systems, which provide accuracies of around 10 metres, Galileo will provide some of its services, like open access navigation, 'free to air' which has the potential to provide real-time positioning accuracy down to the 1 metre level and guarantee availability of the service under all but the most extreme circumstances.

Future GNSS systems, like Galileo, will provide accuracy to a one-metre position and also precisely identify the position of objects in vertical buildings. It will be able to tell that you are sitting on the seventh floor of a 62 storey building in the living room. Creepy!

Google Maps, in 2011, partnered with select organisations to provide in-building navigation. If that hasn't hit home run yet, then consider this: while you are reading this book on your tablet, one of the many satellites orbiting 22,000 miles away in space would have tracked you on your sofa and shared the data you are viewing with organisations of varied interests from government to commercial. The shared data would have profiled you against other location-based information collected on you throughout the day, such as the coffee place you visited, the office in which you work, the lunch place you visited, the gym you went to (or did not go to), the club grocery store you went by and finally the sofa upon which you sit and read this book. Connect the dots and that would make for invaluable information for most advertising companies, but more importantly for government agencies working arduously to prevent the next misadventure. All this is made possible by the omnipresent satellites watching every move you make; well, almost every.

WORLD WAR III: TWO NEW DOMAINS OF CONFLICT

God forbid, if there is to be a World War III, there will be two new domains of conflict additional to the air, naval and land forces where most battles have been fought and won. These two new domains will

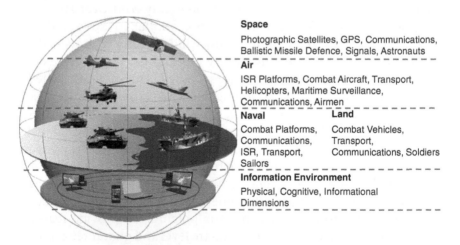

Chart 11.2 **World War III: With advancement in technology, information warfare to be the next domain of conflict**

Source: Frost & Sullivan.

be space and information warfare, also called cyber warfare, with the latter being the first ever man-made domain of conflict while the others were provided by nature.

History shows that the highest aerial position is always a basis of competitive advantage in a conflict, be it for communications, observation, navigation or sniper fire. Militaries globally recognise this and, in the future, most wars will begin with either jamming or shooting down each other's space assets. The nation that can, therefore, most successfully leverage military space and defy the space-based weapons of its enemy will have a key competitive advantage in the war. Space, therefore, provides an inherent military advantage and in the future will move from just being an observation and navigation station to also being a battle station.

The use of space is important for the military, not only for surveillance but also for reconnaissance and communications. In the 1991 Gulf War, the US military utilised 99 Mbps of satellite communications; by contrast, in 2003, a smaller US force used 3200 Mbps of satellite communications, a 60-fold increase per solider. This continues to increase, with some experts indicating a 300-fold increase in data used per soldier by 2030. This increase in demand is mainly driven by the 'futuristic' warfighter programmes such as the increasing use of unmanned systems, soldier modernisation (including electronics and communication needs of the warfighter), strategic and tactical communication, command and control systems, and force protection. To fulfil this requirement the US government has undertaken a two-pronged approach. Firstly, it is investing in creating a reliable and sustainable military satellite infrastructure to meet the evolving needs of the warfighters. Secondly, it is engaging commercial bandwidth to fill in the gaps (which can be considerable; for instance, currently the US military acquires 80% of its bandwidth via commercial satellites).

We have, in the last 24 months, seen enough evidence from nations like Russia and China testing their ability to shoot down satellites and develop an army of hackers, also known as cyber soldiers. China, Iran and North Korea boast of having the world's largest army of cyber hackers. Iran and North Korea claim they can bring down America's systems within 24 hours of an attack. In retaliation, the US military, in May 2010, appointed a four-star general, Keith Alexander, to direct cyber warfare command (USCYBERCOM), a newly established command of over 30,000 cyber soldiers. In December 2011, the US created the 780th Military Brigade from the ground up to support US cyber army commands. In this day and age, you don't see many new brigades being built in this manner. In this case, it was a special new unit; similar to the movie *The Dirty Dozen*, it was hand-picked, purposely recruited and has a clear and defined covert mission, but unlike *The Dirty Dozen*, where the soldiers were criminals, this modern version will be made up of computer geeks.

President Obama realised the importance and vulnerability of digital attack when his campaign strategy for election to the presidency was subject to continuous hacking. On assuming office he immediately appointed a new cyber-security czar, Howard Schmidt, a former Microsoft security executive, and awarded him a budget of approximately $13 billion. Similarly, in the UK, cybercrime is now considered to be one of the biggest security threats facing the nation and the new government has committed £650 million to tackling it despite cuts in defence spending. The US army, as well as many corporate banks and organisations, report a trend of multiple and deliberate attempts to get into their networks almost daily.

The challenge with cyber warfare, compared to other forms of warfare, is that anyone, everyone, anywhere can be an enemy. They don't need to be armed with Kalashnikovs and have structured terrorist training; all they need is a computer and an Internet connection. They are also impossible to find, worse than the guerrilla warfare seen in the Vietnam conflict, as they could be based in Siberia but using an army of hacked computers in multiple countries to direct their attacks. With the rise of BRIC nations and IT graduates in these countries, the cloud computing trend will mean that important and secure data of countries like the UK and US will sit in foreign territory; therefore, it also provides a security risk. As an expert of UK's cyber-security told me, 'Cyber warfare attack will be more difficult to control than a nuclear bomb.'

Next is a description of the main cyber warfare characters and their threats as identified by the US Department of Homeland Security.

MACRO TO MICRO

Despite being a gloomy and fearful scenario, there are some distinct business opportunities within this Mega Trend.

Satellite manufacturing – size matters

Frost & Sullivan analysts predict the satellite manufacturing industry globally to grow at a rate of 10–15% per annum and generate about

Table 11.1 **Cyber characters and threats**

Threat	Description
Bot-network operators	Bot-network operators are hackers; however, instead of breaking into systems for the challenge or bragging rights, they take over multiple systems in order to coordinate attacks and to distribute phishing schemes, spam and malware attacks. The services of these networks are sometimes made available in underground markets (e.g. purchasing a denial-of-service attack, establishing servers to relay spam, phishing attacks, etc.).
Cyber mercenaries	Just like conventional mercenaries, they are lethal and extremely professional. These mercenaries provide a full menu of malware services with guarantees and support packages, from a one-off attack to a sustained, simultaneous attack of several sites. One can even order by the hour from a short one-hour attack on a site to a continuous attack of several hours to as long as it takes to produce a complete meltdown.
Criminal groups	Criminal groups seek to attack systems for monetary gain. Specifically, organised crime groups are using spam, phishing and spyware/malware to commit identity theft and online fraud. International corporate spies and organised crime organisations also pose a threat through their ability to conduct industrial espionage and large-scale monetary theft and to hire or develop hacker talent.
Foreign intelligence services	Foreign intelligence services use cyber tools as part of their information-gathering and espionage activities. In addition, several nations are aggressively working to develop information warfare doctrine, programs and capabilities. Such capabilities enable a single entity to have a significant and serious impact by disrupting the supply, communications and economic infrastructures that support military power – impacts that could affect the daily lives of citizens across the country.
Hackers	Hackers break into networks for the thrill of the challenge or for bragging rights in the hacker community. While remote break-ins once required a fair amount of skill or computer knowledge, hackers can now download attack scripts and protocols from the Internet and launch them against victim sites. Thus, while attack tools have become more sophisticated, they have also become easier to use. According to the Central Intelligence Agency, the large majority of hackers do not have the requisite expertise to threaten difficult targets, such as critical networks. Nevertheless, the worldwide population of hackers poses a relatively high threat of an isolated or brief disruption causing serious damage.

Continued on next page

207

Table 11.1 (Continued)

Threat	Description
Insiders	The disgruntled organisational insider is a principal source of computer crime. Insiders may not need a great deal of knowledge about computer intrusions because their knowledge of a target system often allows them to gain unrestricted access to cause damage to the system or to steal system data. The insider threat also includes outsourcing vendors as well as employees who accidentally introduce malware into systems.
Phishers	They are individuals, or small groups, who execute phishing schemes in an attempt to steal identities or information for monetary gain. Phishers may also use spam and spyware/malware to accomplish their objectives.
Spammers	Individuals or organisations who distribute unsolicited email with hidden or false information in order to sell products, conduct phishing schemes, distribute spyware/malware or attack organisations (i.e. denial of service).
Hacktivists	A hacktivist is an activist who uses the Internet and the tools and techniques of a hacker to disrupt Internet services and bring attention to a political or social cause.
Spyware/malware authors	They are individuals or organisations with malicious intent to carry out attacks against users by producing and distributing spyware and malware. Several destructive computer viruses and worms have harmed files and hard drives, including the Melissa Macro Virus, the ExploreZip worm, the CIH (Chernobyl) Virus, Nimda, Code Red, Slammer and Blaster.
Cyber terrorists	They are terrorists who seek to destroy, incapacitate or exploit critical infrastructures in order to threaten national security, cause mass casualties, weaken the economy and damage public morale and confidence. Cyber terrorists may use phishing schemes or spyware/malware in order to generate funds or gather sensitive information.

Source: Government Accountability Office (GAO), Department of Homeland Security (DHS), United States.[2]

$150 billion in cumulative revenues (including launch services worth around $40 billion) from 2010 to 2020. Geostationary orbit will be the largest market in revenues, not in units, contributing to about half of the total industry's revenues to build and launch satellites in this period. With demand growing for higher-bandwidth communications and finite orbital slots, satellite operators want satellites that are more powerful and flexible than ever before. The wider acceptance of dual-use platforms in the global satellite manufacturing market will bring new opportunities to satellite owners, satellite service providers and satellite manufacturers.

However, the low-cost production capabilities of countries such as India and China challenge the future satellite manufacturing market share of developed countries. The combination of a highly skilled workforce, inexpensive labour and low production costs enables India and China to compete effectively with the established space economies of the West. 'India and China have production costs that are up to 60% lower than those of western space participants,' explains Pannu, adding, 'This encourages strategic international partnerships such as the one between China and Nigeria/Brazil and India's working relationship with Europe and Russia.'

The asymmetric nature of battles that the defence forces across the globe are currently facing, increases the demand for an agile and an operationally responsive force, where the 100-day wars are out and the expeditionary 100-hour battles are the way forward. Space is not isolated to such demands, as is evident from the SMDC-One programme of the US government, wherein nanosatellites are to be launched in order to create an operationally responsive space capability to meet expeditionary requirements of the warfighter. Further to this, the US army is developing the Multipurpose Nanomissile System (MNMS), which has configurable boosters that can be tailored to many specific missions, such as missile defence target vehicle, infrared and radar sensor exerciser, hyper-sonic test vehicle for aerospace components, pop-up reconnaissance system, highly responsive orbital launch vehicle for very small payloads (10 kg to LEO) and even very long-range strike capability with small conventional munitions. Other than the operationally responsive space capability, price is the key driver for the evolution of such a system. The nanosatellites cost between $300,000 and $1 million each, enabling the forces to launch multiple nanosatellites and still keep the entire constellation relatively inexpensive.

The space industry needs to cater to the operationally responsive space environment by developing space infrastructure that is not only reliable but also financially feasible and, more importantly, can be delivered in a short, 'defined' period of time. Frost & Sullivan envisages that by 2030 satellite manufacturers will have created a wide range of commercial off-the-shelf (COTS) subsystems and components to deliver standardised, reliable and quick space systems for meeting the expeditionary needs of the forces. Furthermore, COTS solutions that have a proven track record on terrestrial applications will evolve to be space-qualified, leading to a much lower development cost and hence a more affordable space asset.

Another crucial trend emerging from the militarisation of space would be the emergence of the 'galactic' warfighter. The term 'galactic' warfighter was coined to represent space-operators who control space-based weapons and assets. This may be considered in context with the new age of unmanned aerial systems (UAS) pilots who emerged a decade or so back and who are seen as active contributors to the war theatre today. The use of UAS in Afghanistan and Pakistan is debatable itself. The complexity and danger of deploying space-based weapons can only be extrapolated from UAS missions and experience gathered, at the very least.

Space tourists, space hotels and weddings in space – what next?

If you have $20 million worth of spare change and fancy an ultimate holiday that overlooks the moon, stars and the earth, then you have the chance to spend eight days with that money as a space tourist. And if you can't afford $20 million and don't fancy eight days without civilisation, then with just $200,000, you can join the 430 people who have already signed up for the Virgin Galactic space tourism programme. With just two days of training you can qualify as an astronaut and spend 2.5 hours aboard a plane which will carry six other astronauts like you. Your holiday spacecraft will travel at a speed of Mach 3 to about 109 km above the Earth's surface, which is technically beyond the internationally defined boundary between Earth and space of 100 km. And if you do not trust Sir Richard Branson and think he is just a used-car salesman and would rather go with someone else, you can choose to go with Rocketplane for $250,000 per person or for a budget space holiday with XCOR for approximately $95,000.

This decade will see the commercialisation of space tourism. Virgin Galactic, Boeing, Armadillo Aerospace, XCOR Aerospace, Bigelow

Aerospace, Galactic Suite and Orbital Technologies are some of the companies working progressively towards establishing space tourism as a commercial reality. Some organisations, like the Russian company Orbital Technologies, are going a step further by suggesting that they will have a fully operational space hotel by 2016, with all rooms having a galactic view. For a small sum of about $150,000 you can spend five days in this all-star (literally) space hotel, on top of your flight, which will cost around $750,000. You cannot wine (as per hotel policy), but you can enjoy fine dining along with the best in luxury while listening to your favourite song, 'Hotel California'.

Not only that, if you fancied having your nuptials in space and a wedding vow, 'I promise to be true to you in good times and in bad, in sickness and in health, and in space and on earth', it will also be possible. You can even buy, today, a weightless wedding gown from designer Emi Matsui to go with the wedding.

Industry experts see a space tourism industry potential of around $1 billion per annum by end of this decade. By 2030, one can expect space tourism to become a notable contributor to the overall space industry revenues, with continuing potential to grow further.

The English weather forecast perfected

Having lived in (seldom) sunny England for more than 15 years, I wish regularly, like the rest of the 60 million Brits, for a weather machine. I don't think we will see one in my lifetime, but we can expect to see some more accurate weather forecasts thanks to satellites. In the future, weather forecasts will be generated with 99% accuracy for up to two weeks. Satellites, along with sophisticated supercomputers, will be able to map wind and rain patterns down to less than 10 square metres. Advances in meteorology, thanks to satellites, will also help accurately analyse the impact of long-term global warming and climate modelling will be achieved in far greater detail.

Space-based solar power stations

Space-based solar power (SBSP) satellites are under consideration as a feasible energy alternative. Japan Aerospace Exploration Agency or JAXA plans to launch a small satellite fitted with solar panels in 2015 and test beam the electricity from space through the ionosphere, the outermost layer of the Earth's atmosphere, according to the trade ministry document. The Japanese government hopes to have the solar station fully operational by the 2030s. Under this project, Mitsubishi Electric Corporation and IHI Corporation are leading a $21 billion Japanese project that aims to build a giant solar power generator in space within three decades and beam electricity to Earth. Similarly 'Solar Energy', a private firm, is developing an SBSP system with a similar, if not an earlier, timeline. China has recently unveiled a plan to have a solar power station for commercial use by 2040. It plans to have a sustainable and profitable model in place by 2020 for this launch.

Although SBSP is still nascent, substantial investments by stakeholders (both government and commercial) are driving it towards becoming a crucial source of energy in the long term (as early as 2030). Considering the energy scarcity that the world is faced with, this solution could be a Mega Trend to follow and watch for in the 2030s and 2040s. Other than the technological leaps anticipated in delivering SBSP, satellite manufacturers need to work closely with the key stakeholders developing and promoting this technology to develop satellites that can not only deliver solar energy to Earth but also utilise it to extend the life and power of future satellites. There is a whole set of technologies and product innovations that will drive the successful implementation of this energy solution. This brings new opportunities across the value chain for the space industry, from solar panel innovation to capture and transmission of energy, to creating satellites (and their subsystems) to deliver this solution and, finally, the launch capacity to accommodate/deliver the next-generation satellites.

Service-based satellite business model

The $21 billion space services industry in 2011 is expected to almost double in ten years' time. Space companies like Thales Alenia Space see higher revenue growth rates and increased profits in the space services sector than in manufacturing.

The space services industry can be roughly broken down into five types: Earth observation, network and connectivity, navigation, satellite operations management and ground segment systems, and technical support. Except for the satellite operations management and ground segment, all other services will see healthy growth. Network and connectivity, which contributes to about half of the satellite services revenues, will continue to see high growth driven by the emergence of new applications like satellite broadband solutions, mobile TV (S band), HDTV, 3DTV and military/civil security spending. Navigation will, however, see the highest growth rates driven by need for increased navigation- and location-based services for all forms of mobility and transport solutions. Key stocks to watch out for in satellite services space are those of companies like Astrium Services, Hughes, Vizado, Stratos, Globcast and Telespazio.

One of the satellite services that will find widespread growth will be satellite broadband. Satellite is the only type of broadband Internet service available in less populated areas located outside of cable, digital subscriber line (DSL) and wireless broadband networks. In 2010, according to a Frost & Sullivan study, there were 1.5 million subscribers for this service, and this industry was globally worth $1.26 billion with two-thirds of the market in the United States. Over the next six years, the number of subscribers to satellite consumer broadband Internet will grow to about six million and the industry revenues will double. New higher throughput Ka-band satellites have the potential to revolutionise the satellite broadband Internet industry and compete with DSL Internet services.

Satellite broadband is also now going global. Companies in North America that provide satellite broadband Internet access, such as ViaSat's subsidiary, Wild Blue, and the market share leader, Hughes, have grown in the last several years. Hughes and ViaSat are now selling their Ka-band satellite broadband Internet technology to Avanti and Eutelsat, respectively, in Europe. They will collectively launch three satellites over the next few years. Currently, the market in Europe has less than 100,000 households that depend on satellite service for Internet access, but this will grow to over two million users by 2015.

We will also see more military and government spending with commercial satellite operators. The US government and military outsourced approximately 80% of their satellite communications to commercial satellite operators in 2008. In 2010, that number was projected to be near 90%.The total US government and military spending is projected to almost double to $7.9 billion by 2015 from 2009 levels. Unmanned aerial vehicles and dissemination of satellite communications to the lowest-level personnel within the military are primary drivers in military purchases of satellite communications. More than half of the US government and military spending on commercial satellite capacity and services goes through the Defense Information and Systems Agency (DISA). This trend of spending by the US will spread to other governments and militaries globally, making them an important customer base for this industry.

Overall growth in connectivity will provide a boost to certain niche applications. For example, the machine-to-machine satellite communications market will see explosive growth with its market size doubling in the next five years to become a $1.9 billion market, growing at a healthy 15% CAGR. This will benefit companies like Iridium, Inmarsat, EMS Global Tracking, SkyWave, Globalstar, Qualcomm Omnitracs, Orbcomm, Skybitz, Wireless Matrix and Thuraya. Qualcomm is currently the biggest market player with around 20% global market share.

Implications and opportunities for cyber-security

As the world's population reaches 7.55 billion by 2020 and the number of people who have access to the Internet reaches five billion, the world will see a 20-fold increase in the number of hackers globally. This huge growth in the hacker population presents a huge threat to corporate, civil security and militaries worldwide. Organisations could see attempts to hack into their systems on a daily basis; a few already claim this is happening today.

If one reads of the recent incidents like the attack on Iran's nuclear facilities (a first of its kind where the Stuxnet virus was aimed at industrial programmable logic controllers, most likely by Israel or US or both) or the attack on Sony PlayStation and its online entertainment site (which took the company's network down for about ten days and cost them around $180 million in lost revenues), the situation is worrying. In the so-called Night Dragon cyber-attacks, five oil and gas companies around the world were attacked by hackers who claimed to be from China. Even high-tech Internet giants like Google have become victims of organised cyber-attacks. And these hackers are getting sophisticated – they are saying, 'If you have to hack, why not hack satellites?' The Tamil Tigers in Sri Lanka did just that by hacking and controlling one of Intelsat's satellites for the disbursement of their own propaganda.

So where does this all lead us and what does it mean in terms of market opportunities? As per a study by PwC,[3] global cyber-security spending was approximately $60 billion in 2011 and is expected to grow at close to 10% every year over the next three–five years, with the US accounting for half of this market. In most regions, with the exception of the US, the private sector accounts for the majority of cyber-security spending. A Frost & Sullivan study suggests that organisational spending on IT security has increased by 50% in the last three years alone.

Chart 11.3 shows cyber-security spending by solution segments. The current spending on information protection indicates that network security, security operations and data security are the highest areas of spend. Moving forward, identity and access control, followed by data security, will be the fastest growing segments.

The growth in cyber warfare will see some important changes within the corporate (private) sector environment. We will see the convergence of the physical and information security role within an organisation. Currently, cyber-security is treated primarily as a technology issue and is the responsibility of the Chief Information or Technology office within an organisation. However, with cyber-security becoming critical for a company's survivability, we will see amalgamation of the role of the chief security officer and chief information officer into that of the chief assessment officer (CAO). This CAO will be responsible for all forms of physical and digital security and for physical assets,

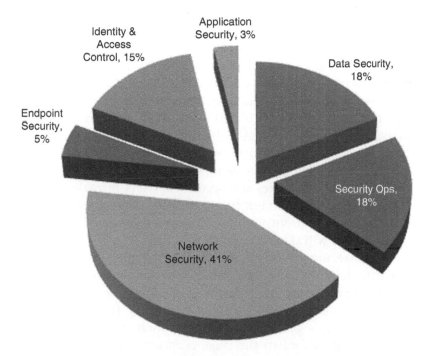

Chart 11.3 **Cyber-security market: Spending by solution segments, 2010**
Source: Frost & Sullivan.

215

as well as for the security of company's products and services. The CAO will work closely with departments like information technology, the R&D and engineering teams, and the security office to ensure zero breaches.

Changes in internal organisation structure of the security office will also lead to evolution of new service-based cyber-security business models. With the development of cloud-based services, and the ability to access data using mobile and tablet PCs, organisations will find it increasingly difficult to manage and protect their own data, thereby driving the outsourcing of the security function as well. Managed security services will thrive in the cyber environment and a new breed of companies will rise to meet this opportunity. Detica is an example of one such company which provides managed security services through an extensive product portfolio of advisory services, suite of technologies, building solutions which physically separate networks (so called air-gapped solutions) and bringing experience of data acquisition and analytics with forensic analysts to detect and thwart cyber-attacks.

As a result of the convergence of roles and functions within an organisation, we are also seeing a convergence in competition within the industry sector. This is likely to drive the emergence of a new breed of companies with the best of capabilities from different specialist areas that focus on IT security, network security and physical security, thereby providing truly end-to-end solutions to the market. We will therefore see an increase in partnerships and mergers and acquisitions within this sector. PwC calculated a cumulative spending on cyber-security M&A (Mergers and Acquisitions) deals since 2008 of nearly $22 billion, an average of over $6 billion in each year. The actors came from a diverse range of sectors which included technology, IT services, defence companies and security services providers as well as financial investors. The majority of the acquisitions included US and UK companies, as currently these are two of the biggest markets, but in the future we will see more cross-border activity.

The cyber-security market also provides opportunity for players to get into new markets and develop new competencies, thereby acquiring new customers. Defence companies like Raytheon and BAE have targeted acquisitions in this industry that provide access to new customers – government agencies such as the CIA, MI6, FBI, etc. – and to get a foot in the huge corporate sector, especially the lucrative banking and insurance sector, as military spending globally declines. On the way, these companies have picked up access to scarce security-cleared personnel, who can be very important in local markets. BAE Systems have spent over $1.8 billion for entry into this industry through acquiring companies like Detica Plc and L-1 Identity solutions. Interestingly, these defence operators have also picked up new business from military as a result. The lack of professional and trained individuals within the military sector is providing new business to these companies that work with the military intelligence communities to support them on their offensive cyber operations.

In the same way, the IT companies see cyber-security as an important evolution of their products and services to not only differentiate themselves from the competition but to also provide their customers with end-to-end solutions. No wonder they have also been engaging in M&A activity notably, and controversially, the biggest being the acquisition of McAfee Inc. by Intel for a whopping $7.8 billion in 2011.

Uncontested white 'space' market opportunities

In terms of blue-ocean, uncontested white space market opportunities in this sector, there are plenty out there in both the space and cyber-security industries.

For a start, satellite manufacturers could find success in developing miniaturised components and subsystems;low-mass, high-strength structural material; and low-mass and low-volume batteries. These enhancements will not only improve efficiency, especially for smaller satellite platforms, but also allow the deployment of these platforms in diverse applications such as high-resolution earth imagery, rapid deployment communications and reconnaissance.

The growth in satellite manufacturing and services revenues will push the industry's transition from being funded mostly by the public to raising funds from the private sector and bring in new business models like public-private partnerships or even private equity funding. This is an important opportunity for the banking as well as the industrial sector to fund these projects. A good example today is the UK's Skynet-5A programme, which is a military communication satellite system whose investor is not the government but Astrium Services (EADS). The UK government purchases the services from Astrium. The US' recent policy developments suggest a similar shift.

The satellites service model will evolve from one that is similar to what we already see in the defence sector to one of through life support (i.e. support through its life cycle operations in the field – for example, in maintenance). Satellite manufacturers will not only build satellites for their customers but also operate them through their life cycle, in some cases using innovating 'power by the hour' business models that provide important bandwidth to the highest payer. The space organisations will, however, need to evolve from being research driven to being more commercially astute.

There are also huge opportunities to work with the 'new space' entrants like India, China and many others, like Brazil, who will join the club soon. Both China and India have gargantuan ambitions to put humans on the moon and launch probes to explore deep space. There are, therefore, opportunities for Western organisations to support those ambitions, although there is a fine dividing line between Chinese military and civilian ambitions.

In the future, the space industry will need to – similar to any competitive industry – reduce its life-cycle cost, development cycle and time-to-market, and provide better performance indicators, like per unit of cost/mass/volume/functionality, to flourish.

There are huge numbers of white space opportunities in the cyber-security market. An obvious one is to target home computer users and small businesses by providing cyber-security packages similar to the anti-virus software consumers currently pay for. I believe a software service provider or even a services provider like a broadband or mobile phone operator can provide a rebranded cyber-security package to customers which protects their assets (like a tablet PC or smartphone) from being hacked, used in a denial of service attack or, when lost or hacked, provides options like locking or wiping out the data remotely. Some apps with basic functionality already exist: for example, WaveSecure Mobile Security offers a $20 annual subscription.

An interesting example of a similar service launched recently by a broadband service provider is called HomeSafe. It is a service built into the broadband network that protects every device connected to your service at home, be it the PC, laptop, iPad or PlayStation. It allows features like parental control, virus alerts and controlling web usage (e.g. the ability to set time limits on specific sites). As of now, the company is using this free service to gain competitive advantage by providing it free to its customers and publishing itself as the UK's safest broadband, but in the future one can expect it to charge for these services.

As more data moves virtual or to the cloud, whether through public, private or hybrid clouds, virtual security of data also becomes hugely important. One needs to first distinguish between a virtual environment and cloud computing, as both technologies share similar uses which, therefore, can cause confusion sometimes. Virtual technologies use software to separate applications from server hardware, allowing a server to have numerous virtual environments that can host multiple applications and operating systems. Therefore, there is a need for virtual security products to safeguard the virtual environment.

Compliance regulations, such as SOX and HIPAA, have not yet established clear requirements for securing these virtual environments. When moving over assets to the cloud environment, security of the data is an aspect that can be overlooked. Just as traditional environments, such as desktops and servers, are susceptible to hacking attempts, so are virtual environments. To combat these efforts by hackers, security vendors have been developing and tuning their virtual security products. These products can be offered as applications within the virtual environment or as applications that work with both physical and virtual infrastructures. Examples of traditional COTS security products offered as virtual appliances and applications include firewalls, anti-virus software, IDS/IPS, security information and event management, and log management appliances. These types of security devices are essential for organisations that are moving to a cloud-based infrastructure.

In 2011, the most common organisations adopting virtual security products happened to be some of the most regulated ones, such as financial services and health care. Other verticals, such as retail, education and government, are good potential targets for the future. For virtual security products, the most typical deployments are in data centres and enterprises. The mid-size market is also expected to experience growth as more businesses adopt virtualisation security or look at combining hybrid cloud infrastructures.

An uncontested market space opportunity in increasingly congested outer space is that of a space Hoover. A Russian company called Energia is actually planning to construct a $2 billion orbital vacuum cleaner that can sweep and suck up satellite and meteoroid debris. Perhaps Sir James Dyson, who revolutionised the vacuum cleaner industry, should consider it a viable market entry.

*

In all previous wars, nations relied on the strength of their conventional military for supremacy, but now the security of a country may depend on the security and quality of its cyber capabilities. So what could be next is a cyber-arms race featuring Kamikaze packets and cyber-bombs with payloads, followed by a Cyberian winter. Some of the prospects one reads are chilling and worrying. What concerns me is that all of this is possible and, sooner or later, we will see some evidence of a large-scale cyber-attack. Watch this space.

12

MACRO TO MICRO

So here we are: the last chapter of the book. As a reader, you might think I have exhausted my list of Mega Trends for this publication. But on the contrary, I originally had around 200 of these Mega Trends to begin with! For the purpose of the book (and for convenient reading), I funnelled those 200 trends into 15 major Mega Trends that were integrated into ten chapters. Some, like Convergence and Connectivity, Space Jam and Cyber Warfare, have been clubbed together. This chapter briefly discusses some of the other major trends which are not covered in the previous chapters but could be game changers, draws the key conclusions from study of these Mega forces, and most importantly, shows how you can apply the Macro to Micro methodology yourself to develop new uncontested market space opportunities.

TRENDS THAT DID NOT MAKE IT INTO THIS BOOK

As once one my colleagues said, 'Forecasting is an imprecise science.'

Absolutely correct! If I could forecast the future, I would not be writing this book; I would be a billionaire already in the stock market. So, although I have made a very calculated effort in identifying the most substantial Mega Trends, there are several major trends out there which I have not written about.

A few of these to watch out for are as follows.

Shale gas

In his 2012 State of the Union Address, President Obama referred to the past 100 years of the United States' dependence upon foreign oil

221

and talked about the need for the country, for the next 100 years, to be dependent upon shale gas, which is already in abundance in America's backyard.

For sure, shale gas will be a game changer. It could make America a net exporter of gas as opposed to an importer. According to a BP study, shale oil and gas reserves, along with other fuel sources, could make the Western Hemisphere completely self-sufficient by 2030, and release Europe from its reliance on political adversaries, like Russia, for gas and oil. So who cares if the Arabs run out of oil? We have shale.

Easier said than done. The extraction of shale gas in Lancashire, UK, was halted after it was linked to a rash of earthquakes. Some countries like France have banned shale gas drilling, possibly more an astute political decision by the French to maintain their nuclear power plant supremacy than a French concern about earthquakes also happening there.

My belief is that shale gas is a future Mega Trend but one for the next decade. It will not be until 2020 that we will be able to come up with technology to safely extract this gas without causing environmental imbalances. Thus, the topic is best left to be addressed in my next book.

Beyond BRIC – the next game changers

I often get asked, 'What are the economies beyond BRIC which will be the drivers of the world's economy once the BRIC countries slow down?' To be honest, there are no countries out there that can be as powerful as the individual BRIC countries. The sheer geographic size and population of the BRIC countries is unmatched and cannot be substituted. However, I strongly believe that there are some regions and countries which will see huge growth in the coming decade.

For a start, I firmly and strongly believe in the African story. In a report completed on Mega Trends in Africa, we were amazed by the potential this continent holds. It has the same population as India but, when looked up from the stars and compared to India, it is a dark continent as only 30% of Africans today have access to electricity. This will change, as GDP in most countries will double or even triple in some cases, and over 70% of Africans will have access to electricity. One can expect lot more integration within the continent, which will become a connected continent with around 1.17 billion phones by 2020. Internet penetration will grow to 800 million by 2020, from 115 million in 2011. Africa will also improve its economic development by beneficiating more raw materials into value-adding components for assembly – this beneficiation can add between 2% and 4% to the continent's GDP growth every year through 2020. It will also benefit from untapped oil and gas resources, making some countries very rich. Our report concluded that there is around $1 trillion on offer in this continent through 2020.

In our analysis, 'Beyond BRIC' includes countries such as Mexico, Argentina, Poland, Egypt, South Africa, Turkey, Indonesia, Philippines and Vietnam. In particular, I believe the ASEAN regions hold huge promise for the future, especially with the development of the ASEAN Free Trade Agreement (AFTA), which will allow organisations to sell and market goods in the whole region similar to what happens in Europe today thanks to the European Union.

Within the boundaries of Europe, I will put my money on Turkey.

Infrastructure spending

As part of our research, we also looked at global infrastructure spending and tried to evaluate which infrastructure sector will fall in the Mega spending category. We looked at spending across sectors like transport, energy, water and air/sea ports. It was especially tough to compare apples to apples when it comes to global spending within these individual sectors. There was also conflicting information. For example, some management consulting companies rate water as an extremely important resource, and as one of the biggest drivers for infrastructure spending.

We completely agree that water is an absolutely important resource, but we found no evidence to suggest it will be the world's number one in terms of infrastructure spending. Water consumption per capita is rising in developing countries but at the same time is more or less flat in countries like the US.

We believe that transport-related infrastructure spending, which includes roads, rails and urban transport, will have the highest infrastructure spend globally driven by urbanisation and the developing world's spend on building new highways and suburban rail systems for their busy, populated cities.

New outsourcing hotspots

Forget Bangalore. The new-age emerging outsourcing hotspots are not in the erstwhile tier 1 cities of developing countries – which offer both the advantages of low cost and fairly developed infrastructure.

The emerging outsourcing hotspots will be in the tier 2 and tier 3 cities of the new world – Indonesia, Vietnam, Philippines, Colombia, Mexico, Africa, Chile, and Argentina, to name a few. These cities will see a rate of growth of development faster than tier 1 cities and will be the focus of infrastructure development and hubs for key projects. These cities will be the centres of niche outsourcing applications such as software application development, contact centres, product development and software testing, and business analytics.

TechVision 2020 – top technologies of the future

The TechVision 2020 Program is a flagship research of Technical Insights (TI), the Technology Research and Consulting division of Frost & Sullivan. It represents a collection of the most exciting technologies that will shape our world in the next ten years.

Chart 12.1 shows the technology clusters that will be important in the future. While each technology cluster is an independent domain demonstrating excellence in global R&D and innovation, all clusters are virtually interlocked. The vast arrays of current and future applications of these dynamic technologies are interdependent and overlapping. These technologies are rapidly evolving and form a vortex of innovation driving new concepts, products and services.

The top ten technologies that Frost & Sullivan believes will be the most innovative and disruptive of this decade are nanotechnology, flexible electronics, advanced batteries and energy storage, smart materials, green IT, solar PV technology, 3D integration, autonomous systems, white biotech and lasers. Each of these technologies possesses unique, innovative properties that could lead to mind-blowing applications and, of course, manifold benefits for consumers and businesses in the coming decade.

One Mega Trend that I often get asked about is 'Will the US still be the world's superpower in 2020?' My answer is yes; but, unfortunately, it will no longer be the sole superpower.

MEGA CONCLUSIONS

Mega Trends are significant forces of change, and since these are forces, they are subject to Sir Isaac Newton's laws of motion. Newton's laws of motion are three physical laws that describe the relationship between

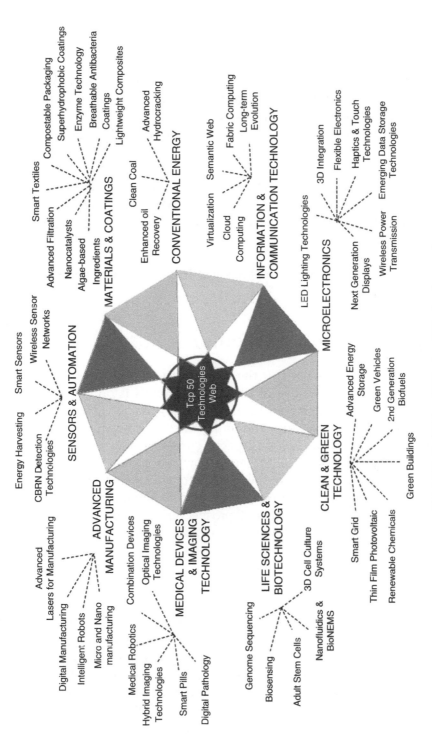

Chart 12.1 **TechVision 2020 – top 50 technology web**

Source: Frost & Sullivan.

the forces acting on a body and its motion due to those forces. They can be applied to Mega Trends as follows:

First Mega Trend law: The impact of a Mega Trend remains constant unless it is acted upon by a significant external force (convergence is driven strongly by connectivity).

Second Mega Trend law: The swiftness and the scale of impact of a Mega Trend is directly proportional to the global force applied to it (e.g. the success of shale gas or eMobility as a fuel for transportation is dependent upon government and public support).

Third Mega Trend law: For every Mega Trend there is an equal and opposite reaction (space jam and cyber warfare, connectivity and convergence).

Chart 12.2 shows how the new Mega Trends can help you identify new opportunities.

MACRO TO MICRO METHODOLOGY

As I start my countdown to the close of the book, I would like to emphasise that knowledge of these Mega Trends is only a first step towards understanding your future opportunities. One must identify these trends, their relevance and importance, build scenarios, analyse impacts, and identify their customers' current unmet needs to reveal future opportunities in 2020. Here is how you do it.

I call this entire exercise the 'Macro to Micro' methodology, and this exercise is important to create uncontested market space opportunities and find the next Facebook prospect or Groupon venture – that very business model which will radically change the dynamics of your business and open it up to new customers.

The Macro to Micro process consists of five key steps, as shown in Chart 12.3:

1. **Identify the Mega Trend and the sub-trends**: For example, it is important to understand that urbanisation has four major sub-trends – Mega-cities, Mega-regions, Mega-corridors and Mega-slums – which will sustain the trend and drive the changes in the society. Most times, these sub-trends are more important than the Mega Trend itself.
2. **Build scenarios**: Once you have identified the sub-trends, evaluate the implications to your industry. It is important, though,

Identify Greenfield Opportunities	Mega Trends enable clients to identify new uncontested marketplace opportunities through growth workshops, consulting engagements and regular research updates.
To Understand the Connectivity and Synergetic Opportunities	Mega Trends are connected and intertwined, which suggests 'synergetic' opportunities exist between them. It is important to understand this synergy and interrelation between trends to maximise growth opportunities.
To Understand the Entire Ecosystem of Growth	In order to understand all-encompassing factors that boost top-line growth, it is important to identify and monitor the ecosystem of the Mega Trend and the elements of the value chain that are the most profitable.
To Identify New Business Models	Mega Trends help identify and understand new and emerging business models that are driven by cross-sectoral synergetic implications and opportunities.
To Sustain Continuous Flow of Innovative New Ideas	It is important to sustain a continuous flow of innovative new ideas arising from futuristic Mega Trends.
To Help Build Contingency Plans	Mega Trends will help build contingency plans based on probable scenarios and market patterns.
To Be Aware of New Competition from Non-traditional Sources	Traditiona approaches to market are no longer working; vendors must change and evolve with end-user needs and industry requirements or become extinct. Mega Trends help you understand new competition arising from innovative and non-traditional sources.
To Emphasise Need for Champions Within an Organisation	Businesses need 'Mega Trend' champions and teams within their organisations to best exploit opportunities, to identify new innovations, to keep up with the accelerating pace of change in technology and to improve business results.
To Help Seek Future Customers	Mega Trends will help innovate to meet expected accelerating changes in future technology and align current strategy to address the needs of the 'Customer of the Future'.

Chart 12.2 **How the new Mega Trends can help you identify new opportunities**

Source: Frost & Sullivan.

227

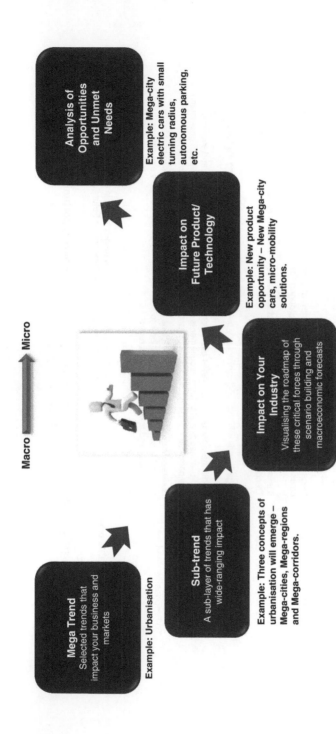

Macro → **Micro**

Mega Trend
Selected trends that impact your business and markets

Example: Urbanisation

Sub-trend
A sub-layer of trends that has wide-ranging impact

Example: Three concepts of urbanisation will emerge – Mega-cities, Mega-regions and Mega-corridors.

Impact on Your Industry
Visualising the roadmap of these critical forces through scenario building and macroeconomic forecasts

Example: People in the future will need 'personal mobility' and not necessarily cars to commute to work. This will lead to the need for integrated mobility, combining all forms of transport, including cars, and possibly car sharing/pooling.

Impact on Future Product/ Technology

Example: New product opportunity – New Mega-city cars, micro-mobility solutions.

Analysis of Opportunities and Unmet Needs

Example: Mega-city electric cars with small turning radius, autonomous parking, etc.

Chart 12.3 **Macro to micro methodology**

Source: Frost & Sullivan.

Note: Examples focus on impact to automotive industry.

to remember here that you need to clearly define what business you are in. Car companies are not in the business of making cars but in the market for providing personal mobility, just like Coca-Cola is in not in the business of 'fizzy' drinks but in the 'drinks' market. Therefore, if you work in the automotive industry, evaluate the impact of the Mega Trends and their sub-trends on personal mobility. Create three extreme scenarios of the Mega Trend (world without oil or oil is $20 a barrel) and brainstorm the implications of these Mega Trends. For example, with cities that have populations of over 15 million, commuters will need integrated, multi-modal transport systems which provide point-to-point journey solutions. Therefore, the car of the future will need to communicate with the infrastructure. In the beverage industry, meanwhile, people's habits are shifting to functional drinks (energy enhancement drinks).

3. **Evaluate implications to the industry**: Once you have created these scenarios, then evaluate their impact on your industry and business in particular and size the market opportunity. Mega-cities could provide opportunities for developing Mega-city cars positioned and targeted to the urban customer. With 60% of the world's population living in cities, and 40–50% of people in cities from developed countries owning cars, it sure can be a lucrative market segment – one in two people could be potentially driving Mega-city cars.

4. **Evaluate implications to your products and to technologies that make up that product**: Once you have defined the product; for example, the Mega-city car in the case of the automotive industry, it is then important to brainstorm technologies that can help you tailor the product to the Mega Trend. It is important here to also understand the linkage of several Mega Trends as most trends are connected and intertwined, which suggests synergetic opportunities. For example, cities of the future, thanks to 1200 satellites in space or 4G, will have wireless access which provides opportunity to provide Internet radio (e.g. Pandora) in city cars or Facebook on wheels, as well as stop/start systems for frequent starts and stops in city traffic.

5. **Identify customers' current unmet needs**: Finally, it is important to understand customers' current unmet needs related to a Mega Trend, and how you can innovate and develop new solutions to satisfy customers' needs. As an urban driver who lives in London and drives an SUV, I always get frustrated with the turning radius of my car. I would like a car with a small turning radius which helps

me turn the car using a two-point turn as opposed to the standard three-point turn designs of car companies, and a car which can park itself in tight parking spaces. London taxis, for several years, have been able to do two-point turns thanks to their short turning radius. Most companies are good at generating new product ideas but poor in understanding customers' unmet needs.

Once you have gone through this first process, you should have a wish list of opportunities. You can then prioritise them into a short and long list by plotting them across two axes – one on impact if successful and a second axis measuring the probability of success:

For the most promising opportunities, which have a high measure of success and probability and fall in the top right-hand quadrant, you can term these as your Mega opportunities (MOs). Work these MOs further to understand their

1. Market attractiveness (market size, your competitive and brand strength)
2. Financial benefit (ROI)

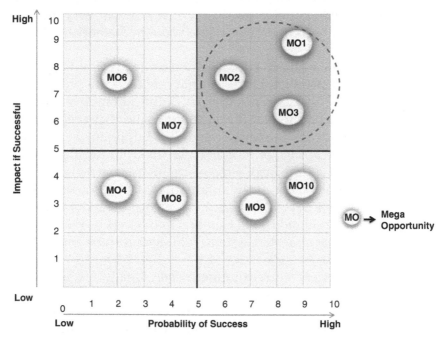

Chart 12.4 **Mega opportunity matrix**
Source: Frost & Sullivan.

Shortlist Top 10–15 Mega Trends which Provide Most Opportunity/Impact to Company

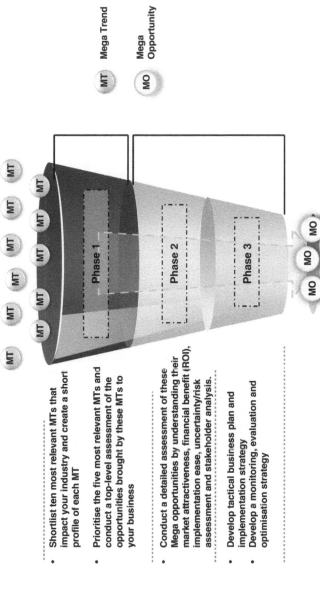

- Shortlist ten most relevant MTs that impact your industry and create a short profile of each MT
- Prioritise the five most relevant MTs and conduct a top-level assessment of the opportunities brought by these MTs to your business

- Conduct a detailed assessment of these Mega opportunities by understanding their market attractiveness, financial benefit (ROI), implementation ease, uncertainty/risk assessment and stakeholder analysis.

- Develop tactical business plan and implementation strategy
- Develop a monitoring, evaluation and optimisation strategy

MT Mega Trend

MO Mega Opportunity

Chart 12.5 **Three-phased approach to identify and analyse Mega Trend-based opportunities**

Source: Frost & Sullivan.

3. Implementation ease
4. Uncertainty/risk assessment
5. Stakeholder analysis

This will then allow you to prioritise the most lucrative MO based on solid external market attractiveness but also your internal organisation's capabilities to implement it and make it successful. Even the most attractive and simplest of market opportunities can fail if you don't have the organisational ability to implement it.

Chart 12.5 shows the process.

Once implemented, do not sit on your laurels, as there is another Mega Trend out there about to swing it away from you.

CONCLUSION

Mega Trends will affect us personally, professionally and socially and will change the way we think, communicate, move, do business and interact with customers, peers, suppliers, colleagues and even communities. The implications of these Mega Trends are not limited in scale – they have the power to change a large city and they have the power to affect the life of a single individual. They can affect revenues, costs and profitability for businesses as well as affect commuting trends, social networking, location of houses and even career choices for individuals.

The most pertinent point to be noted is that not only are all of these Mega Trends interrelated, but that the synergy of the implications and opportunities that arise from it are interrelated too. They have the power to connect people, communities, cities, business, cultures and even countries. For example, urbanization and connectivity are not only interlinked, but the very infrastructure that is involved in integrating future IT platforms will bind people with the city, people with other global cities, people with businesses and, of course, people with people. This will, in turn, affect the way people will live, the services they demand and the solutions cities will in turn deploy to cater to that evolving demand – be it energy or water supply, infrastructure needs, integrated mobility solutions or even geo-location services. And if this is just one example of connecting two Mega Trends in this book, imagine the power of synergy of all Mega Trends that has been featured!

As established earlier, and to stress again, knowledge of these Mega Trends is only a part of the exercise. The entire methodology becomes meaningful only when we see the complete 'Macro to Micro' methodology – to analyse implications of these 'Macro' Mega Trends and convert them to 'Micro' opportunities in the here and now. And this incredible exercise is what will give companies a competitive advantage and will define the winners and game changers of tomorrow.

As Malcolm X noted: 'Education is our passport to the future, for tomorrow belongs to the people who prepare for it today.'

So, now that you are armed and dangerous with your knowledge of the New Mega Trends, are you ready to identify the next Facebook idea?

REFERENCES

2   SMART IS THE NEW GREEN

1. 'European Home Automation Markets', Frost & Sullivan, 2000.
2. 'Global Smart Grid Market', Frost & Sullivan, 2011.
3. 'European Smart Meter Markets', Frost & Sullivan, 2011.
4. 'Smart Energy: Demand Response in Europe', Frost & Sullivan, 2011.
5. 'Large Scale Energy Storage and Opportunities from Growth in Renewable Energy', Frost & Sullivan, 2011.
6. K. LaCommare and J. Eto, February 2006, 'Costs of Power Interruptions to Electricity Consumers in the United States',LBNL-58164, Lawrence Berkeley National Laboratory, Berkeley, CA.
7. Amsmarterdam city. http://www.amsterdamsmartcity.nl/#/en. Accessed in February 2012.
8. Sino-Singapore Tianjin Eco-City Investment and Development Co. Ltd. http://www.tianjineco-city.com/en/index.aspx. Accessed in February 2012.
9. Machine-to-Machine in Government Driving the Smart City Concept, Frost & Sullivan, To be Published.

3   eMOBILITY

1. '360 Degree Perspective of the Global Electric Vehicle Market – 2012 Edition', Frost & Sullivan, 2012.

4   INNOVATING TO ZERO

1. Zero Waste Definition, http://zwia.org/joomla/index.php?option=com_content&view=article&id=9&Itemid=6. Accessed in February 2012.
2. European Pathway to Zero Waste (EPOW), Environment Agency, http://www.environment-agency.gov.uk/aboutus/wfo/epow/123624.aspx, Accessed in January 2012.
3. Executive Order, Federal Leadership in Environmental, Energy, and Economic Performance, Office of the Press Secretary, The White House, 2009,

http://www.whitehouse.gov/assets/documents/2009fedleader_eo_rel.pdf, Accessed in December 2011.

4. N. Duchenaut and L.A. Watts, 2005, 'In Search of Coherence: A Review of Research', *Human–Computer Interaction*, 20: 111–24.
5. Zero Carbon Britain, A New Energy Strategy, Centre for Alternative Technology, http://www.zerocarbonbritain.org/, Accessed in January 2012.
6. Zero Carbon Australia 2020, Beyond Zero Emissions, http://www.beyondz eroemissions.org/zero-carbon-australia-2020, Accessed in January 2012.

5 URBANISATION: FROM MEGA-CITIES, MEGA-REGIONS, MEGA-CORRIDORS AND MEGA-SLUMS TO MEGA OPPORTUNITIES

1. 'Unleashing the Potential of Urban Growth', State of the World Population 2007, UNFPA, http://www.unfpa.org/swp/swpmain.htm, Accessed in November 2011.
2. 'Impact of Urbanization and Development of Megacities on Personal Mobility and Vehicle Technology Planning', Frost & Sullivan, 2010.
3. 'Sustainable and Innovative Personal Transport Solutions – Strategic Analysis of Carsharing Market in Europe', Frost & Sullivan, 2010.

6 SOCIAL TRENDS THAT WILL MODEL OUR FUTURE SOCIETY

1. 'Apple, Google Collect User Data', *The Wall Street Journal*, http://online.wsj.com/article/SB10001424052748703983704576277101723453610.html, Accessed in January 2012.
2. Global Check-ins, Foursquare, https://foursquare.com/infographics/2010infographic, Accessed in February 2012.
3. 'Use Foursquare to Catch a Pair of Jimmy Choos', http://mashable.com/2010/04/27/foursquare-jimmy-choo/, Accessed in January 2012.
4. 'Gigwalk, Work on the Go', http://gigwalk.com/, Accessed in January 2012.
5. Asimo, The World's Most Advanced Humanoid Robot, Honda, http://asimo.honda.com/asimotv/Living-with-robots/, Accessed in December 2011.
6. 'Strategic Analysis of the Global Welding Robotics Market', Frost & Sullivan, 2011.
7. 'NASA – Gen Y Perspectives', http://www.slideshare.net/ashwinl/nasa-geny-perspectives, Accessed in January 2012.
8. 'Capturing the World's Emerging Middle Class', Mckinsey, 2010, https://www.mckinseyquarterly.com/Retail_Consumer_Goods/Strategy_Analysis/Capturing_the_worlds_emerging_middle_class_2639?gp=1, Accessed in January 2012.

7 HEALTH, WELLNESS AND WELL-BEING

1. Human Genome Project Information, Genomics.Energy.Gov, http://www.ornl.gov/sci/techresources/Human_Genome/home.shtml, Accessed in March 2012.
2. '2020 Vision: Global Food and Beverages Industry Outlook', Frost & Sullivan, 2010.

8 BUSINESS MODEL OF THE DECADE – VALUE FOR MANY

1. 'An Update of European Markets for Telematics Based Pay-As-You-Drive Vehicle Insurance', Frost & Sullivan, 2008.
2. 'Etao Launch Report of Tuangou Total 20 Billion Yuan in 2011', http://tech.qq.com/a/20120129/000015.htm, Accessed in February 2012.
3. 'Sustainable and Innovative Personal Transport Solutions - Strategic Analysis of Carsharing Market in Europe', Frost & Sullivan, January 2010.
4. Spotify, www.spotify.com, Accessed in March 2012.
5. Paywithatweet, http://www.paywithatweet.com/, Accessed in March 2012.

9 CONNECTIVITY AND CONVERGENCE

1. Sterling Bruce, *Shaping Things*, 2005, ISBN-10:0-262-69326-7, MIT Press.
2. 'Inside Microsoft's "Future Homes"', http://news.bbc.co.uk/1/hi/8046659.stm, Accessed in February 2012.
3. 'Entering the Zettabyte Era', Cisco Systems, http://www.cisco.com/en/US/solutions/collateral/ns341/ns525/ns537/ns705/ns827/VNI_Hyperconnectivity_WP.pdf, Accessed in February 2012.
4. 'M-commerce to Hit $119B in '15', http://www.marketingcharts.com/direct/m-commerce-to-hit-119b-in-15-18553/, Accessed in February 2012.
5. 'Digital banking to be the norm by 2015', PricewaterhouseCoopers, http://www.pwc.com/in/en/press-releases/digital-banking.jhtml, Accessed in February 2012.
6. '2011 Advertising Forecast', Magna Global, 2011, http://www.neoadvertising.com/ch/wp-content/uploads/2011/06/2011-MAGNAGLOBAL-Advertising-Forecast-Abbreviated.pdf, Accessed in February 2012.
7. 'Report: Google Controls 44 Percent of Global Online Advertising', http://searchengineland.com/report-google-controls-44-percent-of-global-online-advertising-103743, Accessed in February 2012.
8. 'Online Ad Spend to Overtake TV by 2016', http://www.forbes.com/sites/roberthof/2011/08/26/online-ad-spend-to-overtake-tv/, Accessed in February 2012.

9. 'China Internet Advertising Spend Bypassed Newspaper in 2011', http://www.chinainternetwatch.com/1351/online-ad-2006-2015/, Accessed in February 2012.
10. 'The Future of Mhealth Mobile Phones Improve Care in Developing World', http://www.forbes.com/sites/mobiledia/2012/02/10/the-future-of-mhealth-mobile-phones-improve-care-in-developing-world/2/, Accessed in January 2012.
11. 'About Didgets', Bayer, http://www.bayerdidget.ca/About-Didget, Accessed in January 2012.

10 FROM PLANES TO TRAINS – THE ERA OF HIGH-SPEED RAIL

1. 'Japan's Maglev Train Sets Speed Record', CTVglobemedia, 2 December 2003.
2. G. Bisignani, Director General, Business Interview, July 2005.
3. Ministry of Railways, China, n. d.
4. Strategic Analysis of the Global High Speed Rail Market, Frost & Sullivan, June 2011.
5. Arab News, 'SR30.8bn contract for Haramain Railway Phase 2', 15 January 2012, http://arabnews.com/saudiarabia/article563438.ece, Accessed on 6 February 2012.
6. BBC News UK, 'HS2: High-speed Rail Network Gets Go-ahead', 10 January 2012, http://www.bbc.co.uk/news/uk-16478954, Accessed on 6 February 2012.
7. 'Brenner Base Tunnel Wins TEN-T Funding', *Railway Gazette*, 11 January 2008, http://www.railwaygazette.com/news/single-view/view/brenner-base-tunnel-wins-ten-t-funding.html, Accessed on 6 February 2012.
8. 'California High-Speed Rail Program Draft 2012 Business Plan', California High-Speed Rail Authority, 2011, http://www.cahighspeedrail.ca.gov/assets/0/152/431/1a6251d7-36ab-4fec-ba8c-00e266dadec7.pdf Accessed on February 2012.
9. 'Mexico Reviving Travel by Train', azcentral.com, 6 January 2006, http://www.azcentral.com/arizonarepublic/business/articles/0106mextrain06.html?&wired, Accessed on 12 February 2012.
10. 'Brazilian Development Bank to finance $11 bn for High Speed Train', 2009, ANBA http://www2.anba.com.br/noticia_financas.kmf?cod=8866797&indice=50, Accessed Feb 12, 2012.
11. 'Sapsan Train Races Ahead in Profitability for Russian Railways', *RIA Novosti*, 26 October 2010, http://en.rian.ru/business/20101026/161088304.html, Accessed on 12 February 2012.
12. 'High-speed Trains', *Russian Railways*, 2012, http://eng.rzd.ru/isvp/public/rzdeng?STRUCTURE_ID=4054, Accessed on 8 February 2012.

13. 'Strategic Insight on Global Rail Market', Frost & Sullivan, March 2012.
14. 'China Agrees to Major Investments in Argentina's Rail and Metro Lines', thetransportpolitic.com, 15 July 2010, http://www.thetransportpolitic. com/2010/07/15/china-agrees-to-major-investments-in-argentinas-rail-and-metro-lines/, Accessed on 12 January 2012.
15. 'Spain will Build and Operate the High-speed Line between Medina and Mecca in Saudi Arabia', ADIF, December 2011, http://international.adif.org. es/news/spain-will-build-and-operate-the-high-speed-line-between-medina-and-mecca-in-saudi-arabia/12/2011/138, Accessed on 8 January 2012.
16. 'Etihad Rail Signalling and Telecoms Contract Awarded', *Railway Gazette*, 23 January 2012,http://www.railwaygazette.com/nc/news/single-view/view/ etihad-rail-signalling-contract-awarded.html, Accessed on 23 January 2012.
17. 'Etihad Rail orders EMD locomotives', *Railway Gazette*,1 August 2011, http://www.railwaygazette.com/nc/news/single-view/view/etihad-rail-orders-emd-locomotives.html, Accessed on 4 January 2012.
18. 'Etihad Rail Orders CSR Sulphur Wagons', *Railway Gazette*,12 September 2011, http://www.railwaygazette.com/nc/news/single-view/view/etihad-rail-orders-csr-sulphur-wagons.html, Accessed on 4 January 2012.
19. 'European Rail Catenary Systems – Executive Analysis of Copper Requirement for Electrification across Strategic European Markets', Frost & Sullivan, 2010.
20. World Crude Steel Production, World Steel Association, 2011, http:// www.worldsteel.org/dms/internetDocumentList/press-release-down loads/2012/2012-05-production-figures/document/2012-05-production-figures.pdf, Accessed on February 2012.
21. 'Caterpillar to Acquire Electro-Motive Diesel in $820 Million Deal', *Ropes & Gray*, June 2010, http://www.ropesgray.com/ropesrepresentingelectro motive/, Accessed on 11 February 2012.
22. Strategic Analysis of Alternative Powertrain Technologies in the European Diesel Locomotive and Railcar Market, Frost & Sullivan, 2011.
23. 'Railways to Roll Out World's Biggest ERP Project by Aug',http://www. financialexpress.com/news/Railways-to-roll-out-worlds-biggest-ERP-project-by-Aug/316253/, Accessed on 7 February 2012.
24. 'The Bombardier-Alstom Consortium Signs a Contract to Build 468 New Metro Cars for Montréal', 22 October 2010, http://www.bombardier.com/ en/transportation/media-centre/press-releases/details?docID=0901260d 8013a8bc, Accessed on 4 February 2012.
25. 'Strategic Insight on Global Rail Market', Frost & Sullivan, March 2012.
26. 'SELEX Communications has been Awarded a Contract Worth 45 millions of Euro for the Sirth-Benghazi Railway Line', SELEX, 29 July 2009, http:// www.selex-comms.com/internet/index.php?section=CORP&showentry= 11841, Accessed on 1 February 2012.
27. DMIC-Delhi Mumbai Industrial Corridor, n.d., http://delhimumbaiin dustrialcorridor.com/, Accessed on February 2012.

11 NEW BATTLEFIELDS: SPACE JAM AND CYBER WARFARE

1. 'Global Satellite Manufacturing: The Impact of the Evolving Trend', Frost & Sullivan, 2009.
2. 'Role in Critical Infrastructure Protection (CIP) Cybersecurity', May 2005, Government Accountability Office (GAO), Department of Homeland Security (DHS), GAO-05-434 Washington, DC.
3. 'Cyber Security M&A, Decoding Deals in the Global Cyber Security Industry', PricewaterhouseCoopers LLP, HB-2011-09-14-1705-CG_Cyber Security, http://www.pwc.com/en_GX/gx/aerospace-defence/pdf/cyber-security-mergers-acquisitions.pdf, Accessed in January 2012.

ACKNOWLEDGEMENTS

When I ventured into authoring this book, I thought it would be an easy-peasy job and that I would be done and dusted in a couple of months. Two weeks into the process, I realised how wrong I was and that I had really underestimated the job. We still made it in three and a half months, but it was only thanks to the numerous people who supported me.

First and foremost, I need to thank the two true visionaries in the company – the chairman of Frost & Sullivan, David Frigstad, and the global president and managing partner, Aroop Zutshi. Both believed in my idea of creating a Mega Trends research report and then subsequently a dedicated research group. Without their personal support and individual commitments, this book would never have made it.

I thank Archana Amarnath, who I also fondly call 'Mega nath', for her invaluable, mega contribution to this book. She not only contributed by writing major sections in the book but also provided a lot of background research and analysis to support other trends. The challenges of deciphering the trends and their micro implications were made easier by her support. I am also grateful to her for always pushing and challenging me on this book and for constantly pushing the boundaries.

Although I am the author of this book, it is very much a corporate publication of Frost & Sullivan. This work culminates Frost & Sullivan's 51 years of global research. As a company, we publish over 1200 research reports every year, each of which takes about 500 man hours to develop. I am eternally grateful for the access I had to this vast intellectual capital while writing this book. Apart from this wealth of information available to me, I also thank and appreciate the support of the many industry thought leaders who contributed to this book, many of whom even wrote sections or corrected/confirmed my analysis. In particular, I would like to thank Shyam Raman (who even supported me during his wedding preparations and honeymoon in Burma) for his contribution to the High-Speed Rail chapter; Venkat Rajan, Dorman Followwill and Sidharth Saha for their knowledge of and vision for the health care sector; John Raspin, Konkana Khaund and Jonathan Robinson for Smart Energy; Karthik Sundaram for Smart Factories; my personal favourite Programme Manager in the company, Praveen Chandrasekar, for his unbelievable knowledge in the world of smart, intelligent and connected cars; Aman Pannu for his impressive contribution to Space; Michael Jude for his support on Connectivity and Convergence; Richard Sear for his constructive criticism; the Visionary Innovation research group's team members (especially Archana Vidyasekar, Malabika Mandal and Lorena Isla); and – last but not least – the 1700 analysts and consultants in the company who contributed their acumen directly or indirectly to this book.

There are many other individuals who supported me, and I am most obliged to Manoj Menon for his contributions but also for planting the seed for the book two years ago; Mike Malone for helping me create the proposal for the book to submit to publishers; and Papercheck.Com, LLC's senior editor Melissa Weber for not only dotting the i's and crossing the t's, but also for proofreading and improving upon my Hinglish. I also owe thanks to Siemens, Atos and many other corporate organisations that helped create the case studies.

Most importantly, I must thank my dear wife, Julia Saini. She has been a pillar of strength for me and always believes in me and in my abilities – sometimes, perhaps, more than I do myself. She allowed me to steal time from the family and supported me throughout the long haul by looking after my two little ones in the evenings, weekends and during holidays. I thank her for her support, dedication and love.

Ever since I have become a father, I have a lot of respect for parents. I want to, therefore, thank my parents most of all for the sacrifices they made for my education and well-being; especially my mother, who put her children above her own personal life. Without her contributions – especially her willingness to wake me up every morning at 5 a.m. when I was a student – I would not ever have made it to this stage. I did not appreciate those early wake-up calls then, but I certainly do now.

INDEX